For sheer entertainment, for cultural enrichment, or for the development of special talents and interests, nothing surpasses the reading of good books. GOOD READING is dedicated to helping readers find their way through the complex maze of published volumes, both hardcover and paperbound. It is a handy, practical, inexpensive guide, whose usefulness has been tested by several million readers since 1932.

GOOD READING is a descriptive bibliography of about 2000 titles organized in meaningful subject areas; besides author and title, each entry lists editions and prices. Scholars and critics have selected the most important and readable books from all historical and regional cultures, endeavoring to scant no literary type nor any significant phase of the humanities and the sciences. Each chapter is introduced by an authority in the period or field. And there are special sections on how to use GOOD READING, on reference books, on poetry and drama on records, and on science fiction.

From its first edition in 1932, GOOD READING has been edited by the Committee on College Reading, which now includes more than fifty college professors and high school teachers, deans, librarians, editors, and specialists working under the general editorship of J. Sherwood Weber. Since 1946, the project has been counseled by the Advisory Board of distinguished authors. GOOD READING has demonstrated its worth as a helpful companion to the general reader, as a guide to supplementary reading for high school and college courses, and as a reference book in libraries.

Endorsed by
Leading Educational Organizations

Prepared by The Committee
on College Reading

J. Sherwood Weber,
Editor and Executive Secretary

Anna Rothe, Truman M. Talley,
Atwood H. Townsend, Ruth Ulman,
Arthur Waldhorn, Olga Svatik Weber,
Arthur Zeiger, *Assistant Editors*

Good Reading

A MENTOR BOOK PUBLISHED BY
THE NEW AMERICAN LIBRARY

Sponsored by
College English Association

Endorsed by
Adult Education Association of the U.S.A.
American Library Association
Association of College and Research Libraries
National Council of Teachers of English

MENTOR BOOKS are published by
The New American Library of World Literature, Inc.
501 Madison Avenue, New York 22, New York

PRINTED IN THE UNITED STATES OF AMERICA

CONTENTS

Foreword

CARL CARMER

Ever since I, aged eight, held a bamboo pole, string and hook attached, over a curtained aperture at a Sunday School bazaar, and was rewarded by a dangling leather-bound copy of Thomas Moore's *Lalla Rookh*, I have been an outspoken foe of fishpond and grab-bag methods of delivering reading to readers. Though a shy child, I was so articulate on that occasion that my parents and their friends, rather stunned to find a little boy who must really enjoy reading some things since he had such a distaste for reading others, began to consider how best to bend the twig.

A modern physician might have diagnosed my ensuing illness as psychosomatic and attributed it partially at least to my disappointment in the Irish poet's cantos, but Dr. Sutton muttered "pneumonia" and I was put to bed for a stay that lasted eight weeks. During that time I tried to learn to play the violin on an instrument obtained by sending a hundred soap wrappers to a Buffalo firm, and my mother found that she would rather read to me than listen. She soon exhausted the town's supply of books recommended for children. I heard in embarrassed approval *Alice in Wonderland* and *Through the Looking-Glass,* quite annoyed with myself for caring what happened to a girl, and announced firmly that I did *not* care what happened to Elsie Dinsmore or, for that matter, Sara Crewe or the Little Princess. When my mother then patiently picked up *Little Women,* I said I would rather fiddle than hear any more about young ladies.

In desperation she grabbed a volume from the family set of Shakespeare and began to read. The play turned out to be *Macbeth,* and I turned out to be fascinated. The three witches and Lady Macbeth were more in agreement with my concept of females, and the dark melodrama with its horrid spells, its knocking at the gate in the blackness of night, its murders, and its ghost was not just what the doctor ordered but served quite as well. We went through all the tragedies after that and then the chronicles. I shocked my mother by my hearty appreciation of all corpse-strewn stages, my stormy championship of Iago, my desire to keep Romeo alive after the death of Juliet, my hysterical giggles over the bawdy quips of Falstaff and his roistering companions (of which I understood no whit but somehow felt the quality). But, fiddle in sight, she read on.

When I had recovered sufficiently to leave the house, though not to join in a game of one-old-cat, my mother's friend, Mrs. Cole, called to me from her South Main Street doorway one spring day and ushered me into her library. "My children have grown up," she said, "and there is no one to enjoy these books any more. I don't see well enough, and Mr. Cole reads new books. Come to this room as often as you like. I'm not going to tell you what to read here. Find out for yourself."

Even after I could play long and hard I spent hours in the Cole library. The first book I read was *The Original Travels of Baron Munchausen*. My father, native of a country town where taste for oral fiction had been shaped by a great-grandfather known as "the biggest liar in Tompkins County," had already told me tall tales—among them that of a stag he had shot with a cherrystone bullet which had taken root and grown a blossoming tree where antlers had been. I was delighted to find in this volume the story's prototype and immediately demanded of my father that he tell me who was lying, he or Munchausen. Then I met the Robinsons—Swiss Family and Horse-Shoe—finding an equal though dissimilar joy in each, Tom Sawyer, Huckleberry Finn, Pudd'nhead Wilson, The Last of the Mohicans, and I shivered o' nights over Brockden Brown's tale of a ventriloquist whose other voice uttered things even more villainous than those said these days by Edgar Bergen's Charlie McCarthy. Rebellious by nature, I know that had Mrs. Cole told me that reading any of these books would be good for me, I would not have read it. My reading seemed to me entirely haphazard, but in reality it was highly selective. The Cole library had been accumulated by people of taste.

A rather startling incident stimulated my interest in history as the end of my reading in the Cole library drew near. I was earning a quarter a week then carrying stove coal to a little but fiery old lady whose husband had been an upstate New York politician of the 1860's. On the day after Theodore Roosevelt had been for the first time elected President of the United States, she angrily snatched from a shelf a biography of William H. Seward.

"The wrong candidate is always elected," she said bitterly. "This will tell you who should have been President instead of Lincoln."

Having just learned the Gettysburg Address to recite at Friday afternoon "rhetoricals," I could not have been more horrified had she denounced the author of the Sermon on the Mount, but I read the book and increased my understanding of a period.

The reading I did after I had read all that I wished to in the Cole library and before I entered high school was that of all the other boys of my age. We eagerly emulated the speed of an Indian hero named Deerfoot, the business acumen of the protagonists of the Oliver Optic series and the Horatio Alger books, the courage of the Rover Boys, the sport skills of Frank Merriwell; and we tried our best to see in our dogs the qualities described in *The Call of the Wild, A Dog of Flanders,* and *Bob, Son of Battle.* History then found its best interpreters in Cooper and John Fox, Jr., whose *The Little Shepherd of Kingdom Come* I read yearly for a decade. Aside from an effort to dramatize and produce *Evangeline,* which died after the second rehearsal, none of us showed an interest in recommended reading.

Our small town was fortunate, as thousands of American small towns have been and still are, in having a few devoted high school teachers. Salaries were low, though they would buy more then than now, and in some departments, particularly English, the turnover was rapid. We had both good and bad English teachers, but they came and went so quickly that their effect on students was to create a commonplace standard. There were teachers in our town, however, who, come better jobs or lower pay, never intended to leave it. There are among the boys and girls of my graduating class at Albion High School, Albion, New York, farmers, postal clerks, presidents of large businesses, housewives, teachers, who do not forget after more than four decades the rhythmic sonority of scanned Latin verses, the blue of the sunny sea that darkened under cloud shadows, the agony of Dido, the blood of the black bulls of dank Avernus—because Miss Steele, a tall, bespectacled enthusiast, made them into an enchanting brew. Because of her teaching, "Here too there are tears for things, and hearts are touched by the fate of all that is mortal."

Even more inspired was the teaching of the language and literature of another land. Miss Barrett scared us with her stiff discipline and the blaze of her blue eyes when it was threatened, but we learned to read German and we raced through many more of the books-with-vocabularies-in-the-back than were required by the State Board of Regents. We were old enough to have sweethearts then, and the teacher must have been amused by the ardent glances that accompanied our translations of *Hermann und Dorothea* and *Germelshausen* or spiced our discussions of the *ewig weibliche* as we read Goethe's *Faust*.

Reading works that had won the praise of the generations had become a habit before college days but not always the contemplation that leads toward wisdom. I remember with what sudden surprise I found myself in my sophomore year hotly defending the genial and easygoing expounder of the Odes of Horace, who used to stray from his Sabine farm to those spots where Falernian flowed free and come back up College Hill in a series of curving dashes. I had considered myself a righteous champion of temperance in professors, but the Latin poet's tolerance had entered my blood even as the wine had entered my teacher's, and I knew that I would not again smugly denounce members of the faculty whose problems I did not understand. I remember, too, how amazed I was to find an essay of William Hazlitt, in our despised "Assigned Reading," which was a better report of a prizefight than I had read the same morning in a newspaper.

This summary of an average American boy's unplanned but not uninfluenced reading is submitted here not because I consider it admirable, nor because I believe its effects are notable, but simply for the reason that it gave me so much pleasure that I would not want others to miss a similar but far better experience. GOOD READING has been prepared by men and women who have the same feeling and are as capable and devoted to their purposes as were ever Miss Steele or Miss Barrett. It is a kind of reading room into which all readers are invited as I was once invited. It is better chosen and more comprehensive than Mrs. Cole's library, and I am serenely confident of your joy in it as I repeat her kind wise words to me: "I'm not going to tell you what to read here. Find out for yourself."

How to Use GOOD READING

ATWOOD H. TOWNSEND

Reading provides an endless opportunity, an ever-open door to ever-greater mental growth. Practically all the wisdom of the world is in books. No one can ever read all the good books that have been written, but the more one reads, the richer one is in true and useful wisdom.

One excellent way to start using GOOD READING is to check through the whole list, or those parts of it that interest you, putting an "X" before the books you have already read and a check before those you want to read. By continually changing your checks to "X's" you can keep a record of the progress of your own intellectual growth.

If your determination is serious, you will set a standard for yourself and stick to it. A fair minimum is to read one book a week, but anyone who is really well-read averages considerably more than this. No matter how busy you may think you are, you must find time for reading now, or surrender yourself to self-chosen ignorance.

Random reading is usually not as useful as organized reading. An easy way to plan the growth of your knowledge is to follow for a month or more any interesting trail which you happen to start along: perhaps biographies of Presidents, or Greek tragedy, or anthropology. If you like one novel by Balzac or Dostoevski or Steinbeck, almost certainly you will want to read others.

But do not specialize too much. From time to time check the scope of your reading by turning the pages of GOOD READING to see where your large gaps appear. If you find you know very little about the fine arts, or the Orient, or philosophy, you will know what to do.

Always read with a purpose, or rather a succession of

purposes; follow a broad and flexible program, without binding yourself too rigidly to any scheme or system. But also take a chance once in a while: try a book that you happen to see on a library shelf, or that someone casually recommends. Give yourself the opportunity for intellectual lightning to spark your soul.

Never force yourself to read a book that you do not enjoy. There are so very many good books in the world that it is foolish to waste time on one that does not give you pleasure and profit (unless reading it is an arbitrary requirement to pass an examination, or something like that). If you have chosen a book in good faith and have found it dull after a fair try, put it back on the shelf and devote your time instead to reading something else that will pay you richer immediate dividends.

However, if you find yourself bored by a book that many well-informed people regard as important and readable, be honest with yourself and confess that perhaps the shortcoming is not in the book but in you. Often a book which now seems dull or difficult will prove easy to grasp and fascinating to read when you are more mature intellectually. Sometimes young people are puzzled or bored by certain great books because they lack the background and the maturity of mind necessary to meet the book's author on his intellectual level. But this difficulty is one that will correct itself automatically, provided you go on reading and growing mentally.

Not all the material worth reading is in books. Things move so swiftly these days that a consistent reading of a good newspaper such as the *New York Times* or a news magazine such as *Time* is essential. Concentrate on the important national and international news stories, the editorial columns, and letters from readers—not on crime, sports, and comics.

Most American magazines of large circulation are concerned primarily with entertaining their readers and so present few stories or articles of much value. Significant articles are found rather in such general literary monthlies as *Harper's Magazine* and *Atlantic Monthly,* in such journals of opinion as *The Commonweal* and *The Reporter,* and in such organs of special interest as *Business*

Week, School and Society, and *Scientific American.* To read only mass-circulation picture magazines and digests means that you have not grown mentally beyond the level of a high school sophomore.

Anyone who attempts to keep up with intellectual progress needs to read regularly a magazine of book reviews, such as the *Saturday Review* or the Sunday book section of the *New York Times* or the *New York Herald Tribune.* By reading book reviews with some regularity you will discover what new books you want to read and you will have at least some idea about all important new publications, whether or not you have time to read them yourself.

A complete reading program, therefore, should include four factors: at least one good book each week, a newspaper or news magazine, magazines of comment and interpretation, and book reviews. If you keep feeding your intelligence with these four foods, you can be sure your brain cells will not be undernourished. To this must be added the digestive process that comes from your own thinking and from discussion with other people.

It is often desirable to make books that you own personally part of your mind by underlining or by marking in the margin the more important statements. This will help you to understand the book as you first read it, because out of the mass of details you will have selected the essential ideas. It will help you to remember better the gist of the book, for the physical act of underlining, with your eyes on the page, tends to plant the thought firmly into your brain cells. And it will save time whenever you need to refer to the book.

Above all, never forget that creative intelligence is correlation of facts and ideas, not mere memorizing. What counts in what you learn is what you can do with your knowledge by linking it with other things you have read or experienced. If you read Plutarch's life of Julius Caesar, think how his rise to political power paralleled the technique of Hitler or Stalin or of your local political boss. If you read a play by Shakespeare or Arthur Miller, think how the portrayal of one of the characters helps you to understand someone you know. In everything you read, keep in the back of your mind what it means to your life here and now, how it reaffirms or challenges the things you were taught at home, in school, and in church, and how the wisdom you get from books can guide you in your thinking, in your career, in your duties as a citizen, and in your personal values and morals.

To sum up, what you read is both the measure of your intellectual level and the means of raising it to the utmost of your capacity.

100 Significant Books

This list is intended to present, not necessarily the best or greatest works of literature, but simply a representative selection of books that many people have found rewarding to know. Originally prepared for the 1934 edition of GOOD READING, this list has been revised several times by the Committee on College Reading in consultation with the distinguished authors of the Advisory Board.

Ancient Times

Aeschylus—*The Oresteia*
Aristophanes—*Comedies*
Aristotle—*Nicomachean Ethics* and *Politics*
The Bible
Confucius—*The Analects*
Euripides—*Tragedies*
Herodotus—*History*
Homer—*Iliad* and *Odyssey*

Lucretius—*On the Nature of Things*
Marcus Aurelius—*Meditations*
Plato—*Republic* and *Symposium*
Plutarch—*Parallel Lives*
Sophocles—*Theban Plays*
Thucydides—*The Peloponnesian Wars*
Vergil—*Aeneid*

Middle Ages and Renaissance

The Arabian Nights
Bacon—*Essays* and *Advancement of Learning*
Boccaccio—*Decameron*
Cellini—*Autobiography*
Cervantes—*Don Quixote*
Chaucer—*Canterbury Tales*
Dante—*Divine Comedy*
Erasmus—*In Praise of Folly*

Machiavelli—*The Prince*
Malory—*Le Morte d'Arthur*
Mohammed—*Koran*
Montaigne—*Essays*
More—*Utopia*
Omar Khayyám—*The Rubaiyat*
Rabelais—*Gargantua and Pantagruel*
Shakespeare—*Plays* and *Sonnets*

17th and 18th Centuries

Boswell—*Life of Samuel Johnson*
Bunyan—*Pilgrim's Progress*
Burns—*Poems*
Defoe—*Robinson Crusoe*
Descartes—*A Discourse on Method*

Donne—*Poems*
Fielding—*Tom Jones*
Franklin—*Autobiography*
Gibbon—*The Decline and Fall of the Roman Empire*
Hamilton *et al.*—*The Federalist*

17th and 18th Centuries (cont.)

Malthus—*Principles of Population*
Milton—*Paradise Lost*
Molière—*Comedies*
Paine—*The Rights of Man*
Pepys—*Diary*

Rousseau—*Emile* and *The Social Contract*
Smith—*The Wealth of Nations*
Spinoza—*Philosophy*
Sterne—*Tristram Shandy*
Swift—*Gulliver's Travels*
Voltaire—*Candide*

19th Century

Austen—*Pride and Prejudice*
Balzac—*Eugénie Grandet*
E. Brontë—*Wuthering Heights*
Browning—*Poems*
Butler—*The Way of All Flesh*
Byron—*Poems*
Chekhov—*Short Stories* and *Plays*
Darwin—*The Origin of Species*
Dickens—*David Copperfield*
Dostoevski—*Crime and Punishment*
Emerson—*Essays*
Flaubert—*Madame Bovary*
Goethe—*Faust*
Hardy—*Tess of the D'Urbervilles*
Hawthorne—*The Scarlet Letter*

Hugo—*Les Misérables*
Ibsen—*Plays*
Keats—*Poems*
Marx—*Capital*
Maupassant—*Short Stories*
Melville—*Moby Dick*
Poe—*Short Stories*
Shelley—*Poems*
Stendhal—*The Red and the Black*
Thackeray—*Vanity Fair*
Thoreau—*Walden*
Tolstoy—*War and Peace*
Twain—*Huckleberry Finn*
Whitman—*Leaves of Grass*

20th Century

Adams—*The Education of Henry Adams*
Dreiser—*An American Tragedy*
Eliot—*Poems and Plays*
Faulkner—*The Sound and the Fury*
Frazer—*The Golden Bough*
Freud—*Introduction to Psychoanalysis*
Hemingway—*A Farewell to Arms*
Huxley—*Brave New World*

Joyce—*Ulysses*
Lewis—*Babbitt*
Mann—*The Magic Mountain*
Maugham—*Of Human Bondage*
O'Neill—*Plays*
Sandburg—*Lincoln*
Shaw—*Plays* and *Prefaces*
Steinbeck—*The Grapes of Wrath*
Veblen—*The Theory of the Leisure Class*
Wells—*Outline of History*
Wolfe—*Look Homeward, Angel*

THE GOOD READING BOOK LISTS

Key to Paperbound and Other
Inexpensive Editions

The GOOD READING Book Lists use the following abbreviations to indicate titles available in paperbound editions and in the leading hardcover reprint series. The price range given is that of titles in GOOD READING, not that of the publisher's complete list. All normal trade edition book prices are indicated in the appropriate book list entries. If a book is issued in both trade and text editions, the price given is that of the text edition. Some titles marked "o.p." (out of print) are included since they are widely available in libraries.

AA	*Ann Arbor Paperbacks;* University of Michigan Press, Ann Arbor, Mich. $1.25 to $1.95
Ace	*Ace Books;* Ace Books, 23 W. 47th St., New York 36, N.Y. 25¢ to 50¢
Anch	*Anchor Books;* Doubleday & Company, Inc., 575 Madison Ave., New York 22, N.Y. 75¢ to $2.45
Anv	*Anvil Books;* D. Van Nostrand Company, Inc., 120 Alexander St., Princeton, N.J. $1.25
Avon	*Avon Books;* Avon Book Div., The Hearst Corp., 575 Madison Ave., New York 22, N.Y. 25¢ to 75¢
B&N	*Barnes & Noble Paperbacks;* Barnes & Noble, Inc., 105 Fifth Ave., New York 3, N.Y. 50¢ to $2.95
Bal	*Ballantine Books;* Ballantine Books, Inc., 101 Fifth Ave., New York 3, N.Y. 35¢ to 50¢
Ban	*Bantam Books;* Bantam Books, Inc., 25 W. 45th St., New York 36, N.Y. 25¢ to 95¢
Bea	*Beacon Press Paperbacks;* Beacon Press, 25 Beacon St., Boston 8, Mass. 95¢ to $2.75
Berk	*Berkley Books;* Berkley Publishing Corp., 145 W. 57th St., New York 19, N.Y. 25¢ to 75¢
BES	*Barron's Educational Series;* Barron's Educational Series, Inc., 343 Great Neck Rd., Great Neck, N.Y. 50¢ to $2.98
Black	*Black and Gold Library;* Liveright Publishing Corp., 386 Park Avenue South, New York 16, N.Y. $3.50
Calif	*University of California Paperbacks;* University of California Press, Berkeley 4, Calif. $1.25 to $1.95
Cap	*Capricorn Books;* G. P. Putnam's Sons, 210 Madison Ave., New York 16, N.Y. 95¢ to $1.35
Chic	*University of Chicago Paperbacks;* The University of Chicago Press, 5750 Ellis Ave., Chicago 37, Ill. $1.25 to $1.95
CoE	*Collectors' Editions;* Peter Pauper Press, 629 MacQuesten Parkway, Mount Vernon, N.Y. $2.50

Comp	*Compass Books;* The Viking Press, Inc., 625 Madison Ave., New York 22, N.Y. 95¢ to $1.95.
CoNC	*Collins New Classics;* William Collins Sons & Co., 425 Park Avenue South, New York 16, N.Y. $1.65
Corn	*Great Seal Books;* Cornell University Press, 124 Roberts Pl., Ithaca, N.Y. 95¢ to $1.95
Crest	*Crest Books;* Fawcett Publications, 67 W. 44th St., New York 36, N.Y. 25¢ to 75¢
Cro	*Crofts Classics;* Appleton-Century-Crofts, Inc., 35 W. 32nd St., New York 1, N.Y.
Dell	*Dell Books;* Dell Publishing Co., Inc., 750 Third Ave., New York 17, N.Y. 25¢ to $2.95
Dov	*Dover Books;* Dover Publications, Inc., 180 Varick St., New York 14, N.Y. 60¢ to $5
Drama	*Dramabooks;* Hill & Wang, Inc., Publishers, 104 Fifth Ave., New York 11, N.Y. 95¢ to $1.75
Drama-h	*Dramabooks* (hard covers); Hill & Wang, Inc., Publishers. $3 to $3.95
Ever	*Evergreen Books;* Grove Press, Inc., 64 University Pl., New York 3, N.Y. $1 to $3.95
Evman	*Dutton Everyman Paperbacks;* E. P. Dutton & Co., Inc., 300 Park Avenue South, New York 10, N.Y. 95¢ to $1.95
Evman-h	*Everyman's Library—Standard Edition;* E. P. Dutton & Co. $1.85
EvmanNA	*Everyman's Library—New American Edition;* E. P. Dutton & Co. $2.45
Gar	*Garden City Books;* Doubleday & Company, Inc., 575 Madison Ave., New York 22, N.Y. $2.49 to $5.95
Gate	*Gateway Books;* Henry Regnery Company, 64 E. Jackson Blvd., Chicago 4, Ill. 65¢ to $1.95
GB	*Galaxy Books;* Oxford University Press, 417 Fifth Ave., New York 16, N.Y. $1.25 to $2.95
GT	*Golden Treasury Series;* St Martin's Press, 175 Fifth Ave., New York 10, N.Y. $1.25 to $2
GtIl	*Great Illustrated Classics;* Dodd, Mead & Company, Inc., 432 Park Avenue South, New York 16, N.Y. $3.50
HarB	*Harbrace Modern Classics;* Harcourt, Brace and Company, Inc., 750 Third Ave., New York 17, N.Y. $2.25
Harp	*Harper's Modern Classics;* Harper & Brothers, 49 E. 33rd St., New York 16, N.Y. $1.25 and $1.65
Harv	*Harvest Books;* Harcourt, Brace and Company, Inc., 750 Third Ave., New York 17, N.Y. 95¢ to $2.25
Im	*Image Books;* Doubleday & Company, Inc., 575 Madison Ave., New York 22, N.Y. 65¢ to $1.45
Ind	*Midland Books;* Indiana University Press, Bloomington, Ind. $1.25 to $1.95
Lib	*Liberal Arts Paperbacks;* Liberal Arts Press, Inc., 153 W. 72nd St., New York 23, N.Y. 40¢ to $1.75
Lita	Littlefield Adams & Co., 128 Oliver St., Paterson 1, N.J. 50¢ to $3.45
Liv	*Living Library;* The World Publishing Company, 2231 W. 110th St., Cleveland 2, Ohio. $1.65
LLA-Lib	*The Library of Liberal Arts;* Liberal Arts Press, Inc., 153 W. 72nd St., New York 23, N.Y. 40¢ to $1.75

Loeb	*Loeb Classical Library;* Harvard University Press, 79 Garden St., Cambridge 38, Mass. $3.50
Made	*Made Simple Books.* Distributed by Doubleday & Company, Inc., Garden City, N.Y. $1 to $1.50
McGH	*McGraw-Hill Paperback Series;* McGraw-Hill Book Company, Inc., 330 W. 42nd St., New York 36, N.Y. 95¢ to $2.95
Mer	*Meridian Books;* Meridian Books, Inc., 12 E. 22nd St., New York 10, N.Y. $1 to $2.25
ML	*Modern Library;* Modern Library, Inc., 457 Madison Ave., New York 22, N.Y. $1.65
MLCE	*Modern Library College Editions;* Modern Library, Inc. 65¢ to 95¢
MLG	*Modern Library Giants;* Modern Library, Inc. $2.95
MLP	*Modern Library Paperbacks;* Modern Library, Inc. 75¢ to $1.45
ModSA	*Modern Standard Authors;* Charles Scribner's Sons, 597 Fifth Ave., New York 17, N.Y. $1.95 to $3.50
ModSL	*Modern Student's Library;* Charles Scribner's Sons. $1 to $2
MW	*Men of Wisdom Series;* Harper & Brothers, 49 E. 33rd St., New York 16, N.Y. $1.35 to $1.50
NAL	*New American Library;* New American Library of World Literature, Inc., 501 Madison Ave., New York 22, N.Y. 25¢ to $1.95
Nel	*Nelson Classics;* Thomas Nelson & Sons, 19 E. 47th St., New York 17, N.Y. $1.25
New	*New Directions Paperbooks;* New Directions, 333 Sixth Ave., New York 14, N.Y. 95¢ to $1.55
NewC	*New Classics;* New Directions. $1.75 and $2
Noon	*Noonday Paperbacks;* The Noonday Press, 80 E. 11th St., New York 3, N.Y. $1.25 to $2.50
Nort	*The Norton Library;* W. W. Norton & Company, Inc., 55 Fifth Ave., New York 3, N.Y. 85¢ to $4.45
Oce	*Oceana Paperbacks;* Oceana Publications, Inc., 80 Fourth Ave., New York 3, N.Y. 50¢ to $3
Owl	*Owl Press Paperbacks;* The Owl Press, Bay Ridge, Annapolis, Md. $1 and $1.50
Ox	*Oxford University Press Paperbacks;* Oxford University Press, Inc., 417 Fifth Ave., New York 16, N.Y. $1 to $4.80
OxA	*Oxford Standard Authors;* Oxford University Press. $3 to $6
PB	*Pocket Books;* Pocket Books, Inc., 630 Fifth Ave., New York 20, N.Y. 25¢ to 75¢
Pen	*Penguin Books;* Penguin Books, Inc., 3300 Clipper Mill Rd., Baltimore 11, Md. 35¢ to $1.95
Perm	*Permabooks;* Pocket Books, Inc., 630 Fifth Ave., New York 20, N.Y. 25¢ to 75¢
Phoen	*Phoenix Books;* University of Chicago Press, 5750 Ellis Ave., Chicago 37, Ill. $1 to $2.85
Pop	*Popular Library;* Pines Publications, Inc., 355 Lexington Ave., New York 17, N.Y. 25¢ to 50¢
Prem	*Premier Books;* Fawcett Publications, Inc., 67 W. 44th St., New York 36, N.Y. 35¢ to 50¢

Pyr	*Pyramid Books;* Almat Publishing Corp., 444 Madison Ave., New York 22, N.Y. 25¢ to 95¢
Pyroy	*Pyramid Royal Books;* Pyramid Books. 35¢ to 50¢
Ran	*Random House Paperbacks;* Random House, 457 Madison Ave., New York 22, N.Y. 65¢ to $1.75
Refl	*Reflection Books;* Association Press, 291 Broadway, New York 7, N.Y. 50¢
Rine	*Rinehart Editions Reprint Series;* Rinehart & Company, Inc., 232 Madison Ave., New York 16, N.Y. 50¢ to $2.75
RivEd	*Riverside Editions;* Houghton Mifflin Company, 2 Park St., Boston 7, Mass. 65¢ to $1.50
RivLib	*Riverside Library;* Houghton Mifflin Company. $3 to $4
S&S	*Simon and Schuster Paperbacks;* Simon and Schuster, Inc., 630 Fifth Ave., New York 20, N.Y. $1 to $2.50
Saga	*Sagamore Press Paperbacks;* Sagamore Press, Inc., 11 E. 36th St., New York 16, N.Y. $1.25 to $1.95
Scrib	Charles Scribner's Sons, 597 Fifth Ave., New York 17, N.Y. 95¢ to $3
SM	*St Martin's Library;* St Martin's Press, Inc., 175 Fifth Ave., New York 10, N.Y. 95¢ to $3
Torch	*Torchbooks;* Harper & Brothers, 49 E. 33rd St., New York 16, N.Y. 95¢ to $1.95
UL	*Universal Library;* Grosset & Dunlap, Inc., 1107 Broadway, New York 10, N.Y. 95¢ to $1.95
Ungar	*Frederick Ungar Paperbacks;* Frederick Ungar Publishing Co., 131 E. 23rd St., New York 10, N.Y. 65¢ to $2.75
Vik	*Viking Paperbound Portables;* The Viking Press, Inc., 625 Madison Ave., New York 22, N.Y. $1.25 to $1.45
Vik-h	*Viking Portable Library* (hard covers); Viking Press. $2.95
Vin	*Vintage Books;* Alfred A. Knopf, Inc., 501 Madison Ave., New York 22, N.Y. 95¢ to $1.65
WL	*Wisdom Library;* Philosophical Library. Distributed by Book Sales, Inc., 352 Park Avenue South, New York 10, N.Y. 95¢ to $1.95
WoC	*World's Classics;* Oxford University Press, 417 Fifth Ave., New York 16, N.Y. $1.65, $2.50, and $5
Yale	*Yale Paperbounds;* Yale University Press, 143 Elm St., New Haven 7, Conn. 95¢ to $1.45

NOTICE ON PRICES: All book prices quoted above and in the following book lists are correct as of October 1, 1959. Though publishers' prices are subject to change, most should not alter significantly during the life of this edition of GOOD READING.

HISTORICAL AND

REGIONAL CULTURES

1. Greece

JOHN E. HANKINS, *University of Maine*

To know Greece and the Hellenic world is to know the springs of our own culture. In almost every activity of the human mind—in art, architecture, science, philosophy, education, poetry, drama, even in athletics—we are greatly indebted to the ancient Greeks. Nor can we say with assurance that in any of these fields (except natural science) our modern culture has surpassed that of Greece.

The center of Greek intellectual life during the 5th century B.C. was the city-state of Athens. Athenian culture had a threefold foundation: material prosperity, democratic government, and freedom of thought. Athens' role as protector of other states in the Athenian confederacy brought her large sums of tribute money, sums expended on noble public buildings. Her government stimulated pride of citizenship but also had the faults of a democracy—indecisiveness and petty bickering. Her devotion to intellectual freedom made her welcome ideas from the rest of the Mediterranean world, and her eminence as a maritime power kept her in constant touch with other peoples. Foreign scholars flocked to Athens, where they found a willing audience.

Eventually Athens was conquered by Sparta, later by Philip of Macedon, and finally by Rome. Each conquest resulted in the further spread of her superior thought and culture. Philip's son Alexander conquered and Hellenized Egypt and the Near East. Rome adopted Greek culture as her own and spread its influence over Western Europe, North Africa, and the British Isles. Even during the centuries of the Roman Empire, Greek remained the first language of Eastern Mediterranean countries, and Alexandria in Egypt came to rival Athens as a center of intellectual studies. Most cultivated Romans were bilingual: Vergil and Horace took their academic training at Athens. Nor should we forget that the original Greek of the New Testament and the Septuagint translation of the Old Testament made possible the rapid spread of Christianity from a Hebrew sect to an international religion.

Greek genius was interpretive and self-expressive. Other flourishing civilizations preceded that of Greece—Egyptian, Chaldean, Phoenician, Cretan, etc.—but of most of them only fragmentary records survive. The Greeks absorbed much from these earlier cultures as well as from the contemporary world, reinterpreting all that they learned in the clear light of unbiased intellect. In reading the Greek historians, for example, one marvels at their essential fairness and their patriotism without jingoism.

The Socratic dialogues of Plato draw upon a wide range of earlier philosophic theories, harmonizing them, arranging them, and charting a clear course through the intricate maze. Plato's pupil Aristotle was perhaps the greatest systematizer of all time, exercising his analytical genius upon physical and biological science, metaphysics, psychology, poetry, oratory, and human conduct. His perception that every subject can be better understood through rational analysis, systematic arrangement, and reduction to first principles is perhaps the most influential concept in the history of human knowledge.

The same sense of fairness, of harmony, of proportion and balance, is evident in the artistic and literary productions of the Greeks. The Parthenon, designed by Ictinus, is an architectural triumph of grace and symmetry. The Greek tragedians (Aeschylus, Sophocles, Euripides) saw life steadily and whole, portraying without rancor the tragedy of human fate. Homer's *Odyssey*, from an earlier period of Greek history, is a model of a well-designed plot. Perhaps the Greek mind, unwarped

by restraints, vigorous but not prejudiced, tolerant but
not indifferent, came nearer the perception of rational
truth than any people before or since; and this may
account for its continued impact upon our modern
world.

While Homer lived at least 300 years before the Age
of Pericles (5th century B.C.), later Greeks probably knew
less about his times than we do today. Except for his two
great epics and the so-called *Homeric Hymns,* no written
records of his period survive. Archeological excavations
of ancient Troy and Mycenae have taught us a great deal
about Homer's world. Yet *The Iliad,* an epic of war, and
The Odyssey, an epic of travel, tell their own stories in
dramatic human terms which have enthralled readers
throughout the centuries.

The origins of Greek drama are obscure, but it seems
to have emerged from ritual, myth, and dance. In the
form in which we know it, Greek drama began as entertainment for the annual festivals in honor of Dionysus.
At first a single reader chanted epic verse from the stage,
relieved at intervals by choral songs from the dancing
area. When Aeschylus added a second reader or actor,
genuine drama began, but the chorus always remained
a traditional feature of Greek drama. The plays were
performed in outdoor semicircular amphitheaters, which
to this day have acoustical qualities better than those of
most modern theaters.

Greek philosophy was at first in the hands of Sophists,
itinerant scholars who accepted fees for discoursing to
such students as were interested and willing to pay. Later
Plato's Academy, "the world's first university," drew together the best minds in a systematic search for truth.
This arrangement was imitated by the Neo-Platonists of
Alexandria, who extended and refined upon Plato's
more mystical ideas almost to the point of incompre-
hensibility.

Greek history, romance, satire, and lyric verse—also
represented in our reading list—have likewise been influential in many later periods. The reader who would
understand his own civilization should study the Greeks
as a prerequisite to a fuller comprehension of himself
and of the world today.

A. Greek Literature

Collections

The Complete Greek Drama (1938). Ed. by W. J. Oates and Eugene O'Neill, Jr. 47 plays in translation of Aeschylus, Sophocles, Euripides, Aristophanes, and Menander, with useful notes. *Random House 2 vols. $8.50.*

Complete Greek Tragedies. Ed. by David Grene and Richmond Lattimore. A collection of first-rate new translations collected three or four to a volume and provided with excellent introductions. *Chic 9 vols.*

The Greek Anthology (1916–18). Trans. by W. R. Paton. Extensive collection of short lyrics compiled in the 10th century. Epitaphs, epigrams, monument inscriptions, love lyrics drawn from many centuries. *Loeb 5 vols.*

Greek Anthology (1957). Ed. by Dudley Fitts. A good introduction to Greek literature. *New.*

The Greek Historians (1942). Ed. by F. R. B. Godolphin. Complete histories by Herodotus, Thucydides, Xenophon, Arrian; other historical material. *Random House 2 vols. $10.*

Greek Literature in Translation (1944). Ed. by W. J. Oates and C. T. Murphy. Extensive and representative selection in modern translations. *Longmans, Green $6.50.*

Greek Literature in Translation (rev. ed. 1948). Ed. by G. Howe, G. A. Harrer, and P. H. Epps. Collection representing all stages of the cultural history of ancient Greece. *Harper $7.50.*

Greek Poetry for Everyman (1951). Trans. by F. L. Lucas. An excellent selection of Greek verse, including work of minor authors. *Macmillan $4, Bea.*

The Portable Greek Reader (1948). Ed. by W. H. Auden. 726 pages bringing together the high spots of Greek literature from Homer to Galen: 4 complete plays, poetry, philosophy, science, and political writings. *Vik, Vik-h.*

Ten Greek Plays in Contemporary Translations (1958). Ed. by L. R. Lind. An inexpensive collection of first-rate translations presented with solid introductory material. *Houghton Mifflin $3, RivEd.*

Individual Authors

AESCHYLUS 525–456 B.C. *Tragedies.* Best known is the *Oresteia,* a trilogy comprising *Agamemnon, Choephoroe,* and *Eumenides,* a dark tragedy of bloodshed and revenge. The most readable translation is by Vellacott (*Pen*). Others: *Chic 2 vols., Evman-h, Lib, Loeb 2 vols., Nort, Ox, Vik.*

AESOP c. 6th cent. B.C. *Fables.* Animal stories illustrating folk morality with pointed, sometimes cynical, wit. *Lippincott $3.50, Evman-h, Pen.*

ARISTOPHANES c. 448–380 B.C. *Comedies.* Lyrical burlesques, combining boisterous comedy with poetic beauty: on Socrates, *The Clouds;* on politics, *The Knights;* on war and sex, *Lysistrata;* on utopian schemes, *The Birds;* on literature, *The Frogs. Anch, Black, Evman-h 2 vols., Liv, Loeb, Ox, Vik, WoC.*

ARISTOTLE 384–322 B.C. *Nicomachean Ethics.* Moral conduct rationally considered. A major work. *EvmanNA, Loeb, Pen, WoC.*

_____ *Politics.* Influential analysis of the forms and functions of government. *Evman-h, Loeb, ML.*

_____ *Selections. Gate, PB, Scrib.*

_____ *The Basic Works* (1941). Ed. by Richard McKeon. The most comprehensive inexpensive collection. *Random House 2 vols. $6.*

DEMOSTHENES 383–322 B.C. *Orations.* The best in oratory. *Evman-h, Loeb 3 vols.*

DIOGENES LAERTIUS c. A.D. 150 *Lives of Eminent Philosophers.* Interesting biographical material. *Loeb 2 vols.*

EURIPIDES c. 484–408 B.C. *Tragedies and Tragi-Comedies.* Realistic, very human tragedies by the most modern of the great Greek dramatists. Best known: *Alcestis, Hippolytus, Medea, The Trojan Women. Chic 5 vols., Evman-h 2 vols., Lib, Loeb 4 vols., NAL, Nort, Ox, Pen.*

HERODOTUS c. 484–425 B.C. *History.* Shrewd analysis of geopolitics in the ancient world, and lively narrative of the crucial struggle between democratic Greece and totalitarian Persia. *Tudor $2.98, Evman-h 2 vols., Loeb 4 vols., ML, Pen.*

HESIOD c. 770 B.C. *Hesiod and the Homeric Poems.* Myths of the gods, fables, proverbs, social protest, moral advice, prayers, religious chants. *Lib, Loeb.*

HOMER c. 750 B.C. *Iliad.* This great epic of the siege of Troy is still the most universally admired poetry of action ever written. The verse translation by Richmond Lattimore *(Chic)* and the prose version by E. V. Rieu *(Pen)* are highly recommended. Other translations: *Van Nostrand $1.35, Evman-h, Loeb 2 vols., ML, MLCE, MLG, NAL, Nort, SM, WoC.*

_____ *Odyssey.* Return of Odysseus *(Ulysses* in Latin) from the Trojan War to his home in Ithaca. Rousing adventure of individual exploits combined with great human interest. The translations of W. H. D. Rouse *(NAL)* and T. E. Shaw *(Ox)* are particularly good. Others: *Houghton Mifflin $2.48, Van Nostrand $1.35, Evman-h, GB, Loeb 2 vols., ML, MLCE, MLG, Pen, SM.*

LUCIAN c. A.D. 125–210 *Dialogues of the Dead, Dialogues of the Gods.* Pungent and witty satires with philosophic implications. *Oxford Univ. 4 vols. $6.75, Loeb 5 vols.*

PINDAR 522–443 B.C. *Odes.* Chief writer of choral or "Pindaric" odes celebrating Olympic triumphs and special events. *St Martin's $3.75, Univ. of Chicago $3, Loeb, Phoen.*

————— *Some Odes* (1942). Richmond Lattimore's excellent translations of major odes. *New Directions 50¢.*

PLATO c. 427–347 B.C. *Dialogues.* Probing philosophical discussions, with Socrates usually the main speaker. Most interesting are the *Apology* (Socrates' trial), *Phaedo* (Socrates' death), *Symposium* (on love), *Gorgias* (on justice), and *Republic* (on the ideal state). *Random House $7.50, Van Nostrand $1.35, Black, Evman, Evman-h 2 vols., Gate, Lib, Loeb 2 vols., ML, MLP, ModSL, NAL, Ox, PB, Scrib, Vik, Vik-h, WoC.*

PLUTARCH c. A.D. 46–120 *Lives.* Short biographies, paralleling the lives of famous Greeks with the lives of famous Romans. Remarkable character interpretations. *Dell, Evman-h 3 vols., Liv, Loeb 11 vols., MLG, Pen.*

POLYBIUS 204–122 B.C. *Histories.* An outstanding interpretation of Rome's rise to power. *Loeb 6 vols.*

QUINTUS SMYRNAEUS 4th cent. A.D. *The Fall of Troy.* A sequel to the *Iliad,* giving all important events of the Trojan War from the death of Hector to the fall of the city. *Loeb.*

SOPHOCLES 496–406 B.C. *Tragedies.* In the whole range of Greek tragedy, two of his *Theban Plays—Oedipus Rex* for plot, *Antigone* for moral significance—are perhaps the best plays. The best translations are by Fitts and Fitzgerald (*Harv*), Roche (*NAL*), Banks (*Ox*), and Watling (*Pen*). Other translations and other plays: *Chic 2 vols., Evman-h, Lib, Loeb 2 vols., WoC.*

THEOCRITUS c. 300 B.C., BION c. 200 B.C., and MOSCHUS c. 200 B.C. *Idylls.* Pastorals, elegies, love songs, and narratives on mythological subjects. *Cambridge Univ. $2.50.*

THUCYDIDES c. 470–400 B.C. *The Peloponnesian Wars.* An analytical yet stirring account of the fateful struggle between Athens and Sparta. *Oxford Univ. 2 vols. $2 ea, EvmanNA, Loeb 4 vols., ML, MLCE, Pen, WoC.*

XENOPHON 431–355 B.C. *Anabasis.* On the military campaigns of Cyrus, King of Persia, and the retreat of the Greek mercenaries across Arabian deserts to the Black Sea. *McKay $3.50, NAL, SM* (abr.).

————— *Memorabilia, Œconomicus.* The former work sets forth the life and opinions of Socrates. *Loeb.*

B. Books About Greece

BOWRA, C. M. 1898– *The Greek Experience* (1958). Brilliant popular analysis of Greek life, thought, and culture. *World $6, NAL.*

BULFINCH, THOMAS 1796–1867 *Mythology.* The most convenient (and most Victorian) of the many handbooks of mythology. Includes *The Age of Fable* (1855), *The Age of Chivalry* (1858),

The Legends of Charlemagne (1863). *Crowell $3.50, Dell (abr.), MLG.*

BURY, JOHN BAGNELL 1861–1927 *History of Greece* (1900). From prehistory to Alexander the Great. Authoritative and entertaining. *St Martin's $4, MLG.*

DURANT, WILL 1885– *The Life of Greece* (1939). Comprehensive yet most readable survey of Greek civilization from remote times to the Roman conquest. *Simon & Schuster $7.50.*

FARRINGTON, BENJAMIN 1891– *Greek Science* (1939). Illuminating survey of the physical and economic forces and of the speculative minds that laid foundations for modern science. *Pen.*

FINLEY, M. I. 1912– *The World of Odysseus* (1954). The best popular introduction to the world and works of Homer. *Mer.*

FRAZER, SIR JAMES GEORGE 1854–1941 *The Golden Bough* (1915). A basic account of primitive religions and ancient folklores. *Macmillan $6.50 (abr.).*

GRAVES, ROBERT 1895– *The Greek Myths* (1955). The complete story of the Greek gods and heroes assembled—often with fresh insights—into one continuous narrative by a poet and novelist of great ability. *Pen 2 vols.*

———— *Hercules, My Shipmate* (1945). Imaginative reconstruction of the savage, lusty, daring adventures of the Argonauts who sought the Golden Fleece. *UL.*

GUTHRIE, W. K. C. 1906– *The Greeks and Their Gods* (1951). A lucid, nontechnical account of the religious background of the Greek classics. *Bea.*

HADAS, MOSES 1900– *A History of Greek Literature* (1950). A sound comprehensive survey. *Columbia Univ. $4.25.*

HAMILTON, EDITH 1867– *The Greek Way* (1930). Entertaining and stimulating study of Greek writers and their influence in ancient and modern times. *Norton $3.95, NAL.*

———— *Mythology* (1942). Popular, well-written short narrative of the Greek myths. *NAL.*

HARRISON, JANE 1850–1928 *Prolegomena to the Study of Greek Religion* (1955). Fascinating scholarly account of deities, ceremonials, sacrifices, and other elements of primitive Greek religion. Extensively illustrated. *Mer.*

JAEGER, WERNER 1888– *Paideia: Ideals of Greek Culture* (1939). Difficult but highly rewarding study of the development of Greek culture and thought. *Oxford Univ. 3 vols. $6.50 ea.*

KITTO, H. D. F. 1897– *Greek Tragedy* (rev. ed. 1950). Informed, perceptive, illuminating critical analyses of Greek tragedies and their backgrounds. *Barnes & Noble $5, Anch.*

———— *The Greeks* (1954). Social conditions in ancient Greece. *Pen.*

LAWRENCE, ARNOLD WALTER 1900– *Greek Architecture* (1957). Lavishly illustrated history of Greek architecture. *Pen $12.50.*

The Legacy of Greece (1921). Ed. by R. W. Livingstone. Stimulating essays by Gilbert Murray, W. R. Inge, other distinguished scholars on all aspects of Greek life and culture. *Oxford Univ.* *$5.*

LOUYS, PIERRE 1870–1925 *Aphrodite* (1896). Lushly detailed, tragic romance of a priestess of love in rich, corrupt Alexandria, *Avon, Berk, ML, MLP.*

STOBART, JOHN C. 1878–1933 *The Glory That Was Greece* (rev. ed. 1934). Greek life, art, and civilization, profusely illustrated. *Beacon $9.50.*

TOYNBEE, ARNOLD J. 1889– (ed.) *Greek Civilization and Character* (1950). Skillfully edited collection from Greek historians showing various aspects of ancient civilization. *Beacon $3.50, NAL.*

WEBER, J. SHERWOOD 1918– *et al. From Homer to Joyce* (1959). Contains useful popular guides to the understanding of major works of Greek literature: *The Iliad, The Odyssey, Oresteia, Theban Plays, Alcestis, Hippolytus, Medea, Republic, Nicomachean Ethics. Holt-Dryden $1.95.*

2. Rome

NORMAN T. PRATT, JR., *Indiana University*

To modern men, the Romans usually seem like blocks of granite—strong, massive, durable. And with reason, for many of the roads, temples, bridges, aqueducts, amphitheaters they built still survive. But they made other contributions even more enduring. Their configuration of roads and settlements helped give modern Europe its shape. Their language, Latin, was the main source of eight modern languages, including Italian, French, and Spanish. Their political system strongly influenced the founding fathers of America. Their law is the core of one of the two major legal systems in Western civilization. And this list might be greatly extended.

Such accomplishments of the Roman gift for organization are important, but they tend to leave a misleading impression. Efficiency implies hard practicality, perhaps even lack of feeling. Yet the Romans, like other Mediterranean peoples, were also emotional and excitable, as their literature abundantly reveals. Though the Romans did not match the intellectual and artistic originality of the Greeks, their literature has wit, emotional insight and artistic refinement. The uniqueness of Roman literature lies in the fusion of this sophistication with the moral force and seriousness produced by a strong social orientation.

A sampling will show the variety. The comedies of Plautus, written near the beginning of Latin literature, are full of lively humanity. His comic animation and chaotic plots stand in sharp contrast to Terence's quieter, more polished and sensitive comedies of manners.

In the literature of "the Ciceronian period," the first half of the 1st century B.C., the outstanding names are Cicero and Caesar in prose, Catullus and Lucretius in poetry. The orations and letters of Cicero reveal a skilled politician and a consummate orator. The strong and bril-

liant personality of Caesar appears vividly in his accounts
of the Gallic and civil wars. These two writers, enemies
in the political arena, help us to know well a crucial
period in world history. Catullus pictures in his lyrics the
sophisticated society of poets, rakes, and beauties, using
his art for the spontaneous expression of erotic feeling.
Lucretius, a probing thinker, undertakes in *The Nature
of Things* to crush superstition and ignorance with the
scientific thought of Epicureanism.

The following half-century, known as "the Augustan
age," produced equally notable literature. Vergil's *Aeneid*
portrays the cultural mission of Rome with intelligence
and grandeur; this is probably the most significant Latin
book to know. Horace's lyrics—sometimes delicate, sometimes weighty, usually brilliant—and his witty satires
have been enjoyed by countless readers. Ovid's *Metamorphoses* has left endless imprints on later literature.
In a period remembered mainly for its poetry, Livy's
epiclike history of Rome is a prose masterpiece.

The reader will find much that seems modern in the
social criticism that permeates the best literature of the
early centuries A.D. The Roman precursors of the novel,
Petronius and Apuleius, wrote satiric social romances.
Martial mocks his society irrepressibly. The materialism
and immorality of Rome are the targets of Juvenal's
blowtorch satires. Also critical of the times are Tacitus's
devastating historical analysis of the emperors and Seneca's Stoic writings. Stoicism was the source of much social
liberalism, as evidenced in a Senecan letter challenging
slavery: "Just remember that he whom you call your
slave was born from the same seed, enjoys the same sky,
and equally breathes, lives and dies."

The continuous movement from pagan to fully Christian times is reflected in the literature of the 4th to the
6th century. Jerome, whose favorite authors were Plautus
and Cicero, was mainly responsible for the great Latin
translation of the Bible known as the Vulgate. Augustine's *Confessions* records his conversion to Christianity
from and through classical thought. Boethius clings
firmly to the rationality of pagan philosophy as a support
to the faith of Christianity. So new vitality arises from
old.

A. Literature of the Roman Era

Collections

Classics in Translation: Latin Literature (vol. 2, 1952). Ed. by P. L. MacKendrick and H. M. Howe. Roman culture presented through a generous selection of complete works and units, both prose and poetry, mostly in new translations. *Univ. of Wisconsin $5; in set with vol. 1, Greek Literature, $9.*

The Complete Roman Drama (1942). Ed. by G. E. Duckworth. 36 plays: lively comedies by Plautus and Terence which bring the reader close to the life and humor of the Romans; and violent, influential melodramas by Seneca. *Random House 2 vols. $10.*

Latin Literature in Translation (1952). Ed. by K. Guinagh and A. P. Dorjahn. Whole units or substantial sections representative of the writings of all the chief Latin authors. *Longmans, Green $5.*

Latin Poetry in Verse Translation (1957). Ed. by L. R. Lind. An anthology of Latin poetry from the beginnings to the Renaissance, in a variety of translations. *Houghton Mifflin $3.25, RivEd.*

The Latin Poets (1949). Ed. by F. R. B. Godolphin. Complete poems and outstanding passages showing the variety and development of Latin poetry. *ML.*

The Portable Roman Reader (1951). Ed. by Basil Davenport. A compact sampling, including three complete plays (by Plautus, Terence, and Seneca); long units from Lucretius, Vergil, Ovid; and short selections from many others. *Vik-h.*

Roman Readings (1958). Ed. by Michael Grant. A tasteful anthology of Roman poets and prose writers. *Pen.*

Individual Authors

APULEIUS, LUCIUS c. A.D. 160 *The Golden Ass.* The only completely surviving Latin novel, about an adventurer changed to an ass and doomed to fantastic experiences until the goddess Isis allows him to resume human form; an extravagant book containing unusual material, like the initiation into religious mysteries and the famous tale of Cupid and Psyche. *Black, Loeb.*

AUGUSTINE, SAINT A.D. 354-430 *The City of God.* The fall of the Roman Empire and the death of paganism interpreted by a Christian believing in divine providence; one of the most influential early Christian documents. *Evman-h, Im, MLG.*

_____ *Confessions.* A searching autobiography of a brilliant man converted to Christianity. *Regnery $3.75, Black, EvmanNA, Loeb 2 vols., ML, Nel, PB.*

BOETHIUS A.D. 480–524 *The Consolation of Philosophy*. A moving dialogue concerning pagan philosophy and Christianity written by "the last great pagan author." *Lib, Loeb, ML, Ungar.*

CAESAR, GAIUS JULIUS 100–44 B.C. *Commentaries*. The conqueror of Gaul and Britain and victor in civil war gives clear, vivid reports of crucial military campaigns and political struggles. *Evman, Evman-h, NAL, Pen.*

CATULLUS, GAIUS VALERIUS 84–54 B.C. *Poems*. A hypersensitive young artist expresses intense emotion in lyrics moving from personal feeling to contemporary life to the world of myth. His ecstasy and misery with Lesbia make one of the great love stories in literature. *Dutton $3.95, Lib.*

CICERO, MARCUS TULLIUS 106–43 B.C. *Selected Works*. Essays on philosophy and rhetoric, forceful orations, and revealing personal letters, written by a Roman equally active in politics and literature. *Evman-h, ML.*

EPICTETUS c. A.D. 55–135 *Moral Discourses*. Once a slave, later a government secretary under two emperors, Epictetus became one of the foremost teachers of Stoicism. His writings reveal a saintly man interested in practical philosophy. *CoE, Evman-h, Loeb 2 vols.*

HORACE (QUINTUS HORATIUS FLACCUS) 65–8 B.C. *Poems*. Polished lyrics, sophisticated satires, and poetic essays by one who belonged to the court circle but retained independence of mind. His name is synonymous with urbanity and wit. *Evman-h, Loeb, ML, Phoen, SM 3 vols.*

JUVENAL (DECIMUS JUNIUS JUVENALIS) c. A.D. 60–140 *Satires*. Bitter, realistic attacks on vices, abuses, and follies of imperial Rome by an idealist driven to indignation. *Cambridge Univ. $2.50, Evman-h, Ind, Loeb.*

LIVY (TITUS LIVIUS) 59 B.C.–A.D. 17 *History of Rome*. Picturesque account of the growth of the Roman state from the earliest times, emphasizing that the decline of moral values in his time would cause its downfall. *Evman-h 3 vols. o.p., Loeb 13 vols.*

LUCRETIUS (TITUS LUCRETIUS CARUS) c. 94–55 B.C. *On the Nature of Things*. Philosophic poem presenting materialistic Epicureanism as the cure of superstition and human folly; shows how the ancients anticipated such modern concepts as the atomic theory, the conservation of matter, evolution, and the survival of the fittest. *Oxford Univ. $3, Evman, EvmanNA, Loeb, Pen.*

MARCUS AURELIUS ANTONINUS A.D. 121–180 *Meditations*. An emperor and Stoic philosopher records his thoughts as he struggles for composure and order in the face of national disaster and constant enemy pressure upon the frontiers of the Empire. *CoE, Evman-h, Gate, Loeb, WoC.*

MARTIAL (MARCUS VALERIUS MARTIALIS) c. A.D. 40–104 *Epigrams*. Witty, ribald, tender poems by a Spaniard who keenly observed the range of Roman society from garret to imperial court. *Cambridge Univ. $2.75, Loeb 2 vols.*

OVID (PUBLIUS OVIDIUS NASO) 43 B.C.–A.D. 17 *The Art of Love.*
Playful, risqué verses on the devices of love, full of charm and
humor. *Black, Evman-h, Ind, Loeb, UL.*

_____ *Metamorphoses.* Tales of miraculous transformations by
one of the most versatile narrative poets; its broad coverage of
Greek and Roman myth has made it a most influential source
book. The Humphries translation *(Ind),* is first-rate. Others:
Evman-h (abr.), Loeb 2 vols, NAL, Pen.

PETRONIUS, GAIUS d. A.D. 66 *The Satyricon.* Picaresque novel
about the adventures of three rascals, incorporating social and
literary criticism. This hilarious satire also provides important
information about everyday life and, incidentally, about colloquial Latin. The Arrowsmith translation is recommended
(NAL). Others: *Black, Loeb.*

PLAUTUS, TITUS MACCIUS c. 251–184 B.C. *Comedies.* Amusing
farces about tricky servants, young wastrels, braggart soldiers,
courtesans, etc. See *The Complete Roman Drama.* Also *LLA-
Lib (3 plays), Loeb 5 vols.*

PLUTARCH *Lives.* Notable Romans like Romulus, Coriolanus,
Cato, Pompey, Caesar, Cicero, and Antony sketched by a Greek
biographer for pleasure and moral instruction, with many vivid
anecdotes. See page 28.

SENECA, LUCIUS ANNAEUS c. 5 B.C.–A.D. 65 *Works.* Letters and
essays applying Stoic thought to perennial human problems
and conditions of Roman life; melodramas portraying intense
emotion and violence. *Loeb 8 vols.* See also *The Complete
Roman Drama.* Also *Lib (3 plays).*

SUETONIUS, GAIUS TRANQUILLUS c. A.D. 69–140 *Lives of the
Twelve Caesars.* Lively muckraking accounts of the Roman
emperors by a skilled biographer but often injudicious historian. *Loeb 2 vols., ML, Pen.*

TACITUS, CORNELIUS c. A.D. 55–117 *Works.* History of the Roman Empire to A.D. 70 and of Roman occupation in Britain
and Gaul, written from a republican bias, exhibiting ironical
insight as well as literary talent. *ML, Pen.*

TERENCE (PUBLIUS TERENTIUS AFER) c. 195–159 B.C.
Comedies. See *The Complete Roman Drama.* Also *Lib (2 plays),
Loeb 2 vols.*

VERGIL (PUBLIUS VERGILIUS MARO) 70–19 B.C. *Aeneid.* This
great national epic glorifies the historical tradition and cultural
mission of Rome. *Houghton Mifflin $2.48, Anch, Evman-h,
ML, MLCE, Pen, Rine, Scrib, SM (2 trans.), WoC.*

_____ *Eclogues.* Ten pastoral poems blend natural beauty and
the political scene. *Evman-h, MLCE, Pen, WoC.*

_____ *Georgics.* Four books on "tillage, trees, cattle, bees" written by one who knew farming firsthand and respected its rigors
and rewards. *Chicago Univ. $3.75, Evman-h, MLCE, WoC.*

VITRUVIUS POLLIO, MARCUS c. 85–26 B.C. *On Architecture.*
A unique record of Greek and Roman city planning, engineering, and construction of private and public buildings. *Loeb
2 vols.*

B. Books About Rome

BARROW, R. H. 1893– *The Romans* (1949). Clear sketch of their traits, history, achievements, and contributions to modern times. *Pen.*

BRYHER *(pseud.) Roman Wall* (1954). Skillful fictional portrait of the Helvetians warring against the Romans in the 3rd century A.D. *Pantheon $2.75.*

BULWER-LYTTON, EDWARD 1803–1873 *The Last Days of Pompeii* (1834). A colorful historical romance about the life that perished beneath the ashes of Vesuvius. *Evman-h, GtIl, Nel.*

COWELL, F. R. 1897– *Cicero and the Roman Republic* (1948). A substantial book which uses Cicero as the focus for portraying the development and nature of the Republic. *Pen.*

DE BURGH, W. G. 1866–1943 *The Legacy of the Ancient World* (1947). Comprehensive treatment of our cultural legacy from the Hebrews, Greeks, and Romans. *Pen 2 vols.*

DUGGAN, ALFRED 1903– *Winter Quarters* (1956). Competent historical novel concerning the experiences of two Gallic nobles serving in the Roman army. *Coward-McCann $3.75.*

DURANT, WILL 1885– *Caesar and Christ* (1944). Well-informed cultural history of Rome and Christianity from their beginnings to A.D. 325. *Simon & Schuster $7.50.*

GIBBON, EDWARD 1737–1794 *The Decline and Fall of the Roman Empire* (1776–1778). Masterful work of great analytical power which has become a historical classic. *Evman-h 6 vols., MLG 3 vols., Torch (selected chapters), Vik (abr.), Vik-h (abr.).*

GRAVES, ROBERT 1895– *I, Claudius* (1934). Fictional autobiography of a strange emperor, which makes excellent use of the historical sources. *ML.*

HADAS, MOSES 1900– *A History of Rome* (1956). Short, readable. *Anch.*

HAMILTON, EDITH 1867– *Mythology* (1942). See page 29.

———— *The Roman Way* (1932). A readable portrayal of Rome and the Romans during four centuries. *Norton $3.50, NAL.*

HIGHET, GILBERT 1906– *The Classical Tradition* (1949). Authoritative, engaging analysis of classical influences upon Western literature. *Oxford Univ. $7.50, GB.*

KOESTLER, ARTHUR 1905– *The Gladiators* (1939). The revolt of slaves, farmers, and gladiators under Spartacus realistically recreated in a historical novel. *Macmillan $3.75.*

MACKENDRICK, PAUL 1914– *The Roman Mind at Work* (1958). Identifies Roman attitudes and qualities, and illustrates them with translated readings from Greek and Latin sources. *Anv.*

PATER, WALTER H. 1839–1894 *Marius the Epicurean* (1885). Many-sided picture of Roman life and thought in the 2nd century A.D. as seen by a young patrician. *Evman-h.*

RADIN, MAX 1880–1950 *Epicurus My Master* (1949). The imaginary but soundly conceived memoirs of Atticus, a refined Epicurean friend of Cicero. *Univ. of North Carolina $2.75.*

RENAN, ERNEST 1823–1892 *The Life of Jesus* (1863). A moving, skeptical portrayal of the Great Teacher against the background of Roman Judaea. *Evman-h, ML.*

SIENKIEWICZ, HENRYK 1846–1916 *Quo Vadis?* (1896). Melodramatic tale of the burning of Nero's city, gladiatorial combats, and Christian martyrdom which distorts the picture of Rome in a manner made familiar by Hollywood. *Grosset $1.98, Little, Brown $5, Evman-h, GtIl, Nel.*

WALLACE, LEW 1827–1905 *Ben Hur, A Tale of the Christ* (1880). Charioteers in mad races, galley slaves chained to their oars, proud and profligate aristocrats. *Ban, Dell (abr.), NAL.*

WILDER, THORNTON 1897– *The Ides of March* (1948). The assassination of Julius Caesar brought to life through imaginary letters and documents. *Harp, UL.*

YOURCENAR, MARGUERITE *Hadrian's Memoirs* (1954). Brilliant recreation of an intelligent emperor's reflections on the world of his time. *Farrar, Straus & Cudahy $4, Anch.*

3. The Middle Ages

JULES ALAN WEIN, *Pratt Institute*

The thousand years of the Middle Ages are convention-
ally dated from the fall of Rome in the 5th century to
the fall of Constantinople (Istanbul) in the 15th. The
first half of this period, often called the Dark Ages, used
to be regarded as a "long Gothic midnight," because the
Europe-wide organization of the Roman Empire had
disintegrated and because we inherit from those five
centuries few noteworthy architectural monuments and
relatively little of value in art and literature.

But nowadays we realize that the so-called Dark Ages
were not a blackout of civilization, but a long period of
incubation during which a fusion of classical and "bar-
barian" cultures prepared the way for the great achievements of the later Middle Ages. Greco-Roman society
was dying of its own defects long before the incursion of
alien peoples administered the *coup de grâce*. It was
those vigorous and independent peoples, aided by a store
of classical knowledge preserved in monasteries and in
daily productive work, who created the basis for social
progress far beyond the capability of the ancient world.
Not least among their organizational accomplishments
was the replacement of the defunct international system
of the Roman Empire by the international structure and
ideology of the Roman Church.

Some of the notable literature of the five centuries of
incubation—such as Augustine's *City of God* and Boethius's *Consolation of Philosophy*—drew inspiration from
Plato and the Greco-Roman past, interwoven with the
doctrines of Christianity. Other literary documents—such
as *Beowulf, The Song of Roland,* the legends of King
Arthur, and numerous Norse, Icelandic, and Teutonic
sagas, eddas, and lieder, chanted by scops, bards, min-
strels—reflect the injection into the old culture of new
peoples with new values and a characteristic cult: glorification of the conquering hero.

The medieval tales of most appeal to the modern reader are the Icelandic and Norse sagas, especially the *Njal Saga*, the *Heimskringla*, and, of course, the Old English *Beowulf*. They present with vivid realism and narrative skill the seafaring adventures, family feuds, personal duels, and political history of the Scandinavian peoples from the 9th to the 12th century.

The later Middle Ages witnessed the full development of feudalism, the gallantry and sordidness of the Crusades, the struggle between popes and emperors for control of Christendom, the fragmentation of the West into segments approaching nationhood, the formation of modern European languages, and the economic progress that provided material basis for the Renaissance. This is the great period of theological philosophy, of religious art and architecture, of chivalric romance, and of the troubadour poetry and religious idealism that found their consummation in Dante's *Divine Comedy*.

The subject of the *Divine Comedy* is the Christian drama of sin and redemption, of that salvation to which man is led by his love for woman, his Reason, and God's Revelation. Christian in inspiration and form, it speaks to all men in the magnificence of its poetry and the universality of its human insight. Here, and (in miniature) in *The Pearl*, a 14th-century English poem, are movingly recorded medieval man's noblest aspirations.

Medieval readers had large appetite for miscellaneous information along with their stories. Like the encyclopedic *Divine Comedy*, many of Chaucer's poems abound in information. But this serves only to enrich the effect of Chaucer's imaginative power in works like *Troilus and Criseyde* (a superb psychological narrative poem adapted from Boccaccio's *Filostrato*) and the incomparable *Canterbury Tales*, with its brilliant portraiture, lusty realism, and healthy humor. Chaucer was an avid reader and liked to share his harvest. In fact, he claimed to have learned about love by reading old books of romance rather than by experience. Read "The Friar's Tale" and the whole account of the Wife of Bath, and see if you believe him.

Boccaccio, in mid-14th-century Italy, was a transitional figure—an inheritor of the Middle Ages and a shaper of

the Renaissance. Poet and author, classical scholar and
social philosopher, he wrote in almost every literary form
available and invented others, including the psychological
novel (the autobiographical *La Fiammetta*). But he is
best known for the *Decameron,* a masterpiece of literary
art. In form the *Decameron* is a typically medieval collection of short stories, but in substance it embodies a
penetrating critique of medieval values and institutions.
Though the *Decameron* is most famous for its tales of
illicit love, some amusing and some tragic, less than a
third of its hundred stories deal with sex relations, and
even these are integral to the social and philosophical
themes of the work as a whole.

As Boccaccio created the realistic prose fiction of the
Renaissance, so his older contemporary, friend, and mentor, Petrarch, set the pattern for Renaissance love poetry.
Emulating Dante's literary passion for Beatrice, Petrarch
produced, in the *Sonnets* to Laura, one of the greatest
lyrical sequences in the long tradition that culminated in
Shakespeare's sonnets. His place is also secure in intellectual history, for if any individual can be styled the
"father" of the Renaissance, Petrarch is the man. A tire-
less scholar, writer, and searcher for ancient manuscripts,
he led and inspired the generations of humanists who
recovered classical letters for the modern world.

But perhaps the medieval poet who speaks to us with
the most modern accent is François Villon, vagabond-
poet of 15th-century Paris. Read about his life and works
in D. B. Wyndham Lewis's fascinating biography, and
you will find a timeless, ageless character who is yet an
epitome of the medieval temper, with its strange mixture
of love-gallantry and religious ribaldry, of piety and gay
wit, of gusto in sinning and lust for repentance. The side
of the Middle Ages that Henry Adams omits from his
Mont-Saint-Michel and Chartres (greatest single American book on the Middle Ages) you will find in Villon.
Like Petrarch, Boccaccio, and Chaucer, this French poet
had one foot in the future. So did the earnest English
cleric who wrote *Piers Plowman.* In his search for truth
and justice, Langland's *Piers* is a symbol of man's eternal
yearning for a social order in which to live a life fit for
man. And that is still the search of the modern world.

A. Medieval Literature

The Age of Belief (1954). Ed. by Anne Fremantle. Excerpts from the medieval philosophers from Augustine to Ockham, with lucid commentary by the editor. *Houghton Mifflin $3, NAL.*

The Arabian Nights (8th to 15th century). Colorful tales of adventure, intrigue, and magic. See page 75.

Aucassin and Nicolette, and Other Medieval Romances (13th to 16th century). Delightful stories of love and adventure in the days of the troubadours. *Evman, EvmanNA.*

AUGUSTINE, SAINT *The City of God* and *Confessions.* Influential early Christian writings. See page 33.

Beowulf (8th century). Anglo-Saxon epic of the heroic deeds of a legendary hero. *Appleton-Century Crofts $1.75, Barnes & Noble $2.75, Cambridge Univ. (in prep.), Oxford Univ. $3.50, Pen.*

BOCCACCIO, GIOVANNI 1313–1375 *Decameron* (c. 1348–53). A lusty age and a philosophy of life brilliantly delineated in 100 tales of love, intrigue, and adventure. *Black, CoE, Gar, Evman-h 2 vols., Liv, ML, PB (abr.).*

BOETHIUS *The Consolation of Philosophy.* The last great pagan ponders life's meaning. See page 34.

Burnt Njal Saga. Realistic, grimly humorous story of a 12th-century Icelandic judge who could rule the republic by his justice, but could not keep his wife from feuding with beautiful neighbor Hallgerda, to Njal's undoing. *Evman o.p.*

CHAUCER, GEOFFREY 1340?–1400 *The Canterbury Tales* (1387–1400). Medieval English life and thought entertainingly compounded in stories touched with wit, pathos, common sense, and superb literary art. *Evman-h, ML, ModSL, WoC.* For excellent versions in modern English, see the translations by J. U. Nicolson *(Gar)*, Nevill Coghill *(Pen)*, and R. Lumiansky *(Rine)*. V. F. Hopper has done an interlinear translation *(BES).*

————— *The Portable Chaucer.* Contains selections from *The Canterbury Tales, Troilus and Criseyde* (a "psychological novel in verse"), shorter poems, and selections from other long poems in modern translations. *Vik, Vik-h.*

DANTE ALIGHIERI 1265–1321 *The Divine Comedy* (1300–21). An epic journey through Hell, Purgatory, and Paradise, the poem is a compendium of medieval Catholic philosophy and religion, embraced in a timeless love story. *Evman-h, ML, MLCE, MLP, OxA, Pen, Rine, Vik, Vik-h, WoC.* The translation of the "Inferno" ("Hell") by John Ciardi is particularly good *(NAL).*

English Drama before Shakespeare. Famous medieval miracle plays and interludes, variously anthologized and titled by different publishers. *Evman, Evman-h, Rine.*

FRANCIS OF ASSISI, SAINT 1182–1226 *The Little Flowers.* A beautiful record of the kind hearts of "Il Poverello" and his friends. *British Book Centre $1.50, CoE, Evman, EvmanNA, Pen, WoC.*

FROISSART, JEAN 1333?-1400? *Chronicles of England, France, and Spain* (1373-90). The classic contemporary history of the first half of the Hundred Years War. *Evman o.p.*

GEOFFROY DE VILLEHARDOUIN 1160?-1212? and JEAN DE JOINVILLE 1224?-1317? *Memoirs of the Crusades* (c. 1207 and 1309). Vivid and fascinating firsthand accounts of the 4th and 7th Crusades. *Evman, Evman-h.*

GEOFFREY OF MONMOUTH 1100?-1154 *Histories of the Kings of Britain* (c. 1136). Idealized, often imaginary, history that underlies much of Arthurian romance. *Evman.*

LANGLAND, WILLIAM 1332?-1400? *Piers Plowman.* A powerful social protest in vigorous verse. *Oxford Univ. $1 & $2.25, Evman-h, Pen.*

MALORY, SIR THOMAS 1430?-1471 *Le Morte d'Arthur* (1485). Sometimes lusty, sometimes idealized picture of chivalric combat and courtly love. *Appleton-Century-Crofts $1.75, Evman-h 2 vols., Rine (abr.).*

MANDEVILLE, SIR JOHN d. 1372 *Travels* (1371). An enjoyable compound of geographical facts and legendary marvels. *Evman.*

Medieval Latin Poetry. Delightful verse translations of medieval songs and satires are presented in two sound scholarly anthologies: HELEN WADDELL 1889- *Mediaeval Latin Lyrics* (1929), *Barnes & Noble $3;* and GEORGE F. WHICHER 1889-1954 *The Goliard Poets* (1949), *New Directions $7.50.*

Medieval Philosophers, Selections from (1930). Two volumes of selections from Augustine to Ockham, with introductions by Richard McKeon. *ModSL 2 vols.*

Medieval Reader, The Portable (1949). Ed. by James B. Ross and Mary M. McLaughlin. The world of the Middle Ages in 690 pages of selections from biography, history, science, theology, and poetry. *Vik, Vik-h.*

MOHAMMED *The Koran.* The scriptures of Islam. See page 76.

OMAR KHAYYAM *Rubaiyat.* Pleasant Persian skepticism. See page 76.

PETRARCH (FRANCESCO PETRARCA) 1304-1374 *Sonnets and Songs.* Justly admired for centuries as the first great poet of romantic love. *O.p.*

POLO, MARCO 1254?-1324? *Travels* (1300-24). Colorful autobiographical account of the adventures of a Venetian merchant who visited the countries of the great Kublai Khan. *Black, Evman-h, ML, Pen.*

The Romance of Tristan and Iseult (12th century). The great medieval legend of tragic love. *Columbia Univ. $3.50, Anch.*

THOMAS A KEMPIS 1380-1471 *The Imitation of Christ* (c. 1471). A famous devotional work reflecting the ideals of the medieval church. *British Book Centre $1.50, Bruce $1.50, Grosset $1, Harper $2, McKay $1, Macmillan $2.50, Newman $2.50, Sheed $2, Winston $1.50, CoNC, Evman-h, Im, NAL, Nel, PB, Pen, WoC.*

THOMAS AQUINAS, SAINT 1225?–1274 *Writings.* The greatest
Catholic philosopher and theologian writes about God, man,
and man's pursuit of his destiny. *Random House 2 vols. $10,
EvmanNA, ML.*

————— *On the Truth of the Catholic Faith.* A new translation of
the *Summa Contra Gentiles,* classic manual of Christian doctrine. *Im 4 vols.*

VILLON, FRANÇOIS 1431–1463? *Poems.* The singing rogue of old
Paris. *Ban, Black.*

B. Books About the Middle Ages

ADAMS, HENRY 1838–1918 *Mont-Saint-Michel and Chartres* (1904).
Penetrating, sensitive analysis of the medieval spirit in architecture and literature. *Houghton Mifflin $6, Anch.*

The Age of Chaucer (1954). Ed. by Boris Ford. Vol. 1 of *The Pelican
Guide to English Literature,* containing short essays on the
literature of the period and an excellent anthology of the poems
and plays. *Pen.*

ANOUILH, JEAN 1910– *The Lark.* A thoughtful dramatic treatment of St. Joan, to be compared with Shaw's version. Trans.
by Christopher Fry, *Oxford Univ. $3;* adapted by Lillian Hell-
man, *Random House $2.95.*

BALZAC, HONORE DE 1799–1850 *Droll Stories* (1837). Imitations
of the broadly humorous fabliaux popular in the Middle Ages.
Black, ML.

CHUTE, MARCHETTE 1909– *Geoffrey Chaucer of England*
(1946). Delightful and meaty introduction to the poet and his
time, with illuminating analyses of his major poems. *Dutton
$5, Evman.*

COULTON, G. G. 1858–1947 *Medieval Panorama* (1947). Richly detailed survey of the English scene from the Norman Conquest
to the Reformation. *Cambridge Univ. $6.50, Mer.*

DURANT, WILL 1885– *The Age of Faith* (1950). Clear, vivid
history of 1000 years of medieval civilization–Christian, Judaic,
and Islamic–written for the general public. *Simon & Schuster
$7.50.*

HUGO *The Hunchback of Notre Dame.* Masterful historical novel
set in 15th-century Paris. See page 91.

KELLY, AMY 1878– *Eleanor of Aquitaine and the Four Kings*
(1950). Wife of Louis VII of France and Henry II of England,
mother of Richard the Lion-Hearted and King John, Eleanor
made history as a mistress of political intrigue. First-rate biography and history. *Harvard Univ. $5.50, Vin.*

KOSSAK, ZOFIA 1890– *Blessed Are the Meek* (1944). A moving
novel based on the Children's Crusade, with St. Francis of
Assisi as a central character. *Roy $3.*

LAMB, HAROLD 1892– *Charlemagne* (1954). One of the world's greatest kings and conquerors brought to life in a striking biography. *Doubleday $4.50, Ban.*

_____ *The Crusades.* One-volume edition combining *Iron Men and Saints* (1930), the best popular account of the First Crusade, and *The Flame of Islam* (1931), the story of 150 years of struggle for supremacy between the Saracens and the West. *Doubleday $6.*

LEFF, GORDON 1926– *Medieval Thought from St. Augustine to Ockham* (1958). Concise survey of the philosophers and philosophies of the Middle Ages. *Pen.*

LEWIS, D. B. WYNDHAM 1894– *François Villon* (1928). A fascinating biography of the great 14th-century vagabond-poet, with generous selections from his poetry. *Anch.*

MOORE, GEORGE 1852–1933 *Héloïse and Abélard* (1921). Fictionized version of a famous medieval love affair. *Tudor $3.50.*

MUNTZ, HOPE *The Golden Warrior* (1950). A distinguished and beautiful novel about Harold, last of the Saxon kings, and his gallant fight against William the Conqueror. *Scribner $3.95, ModSA.*

PAINTER, SIDNEY 1902– *Mediaeval Society* (1951). The complex system of medieval life lucidly summarized in a short essay. *Cornell Univ. $1.25.*

PIRENNE, HENRI 1862–1935 *Economic and Social History of Medieval Europe* (1937). Clear and penetrating; a rapid sketch but a classic in its field. *Harv.*

_____ *Mohammed and Charlemagne* (1939). The history of the Mediterranean world from the 5th to the 9th century, in concise and creative analysis. *Barnes & Noble $3.50, Mer.*

POWER, EILEEN 1889–1940 *Medieval People* (1924). Fine scholarship and stylistic grace recreate six medieval lives in memorable fashion. *Anch.*

READE, CHARLES 1814–1884 *The Cloister and the Hearth* (1861). Vigorous, realistic novel set in Flanders, France, Germany, and Italy toward the end of the Middle Ages. *CoNC, Evman-h, GtIl, ML, Nel, SM.*

SCOTT, SIR WALTER 1771–1832 *Ivanhoe* (1819). Romance of Old England, with Richard the Lion-Hearted, Robin Hood, tournaments, love, and robber barons. *CoNC, Evman-h, GtIl, MLG, (with Quentin Durward), Nel, PB, RivEd.*

_____ *Quentin Durward* (1823). A young Scottish adventurer in France wins the king's favor and a bride. *CoNC, Evman-h, GtIl, MLG, Nel.*

SHAKESPEARE *Henry IV, Henry V, Macbeth, Richard II, Richard III, King John.* These great historical dramas reflect the glories and crudities of feudal times. See page 54.

SHAW, GEORGE BERNARD 1856–1950 *Saint Joan* (1923). A modern chronicle play with Jeanne d'Arc as its heroine. *ML, Pen.*

TAYLOR, HENRY OSBORN 1856–1941 *The Mediaeval Mind* (4th ed. 1925). The standard scholarly exposition of medieval intellectual history. *Harvard Univ. 2 vols. $15.*

UNDSET, SIGRID 1882–1949 *Kristin Lavransdatter* (1920–2). A trilogy of medieval Scandinavia: the passion of Kristin's bridal wreath, the tragedy of her married life at Husaby, and the cross she bore to the end. *Knopf $5.75.*

VALENCY, MAURICE 1903– *In Praise of Love* (1958). A brilliant analysis of the poetic tradition of the troubadours in its historical, social, and psychological setting. *Macmillan $6.50.*

VOSSLER, KARL 1872–1949 *Mediaeval Culture: An Introduction to Dante and His Times* (1929). Definitive study of the religious, philosophical, political, and literary background of Dante's poetry, with analysis of *The Divine Comedy*. An education in itself. *Ungar 2 vols. $9.*

WADDELL, HELEN 1889– *Peter Abelard* (1933). A scholarly yet graceful romance stressing the theological aspects of a haunting medieval tragedy of love. *Comp.*

———— *The Wandering Scholars* (1927). The life and art of the lyric poets of the Latin Middle Ages, with selections from the poetry in the original and in charming translations. *Barnes & Noble $3, Anch.*

4. The Renaissance

ON THE CONTINENT

LOUIS C. ZUCKER, *University of Utah*

The Renaissance nurtured the seeds of our modern culture: our art, our science, our literature. During the Middle Ages the great painters had been committed to religious symbolism: Madonna and Child, Descent from the Cross, saints and saints and saints again, rendered with pious zeal. In the Renaissance, the artists became absorbed with this world rather than the next, with humanity rather than divinity. They rediscovered what the Greeks had known and enjoyed: the eloquence of the human body and the deep delights of nature. As a result, in the painting which reached a climax with da Vinci, Michelangelo, Raphael, and Titian (even when they dealt with stock religious subjects) we find a passion for the magnificent textures of the world about them and for the beauty of mankind. Like Shakespeare's Miranda, they seem to cry:

> How beauteous mankind is! O brave new world
> That has such people in't!

Fortunately for us, several of the greatest Renaissance artists were also writers. Cellini's *Autobiography* is perhaps the best single record of the virtù—the bold self-assertiveness of the period. Da Vinci's *Notebooks* with their fascinating drawings show the proverbial yet incredible range of Renaissance genius. And a lesser artist of the period, Vasari, gives us in his *Lives of the Painters* an intimate, gossipy glimpse into the lives of the great men who wrought the new beauty.

As in art, so in science. Heroic navigators—Vasco da Gama, Columbus, Vespucci, Magellan—opened new horizons on earth and in the minds of men; they were rapidly followed by that astonishing swarm of explorers and colonizers who opened the continent on which we live. Similarly, Copernicus and Galileo discovered new vistas in the heavens. Da Vinci and Vesalius pioneered the new science of anatomy, helping men to learn more about their bodies and hence about themselves. All these discoveries might have been largely wasted but for one Renaissance craftsman, Gutenberg, who invented the art of printing from movable type. From 1475 to 1500 ten thousand editions of books poured from the presses in Italy alone. For most people, without printing there would have been no books to read; mass education and modern democracy would have remained the most visionary of dreams. Altogether, Renaissance science was profound in its effects and magnificent in its scope, embracing the heavens, earth, and man.

The Renaissance was speeded by the revival of ancient culture. But, like its art and science, its literature arose from that extraordinary release of creative energy which thrilled first through Italy, later through France, Spain, England, and beyond.

Consider, for instance, what lies behind such modern phrases as "a Machiavellian schemer" and "a Rabelaisian wit." The first phrase reflects the fame of a Florentine statesman, Niccolò Machiavelli, whose brief volume *The Prince* is surely the most perceptive analysis ever written of the methods of power politics. Almost simultaneously, the counterpart of *The Prince,* More's *Utopia,* projected the soaring Renaissance dreams of social perfection.

The phrase "a Rabelaisian wit" recalls the unique comic genius of a Renaissance Frenchman, François Rabelais. A physician and an irrepressible jester, Rabelais had his joke even in his will, which reads: "I owe much; I have nothing; I give the rest to the poor." His *Gargantua* and *Pantagruel* are the meaningfullest and tallest tall tales in literature. Rabelais was the earthiest writer of an earthy age: fanciful word inventions, ribald jests, and lusty adventures poured from him in a torrent, while he was hugely amused by the body's appetites and functions.

Meanwhile Montaigne, Rabelais's younger and more

urbane contemporary, set forth in his *Essays* a timeless appraisal of men, morals, and manners. Except for Shakespeare, no man of his age plumbed human motives more cannily. "Others form man," Montaigne wrote; "I only report him." And he reported himself with a poise and veracity that make him still the delight of adults the world over. To Montaigne, a balanced skepticism guided by the great pagan classics was the way to learn about and enjoy life. Though a conforming Catholic, he doubted that any philosopher or theologian had found ultimate truth.

To see man through the eyes of a Michelangelo or a da Vinci; to pierce the uncharted seas with Columbus; to explore the universe with Copernicus or Galileo; to meet Rabelais and Montaigne face to face—this is to sample the range, the depth, the brilliance, of the Renaissance. In its creative energies set free we mark for the first time in history the limitless potentialities of the modern mind.

A. Continental Renaissance Literature

CASTIGLIONE, BALDASSARE 1478–1529 *The Courtier* (1528). Delineates the Renaissance ideal man, in spirited dialogue and story. *Scribner $2* (bound with *The Prince* and *Utopia*), *Anch, Evman-h, Ungar.*

CELLINI, BENVENUTO 1500–1571 *Autobiography* (first pr. 1728). A vivid portrayal of an unscrupulous genius. Entertaining sidelights on popes, nobles, kings, and artists. *Ban, Black, Evman-h, ML, Pen, WoC.*

CERVANTES *Don Quixote.* A great novel, ranging from farce to philosophy. See page 60.

DA VINCI, LEONARDO 1452–1519 *The Notebooks.* Text and drawings mirror Leonardo's comprehensive genius as painter, sculptor, architect, engineer, inventor. *Braziller $7.50, ML* (abr.).

ERASMUS, DESIDERIUS 1466–1536 *In Praise of Folly* (1512). Witty satire of monkish superstitions, theological squabbling, learned ignorance, war, and other human vagaries by a great humanist. *Hendricks $1.75, Princeton Univ. $3.75, AA, WL.*

Famous Utopias of the Renaissance (1946). Ed. by Frederick R. White. Presenting with brief but helpful notes MORE'S *Utopia* (1516), RABELAIS'S "Abbey of Thélème" from *Gargantua* (1535), CAMPANELLA'S *City of the Sun* (1623), and BACON'S *New Atlantis* (1676). *Hendricks $2.*

MACHIAVELLI, NICCOLO 1469–1527 *The Prince* (1513). Assumes a deep, unvarying self-interest as the core of human nature. A realistic manual of methods followed by Renaissance despots.

Hendricks $2, Scribner $2, Cro, Evman-h, Gate, ML, MLCE, NAL, WoC.

MONTAIGNE, MICHEL DE 1533–1592 *Essays* (1580, 1588). Delightful, rambling, richly urbane discourses on men, manners, morals, and books. Complete: *Knopf 3 vols. $15, Oxford Univ. $3.50, Stanford Univ. $5.75.* Selections: *Harper $1.75, Van Nostrand $1.35, Cro, ML, NAL, PB, Pen.*

PETRARCH *Sonnets and Songs.* See page 42.

RABELAIS, FRANÇOIS 1494?–1553 *Gargantua* (1535) and *Pantagruel* (1533). The fabulous giant-heroes fight, eat, drink, jest lustily; but their saga includes the learning and the expansive humor of Renaissance France. *Evman-h 2 vols., MLG, Pen, Vik (abr.), Vik-h (abr.).*

Renaissance Reader, The Portable (1953). Ed. by James B. Ross and Mary M. McLaughlin. The Continental Renaissance in 756 pages, chosen to represent all the writings of that teeming time. *Vik, Vik-h.*

VASARI, GIORGIO 1511–1574 *The Lives of the Painters* (1550). Lively anecdotal accounts of the great Italian artists, by a contemporary. *Noon (abr.).*

B. Books About the Continental Renaissance

BERENSON, BERNARD 1865–1959 *Italian Painters of the Renaissance* (1932). Essays on the Venetian, Florentine, Central Italian, and North Italian painters. *Doubleday $8.50, Oxford Univ. $3.40, Mer.*

BURCKHARDT, JACOB 1818–1897 *The Civilization of the Renaissance in Italy* (1860). Pioneer yet still definitive work on the cultural history of the period. *Doubleday $2.95, Torch 2 vols., ML.*

CORVO, FREDERICK, BARON (*pseud.*) 1860–1913 *History of the Borgias* (1901). The story of a powerful and wicked family, told in a style at once brilliant and exciting. *ML.*

DURANT, WILL 1885– *The Renaissance* (1953). A panorama of our Renaissance heritage and of the men who made it, stressing Italy and its art. *Simon & Schuster $7.50.*

ELIOT, GEORGE 1819–1880 *Romola* (1863). A novel portraying moral deterioration and picturing 16th-century Florence. *Evman-h, WoC.*

LAMB, HAROLD 1892– *Suleiman the Magnificent* (1951). Biography of the 16th-century ruler of the Ottoman Empire, called "The Lawgiver" by his own people. *Doubleday $5.*

LUCAS, HENRY S. 1889– *The Renaissance and the Reformation* (1934). Dependable summary of this most significant period of history. *Harper $6.*

MADARIAGA, SALVADOR DE 1886– *The Heart of Jade* (1944). A colorful tapestry of 16th-century Spaniards and Aztecs. *Farrar, Straus & Cudahy o.p.*

MATTHEWS, GEORGE T. 1917– (ed.) *News and Rumor in Renais-*

sance Europe (The Fugger Newsletters) (1958). About the great German family of merchant princes, the richest family in Renaissance Europe. *Cap.*

MATTINGLY, GARRETT (1900–) *The Armada* (1959). A masterful piece of historical writing, as readable as a novel, about the Spanish effort to invade Elizabethan England. *Houghton Mifflin $6.*

MEREJKOWSKI, DMITRI 1865–1941 *The Romance of Leonardo da Vinci* (1902). A brilliant imaginative portrait of da Vinci and a panoramic pageant of his times. *Heritage $3.95, ML.*

MORISON, SAMUEL ELIOT 1887– *Admiral of the Ocean Sea* (1942). Scholarly but very readable biography of Columbus, stressing his practical seamanship. *Little, Brown $8.50.* Revised edition published as *Christopher Columbus, Mariner. NAL.*

MOTLEY, JOHN L. 1814–1877 *The Rise of the Dutch Republic* (1856). A brilliant history of the Netherlands from 1555 to 1584. *Evman-h 3 vols., WoC.*

PANOFSKY, ERWIN 1892– *Meaning in the Visual Arts* (1955). Describes life and art during the later Middle Ages and the Renaissance. Sound and stimulating. *Peter Smith $3.50, Anch.*

PATER, WALTER 1839–1894 *The Renaissance* (1873). Deeply felt impressions of a great era by a great critic. *ML, NAL.*

PRESCOTT, WILLIAM H. 1796–1859 *Conquest of Mexico* (1843) and *Conquest of Peru* (1847). The impact of Renaissance Spain on the New World. *MLG.* Latter alone: *NAL.*

The Renaissance Philosophy of Man (1956). Ed. by Ernst Cassirer *et al.* Selections from the major thinkers of the early Italian Renaissance on the nature of man. *Phoen.*

ROEDER, RALPH 1890– *The Man of the Renaissance* (1933). Aretino with his lust for living; Castiglione, the gentle knight; Machiavelli, shrewd and subtle; Savonarola, puritanical monk—dissected to interpret the era. *Mer.*

SCOTT, GEOFFREY 1885–1929 *The Architecture of Humanism* (1914, 1954). An eloquent vindication of Renaissance architecture based on the styles of Greece and Rome. *Anch.*

SYMONDS, J. A. 1840–1893 *Life of Michelangelo* (1893). A dynamic study of the greatest sculptor between Phidias and Rodin. *ML.*

SYPHER, WYLIE 1905– *Four Stages of Renaissance Style* (1955). Integrating the fine arts and literature, the author describes and interprets their transformations from 1400 to 1700. *Anch.*

WEBER, J. SHERWOOD 1918– *et al. From Homer to Joyce* (1959). Contains guides to the reading of masterworks by Boccaccio, Chaucer, Machiavelli, Rabelais, Montaigne, Shakespeare, and Cervantes. *Holt-Dryden $1.95.*

YOUNG, GEORGE F. 1846–1919 *The Medici* (1910). The Florentine merchant princes and their artists. *ML.*

ZWEIG, STEFAN 1881–1942 *Erasmus of Rotterdam* (1934). Readable, authoritative biography of the great Dutch humanist, the epitome of the Renaissance man of culture. *Comp.*

IN TUDOR ENGLAND

LESLIE M. OLIVER, *Lesley College*

Foremost among the forces that shaped the Renaissance in England were the Tudor monarchs themselves: Henry VII, who ended the Wars of the Roses and founded the Tudor dynasty; Henry VIII, whom we remember for his six wives and his split with Rome, but who in his youth was a humanist of parts and a patron of learning; the sickly child Edward VI; Mary—"Bloody Mary" to many—half Spanish, wholly Catholic; and, of course, Elizabeth, greatest of her family, who ruled England for nearly half a century (1558–1603) and gave her name to its golden age.

It was a time when great things had their beginnings, a time when great things came to climax and fruition. The titanic political and doctrinal struggle between England and the Catholic Church was fought out across the century; the Armada expedition was its last great outward action. It was a time of fierce intolerance and equally fierce loyalties, a time when men died for their beliefs or ate out their hearts in the slow death of exile. The same period saw planted the seeds of the next century's Puritan Revolution, seeds which lay dormant while Elizabeth, the strong-minded compromiser, held the throne.

The Tudor period was also a time of exploration, but not of conquest or settlement. The English, in their handy little ships, were half sea rovers and half pirates. Drake and Hawkins harried the Spanish treasure fleets and "singed the King of Spain's beard" in his own harbors. Drake sailed his little vessel clear around the world. And English seamen in English ships, boldly at bay before the greatest sea power in the world, saw the humbling of the Spanish Armada when "the Lord sent His wind, and they were scattered."

It was a time when men's minds reached eagerly back into the past to seize and use the beauty and wisdom of the ancients; when not only universities but also kings' courts and bishops' palaces were centers of enthusiastic study of Greek and Latin and Hebrew—of what we call the humanities. It was a time when everyone sang: glees, roundelays, madrigals, ballads; a time when English poetry found its voice in the sonnets of Sidney, Daniel, and Shakespeare, in a host of delightful, singable lyrics, and in the mighty blank verse of the Elizabethan playhouse.

Above all, it was a time of the enthusiastic writing of books. Some of them were translations; English scholars freely, almost piratically, turned into English verse and prose whatever of the world's great books they thought they might require: Homer, Seneca, Plutarch, Montaigne. The Bible itself received during this century the essential English form in which we commonly know it today. Some books—Bacon's *Novum Organum* and *The Advancement of Learning,* for instance—boldly ventured into new seas of thought.

Other books were histories; for Englishmen were keenly conscious and fiercely proud of their island, and they wrote chronicles that traced their blood lines back to the Trojans and sang all the glories of their island's past. Of these, Holinshed's *Chronicles* are best known to us because Shakespeare drew on them for his history plays.

But if everything else were forgotten, we would still remember this century in England for its theater. Shakespeare was not a solitary genius, a lone peak rising from a plain, but rather the greatest among the great, the tallest eminence in a range of towering mountains. When the period opened there was already a well-developed native drama, given largely to religious and didactic themes. This expanded into secular fields, enriched by classical and foreign influences, and culminated between 1590 and 1620 in the world's richest and most varied drama.

The Elizabethans were fully aware that they were living in a great age. In the last year of the 16th century, Samuel Daniel made a proud prophecy:

And who in time knows whither we may vent
The treasure of our tongue? To what strange shores
This gain of our best glory shall be sent,
T'enrich unknowing nations with our stores?
What worlds in th' yet unformed Occident
May come refin'd with th' accents that are ours?

A. Tudor Literature

Anthology of English Drama Before Shakespeare (1952). Ed. by Robert B. Heilman. Interesting and representative early plays showing how the drama developed before it reached its climax in Shakespeare. *Rine.*

BACON, FRANCIS 1561–1626 *The Advancement of Learning* (1605). An outline of the inductive system of reasoning, and an argument for adoption of the scientific method. *Evman-h, WoC.*

——————— *Essays* (1597, 1612, 1625). Project a shrewd, practical estimate of human life; Macaulay says these essays have "moved the intellects that have moved the world." Selections: *Houghton Mifflin $2, Odyssey $2.50, Evman-h, Nel, SM, WoC.*

——————— *The New Atlantis* (1624). A utopian vision displaying Bacon's keen interest in the possibilities of science. *Van Nostrand $1.35.*

DONNE, JOHN 1573–1631 *Poems* (1633). First of the so-called metaphysical poets, and still first among English poets in the brainy, sinewy quality of his verse. Don't try to read Donne unless you like to think. *Hendricks $2.50, Macmillan $1.50, Oxford Univ. $1.40, Evman-h, ML, MLG, Nel, OxA, Pen.*

Eight Famous Elizabethan Plays (1932). Ed. by E. C. Dunn. Dramas by MARLOWE, DEKKER, HEYWOOD, JONSON, WEBSTER, BEAUMONT and FLETCHER, MASSINGER, and FORD. No one knows Shakespeare who knows Shakespeare only; these contemporaries, first-rate playwrights by any standard, will add a new dimension to your understanding and appreciation of Shakespeare and of his period. *ML, MLCE.*

Elizabethan Reader, The Portable (1946). Ed. by Hiram Haydn. The best small anthology of Tudor writing. *Vik, Vik-h.*

HAKLUYT, RICHARD 1552–1616 *Voyages* (1598–1600). Selected reports of English voyagers and explorers, real and legendary. Often fascinating reading. *Evman-h 2 vols.*

HOLINSHED, RAPHAEL d. 1580? *Chronicles* (1577, 1586). One of several contemporary histories of England, best known today because Shakespeare used it as a source. *Evman-h.*

JONSON, BEN 1573?–1637 *Plays.* Next to Shakespeare, the best and most interesting of Elizabethan dramatists. His chief plays are *The Alchemist, Every Man in His Humour,* and *Volpone. BES, Drama, Drama-h, Evman-h 2 vols., WoC.*

MARLOWE, CHRISTOPHER 1564–1593 *Plays.* If this brilliant poet-dramatist had lived longer, he might well have been a close second to Shakespeare. *Oxford Univ. $2.80, BES, Drama, Drama-h, EvmanNA, Nel, WoC.*

MORE, SIR THOMAS 1478–1535 *Utopia* (Latin 1516, English 1551). In this satire More pictures an ideal nation founded on liberty, toleration, and public welfare. One of the classic visions of what society might be. *Cambridge Univ. $1.75, Oxford Univ. $1.20, Evman-h.*

NASHE, THOMAS 1567–1601 *The Unfortunate Traveller* (1594). Picaresque forerunner of the modern novel. *Cap, Evman-h, Rine.*

SHAKESPEARE, WILLIAM 1564–1616 *Plays.* The finest drama of the Christian world—infinitely various. Perhaps the most popular plays are *As You Like It, Hamlet, Henry IV, King Lear, Macbeth, A Midsummer Night's Dream, Othello, Romeo and Juliet, The Taming of the Shrew, The Tempest,* and *Twelfth Night. Grosset $3.95, Harper $5.25, Houghton Mifflin $7.50, Oxford Univ. $3, Random House $4.75, Scribner $6, Winston $3.50, Dell, Evman-h 3 vols., Gar, Nel 3 vols., PB 3 vols., Pen, Rine, Vik, Yale.*

——— *Sonnets* (1609). An uneven and puzzling sonnet sequence containing some of the world's finest sonnets and raising several seemingly unanswerable questions about their author and his subjects. Included in most editions of his works listed above.

SIDNEY, SIR PHILIP 1554–1586 *Astrophel and Stella* (1591). The first and perhaps the finest English sonnet sequence. Not now in print, it is worth a trip to the library. His *Defense of Poesy* is a classic of English criticism. *Cambridge Univ. $1.25, SM.*

SPEED, JOHN 1552–1629 *An Atlas of Tudor England and Wales* (1951). Ed. by E. G. R. Taylor. Contains reproductions of 44 plates from Speed's Pocket Atlas of 1627. *Pen.*

SPENSER, EDMUND 1552–1599 *Poems.* The first major English poet after Chaucer. His technical skill and rich imagery have made him the poet's poet. *Cambridge Univ. 2 vols. $1.50 ea., Oxford Univ. 2 vols. $1.15 ea., Evman-h 3 vols., OxA, Rine.*

B. Books About Tudor England

ADAMS, JOSEPH QUINCY 1881–1946 *A Life of William Shakespeare* (1923). Scholarly, compact, lively, and not dated. *Houghton Mifflin $4.75.*

ANDERSON *Elizabeth the Queen* (1930) and *Mary of Scotland* (1934). Poetic dramas about two extraordinary women. See page 152.

BINDOFF, S. T. 1908– *Tudor England* (1950). Readable and informative history of the period, "with the politics put in." *Pen.*

BRADLEY, A. C. 1851–1935 *Shakespearean Tragedy* (1904). Extremely thorough and helpful studies of *Hamlet, Othello, Lear,* and *Macbeth. Mer.*

CHAMBERS, E. K. 1866–1954 *Shakespeare, A Survey* (1925). A great Elizabethan scholar wrote these essays as introductions to the plays. *Macmillan $3, Drama.*

CHUTE, MARCHETTE 1909– *Shakespeare of London* (1949). The best popular biography. A brilliant researcher lets the facts speak for themselves. *Dutton $5, Evman.* See also her fine *Ben Jonson of Westminster* (1953), *Dutton $5,* and *Introduction to Shakespeare* (1951), *Dutton $2.50.*

COLERIDGE, SAMUEL TAYLOR 1772–1834 *Lectures on Shakespeare* (1849). A great poet exercises his critical judgment on the great dramatist. *Cap, Evman-h.*

CRAIG, HARDIN 1875– *Introduction to Shakespeare* (1952). Craig is probably the foremost American editor of Shakespeare. This book contains the introduction and critical essays from his edition of the complete plays. *Scott, Foresman $2.75.*

DEAN, LEONARD F. 1909– (ed.) *Shakespeare: Modern Essays in Criticism* (1957). A good collection of about thirty critical essays by modern authorities. *Ox.*

ELIOT, T. S. 1888– *Essays on Elizabethan Drama* (1932). One of our most respected, and respectable, poets writes on one of his chief interests. *Harv.*

FORD, BORIS *The Age of Shakespeare* (1955). A broad and thoughtful analysis of the whole period and of its principal literary figures. *Pen.*

GRANVILLE-BARKER, HARLEY 1877–1946 *Prefaces to Shakespeare* (1946–7). A great producer-director of Shakespeare writes shrewd and sensitive analyses of plot, character, and language. *Princeton Univ. 2 vols. $6 ea.* Separate *Preface to Hamlet, Drama;* to *Othello, Princeton Univ.*

HACKETT, FRANCIS 1883– *The Personal History of Henry VIII* (1929). Rounded portrait of a lusty monarch who ran the British nation as his private business and established the "balance of power" principle as the basis of English diplomacy. *Ban, Black, ML.*

HARBAGE, ALFRED B. 1901– *Shakespeare and the Rival Traditions* (1952). Rich in understanding of the world of the London theater. *Macmillan $6.*

HARRISON, G. B. 1894– *Introducing Shakespeare* (1939). The best layman's handbook on the dramatist, his theater, and his plays. *Pen.* Harrison's *Elizabethan Plays and Players* and *Shakespeare at Work* are also good background studies. *AA.*

KINGSLEY, CHARLES 1819–1875 *Westward Ho!* (1855). Bitterly anti-Jesuit, but a thrilling adventure story of the time when Elizabeth knighted sea captains for piracy against the Spaniards. *Scribner $1.50, Evman-h, GtIl, Nel.*

Life in Shakespeare's England (1911). Ed. by John Dover Wilson. Selected readings in Elizabethan prose to represent the tenor of the times. *Cambridge Univ. $2, Pen.*

PARROTT, T. M. 1866– *William Shakespeare: A Handbook* (rev. ed. 1955). Excellent factual and background material. *Scribner $2.50.*

PARTRIDGE, ERIC 1894– *Shakespeare's Bawdy* (rev. 1955). This often fascinating study of Shakespeare's bawdy vocabulary will increase the reader's understanding of almost any Elizabethan text. *Dutton $5.*

ROWSE, A. L. 1903– *The England of Elizabeth* (1950) and *The Expansion of Elizabethan England* (1955). The first two of a projected 3-volume history of the period by its foremost modern historian. Vol. 1, *Macmillan $8.50;* vol. 2, *St Martin's $5.75.*

SCOTT, SIR WALTER 1771–1832 *Kenilworth* (1821). *CoNC, Evman-h, GtIl, MLG, Nel.* *The Abbot* (1820), *o.p.* *The Monastery* (1820), *o.p.* Full-dress historical novels, by the father of the type, about Amy Robsart and Mary Queen of Scots, two women in Elizabeth's life.

Shakespeare's England (1917). Ed. by Sir Walter Raleigh. The standard reference, rich in colorful detail about clothes, homes, sports, trade, manners, and a host of other things. *Oxford Univ. 2 vols. $11.20.*

SITWELL, DAME EDITH 1887– *Fanfare for Elizabeth* (1946). The future queen's childhood on the periphery of the romantic and terrible court of Henry VIII. *Macmillan $3.*

STRACHEY, LYTTON 1880–1932 *Elizabeth and Essex* (1928). A subtle portrayal of Queen Elizabeth, Essex, Raleigh, Burghley, Bacon, Tyrone of Ireland, Philip of Spain, and of their effect on one another. *HarB.*

VAN DOREN, MARK 1894– *Shakespeare* (1953). Valuable critical material, helpful to an understanding of the plays. *Anch.*

WEBSTER, MARGARET 1905– *Shakespeare Without Tears* (rev. ed. 1955). America's foremost Shakespearean stage director tells of her experiences in staging the plays. *World $4.50, Prem.*

WINTER, CARL 1906– *Elizabethan Miniatures* (1943). Splendid color reproductions of an almost forgotten art. *Pen.*

5. The 17th Century

JOSEPH A. BYRNES, *New York University*

Between the Renaissance and the Age of Reason, prolonging one and preparing for the other, came the politically turbulent, intellectually active 17th century. In science, the age began with the new cosmology of Copernicus and Galileo, and ended with Newton's law of gravitation. The experimental method established by Bacon, the founding of the English Royal Society and the French Academy of Sciences, the invention of the telescope and the microscope, and the discovery of the calculus, logarithms, and, in biology, Harvey's "Motion of the Heart and the Blood"—all materially furthered man's enlightenment. In the arts, painting produced Rembrandt, Hals, Rubens, Van Dyck, Vermeer. Music developed from polyphony to harmony, from madrigal to opera; Monteverdi, Corelli, Lulli, and England's greatest native-born composer, Purcell, established the baroque style.

These peaceful accomplishments were achieved at a time when Europe was torn by political, economic, and religious strife. During the Thirty Years War (1618–1648), pious Catholic and pious Protestant thoroughly devastated most of Germany. Victims of religious persecution fled: many, like the Huguenots and the Pilgrim Fathers, sought liberty of conscience in the wilderness of the New World. Spain's power was weakening; in France, the monarchy, aided by able administrators like Richelieu and Mazarin, acquired supreme power over the rest of the nation, although on an uncertain financial basis. The English, during and after the Civil War (1642–1649), modified their government—in part by killing one king, expelling another, and importing a third, and in part by applying the liberal political tenets of men like Milton and Locke. Europe's merchant classes made weapons of their wealth in their vigorous struggle for power, nowhere with more success than in England. Energetic, practical, "forward-looking," predominantly radical-

Protestant, they eventually triumphed over the conservative aristocrats.

Religion, long a source of bitter controversy, found itself harassed from a new quarter by doubts induced by the "new science." The issue of faith versus reason began increasingly to trouble men's minds. Although the bulk of partisan religious writing is unreadable today, not all religion was acrimonious. Among Englishmen, Fox and Bunyan explored serene, personal approaches to God; Donne and Herbert spoke for Anglican moderation.

Philosophy was concerned with its perennial problems, but especially with religion and politics. Descartes radically commenced with complete skepticism; Hobbes postulated man's inhumanity to man, advocating absolutism as the safeguard of domestic tranquillity. Locke's *Two Treatises of Government* formed part of the liberal intellectual heritage of America's founding fathers. The pantheist Spinoza re-examined the fundamentals of religion; Pascal, moralist and mathematician, exalted faith alone. The Moravian pedagogue Comenius empirically developed his idealistic project for universal free education.

Cervantes' comic knight and the works of Calderón and Lope de Vega are Spain's foremost contributions to European letters. The French drama found its most sublime classical formulation in Corneille and Racine, and its supreme comic vision in Molière. English literature began the century with Shakespeare and the Jacobean dramatists, and with Donne and his fellow metaphysical poets, who compressed their world into intense, striking images. Unlike the metaphysicals, the greatest Puritan literary spokesman, Milton, was deeply committed to active politics as well as to his attempt to "justify the ways of God to men." His rejection of royal absolutism and his fervent plea in the *Areopagitica* for the free exchange of ideas unhampered by censorship are seminal propositions in the British and American view of democratic life.

After years of godly Puritan repression, the Restoration ushered in a reaction well characterized by its witty, rationalistic comedies about eager gentlemen in pursuit of equally eager mistresses. Life in the England of Charles

II was reported with humor and frank self-revelation by that prince of diarists, Pepys. The dominant verse form became the iambic pentameter, and the varied stanzas and delicate lyrics of the metaphysicals, Herrick, and the Cavaliers were replaced, at the hands of a master like Dryden, by pointed, balanced, rational couplets. English prose, the best of it nonpolemic, developed rapidly. What the English sentence lost in exuberant Elizabethan length, it gained in power, precision, and suppleness. The magnificent phrasing of the King James Bible, the cadences of Sir Thomas Browne, the devotional simplicity of Bunyan, the rational power of Dryden's prefaces—all helped to shape the future of our language.

If, during the Renaissance, man reached the threshold of the modern world, he stepped fully into it when he entered the 17th century with its conflicts and confusions —some of which still plague us today. In coping with his problems, he forged many of the scientific and philosophic principles we live by, leaving us an enduring literary record of the agonies, delights, and accomplishments of his passage.

A. 17th Century Literature

AUBREY, JOHN 1626–1697 *Brief Lives* (1813). Informal, revealing sketches of a host of 17th-century persons. *Univ. of Michigan $5.95.*

Authorized Version of the Bible (King James translation, 1611). "The noblest monument of English prose." Countless editions.

BACON *Advancement of Learning* and *Essays.* A product of the Renaissance and a prophet of modernism. See page 53.

_____ *Novum Organum* (1620). *Lib.* Contained in *English Philosophers from Bacon to Mill,* MLG.

BEAUMONT, FRANCIS 1584–1616 and JOHN FLETCHER 1579–1625 *Selected Plays.* Excellent theater, violent and exotic; elegant, poetic, witty. *Hill & Wang* 2 vols. *$3 ea., Evman-h.*

BEHN, APHRA 1640–1689 *Selected Writings of the Ingenious Mrs. Aphra Behn* (1950). Witty, clever, sometimes sentimental, sometimes indelicate novellas by England's first professional lady of letters. *Ever.*

BOYLE, ROBERT 1627–1691 *The Sceptical Chymist* (1661). An empirical researcher demolishes alchemy and other pseudo "chemistry," and inaugurates the science of chemistry. *Evman-h.*

BROWNE, SIR THOMAS 1605–1682 *Religio Medici* (1643). Memorable for the reasonable liberalism of a physician's faith and for the style: stately, cadenced, lucid, personal. *Cambridge Univ. $1.75 EvmanNA, Gate, SM.*

BUNYAN, JOHN 1628–1688 *Pilgrim's Progress* (1678). A visionary tinker's allegory of the Christian's journey to self-fulfillment; the most abiding scripture of English Puritanism. *Macmillan $2, Winston $2.50, CoE, CoNC, Evman-h, Nel, OxA, PB, Rine, WoC.*

BURTON, ROBERT 1577–1640 *The Anatomy of Melancholy* (1621). Ed. by F. Dell and P. Jordan-Smith (1927). A monumental accumulation of 17th-century science and amusing pseudo-science, elaborately organized in a remarkable style. *Tudor $3.95.*

CERVANTES SAAVEDRA, MIGUEL DE 1547–1616 *Don Quixote* (1605–15). Kindly, mad satire on the delusions inspired by chivalric romance, and, implicitly, on too much and too little idealism. Two new translations—by Samuel Putnam (*Vik, Vik-h*) and by J. M. Cohen (*Pen*)—are superior to any others in English for vividness and ease of reading. Other editions: *Dodd, Mead $3, Houghton Mifflin $2.60, Knopf $3, BES (selections), Evman-h 2 vols., ML, MLCE, MLG, NAL (abr.), PB (abr.).*

Colonial American Writing (1950). Ed. by R. H. Pearce. Original, wide-ranging anthology marking the progress from Old England to the American Enlightenment. *Rine.*

CONGREVE, WILLIAM 1670–1729 *Comedies.* Satire on, and for, Restoration society. Brilliantly cynical situations; dialogue of amazing finish and verve. *Drama, Drama-h, WoC.*

CORNEILLE, PIERRE 1606–1684 and JEAN RACINE 1639–1699 *Six Plays.* The pre-eminent classical drama of the Renaissance; the age-old tension between reason and passion, illustrated always in polished verse and mostly in Greco-Roman costume. *ML.* Especially recommended are Corneille's *The Cid* (*Cambridge Univ. $1.25, BES, SM*) and Racine's *Andromache* (*BES, SM*).

DESCARTES, RENE 1596–1650 *Discourse on Method* (1637). Established scientific doubt and mathematical logic as the bases for modern rationalism. *Dov, EvmanNA, Lib.*

DONNE *Poems.* Sensual and transcendent and desperate; highly versatile. A strong tone-giver to poetry in our time. See page 53.

DRYDEN, JOHN 1631–1700 *Poems.* A titan of 17th-century English literature, as satirist, critic, translator, dramatist, and lyric poet. *Evman-h, Nel, OxA, Pen, Rine.*

EVELYN, JOHN 1620–1706 *Diary* (Selections). More staid than Pepys, Evelyn set down wide-ranging observations covering his whole life span. *Evman-h 2 vols.*

FOX, GEORGE 1624–1691 *Journal* (1694). The Quaker leader traces his 34 years of "enlightening" the people, in house and garden, with Christ's light and love. *Evman-h.*

HERRICK, ROBERT 1591–1674 *Poems* (1648). Lyrics of Latin perfection, piquant and poignant, whether Epicurean or devout. *CoE, OxA, WoC.*

HOBBES *Leviathan.* Glorifying authoritarianism. See page 211.

LAFAYETTE, MADAME DE 1634–1693 *The Princess of Cleves.*
New trans. by Nancy Mitford (1951). Profound, delicate psychological novel about a woman in a triangle. *Cambridge Univ.*
$1.25, NewC.

LA FONTAINE, JEAN DE 1621–1695 *Fables* (1668, 1693). Stories of
all-too-human animals from Aesop and other sources adapted
to the not-too-nice world of Louis XIV. *Cambridge Univ. $1,*
Grosset $1.95, Holt $3, Oxford Univ. $1, Evman-h.

LA ROCHEFOUCAULD, DUC DE 1613–1680 *Maxims* (1665). Deft
phrasing of cynical wisdom. *Cambridge Univ. $1.75, Gate.*

LEIBNIZ, GOTTFRIED WILHELM VON 1646–1716 *Selections.*
Rationalized optimism. *B&N, Evman-h, Scrib.*

LOCKE, JOHN 1632–1704 *An Essay Concerning Human Understanding.* An extremely influential book. See page 187.

_____ *On Politics and Education.* Basic writings of a pivotal
writer. *Van Nostrand $1.35.*

_____ *Two Treatises of Civil Government.* See page 211.

MARVELL, ANDREW 1621–1678 *Poems.* A Puritan politician
known not only for a remarkable political ode, but also for one
of the greatest love poems in English. *Harvard Univ. $2.50.*

Masterpieces of the Spanish Golden Age (1957). Ed. by Angel Flores.
Works tragic and comic, with noble heroes and engaging rascals,
illustrating the great range and power of Cervantes' contemporaries and successors. *Rine.*

Metaphysical Lyrics and Poems of the Seventeenth Century (1921).
Ed. by H. J. C. Grierson. An excellent introduction to some
difficult but delightful verse. *GB.*

MILTON, JOHN 1608–1674 *Areopagitica* (1644). The most impassioned defense in English of free speech, founded on the principle that social responsibility needs freedom in which to grow.
Oxford Univ. $1.20, Evman-h, SM.

_____ *Poems.* By some ranked next to Shakespeare. *Evman-h,*
ML, MLCE, Nel, OxA, Rine, WoC.

_____ *The Portable Milton* (1949). Ed. with an excellent introduction by Douglas Bush. Includes *Paradise Lost,* sonnets, other
poems, *Areopagitica,* other prose. *Vik, Vik-h.*

MOLIERE (JEAN BAPTISTE POQUELIN) 1622–1673 *Comedies.*
Comic genius, expert theatricalism, and classical art united in a
satiric portrayal of 17th-century society. *BES (one play in each*
of 5 vols.), Evman-h 2 vols., ML, MLCE, Pen.

NEWTON, SIR ISAAC 1642–1727 *Principia* (1687). The foundation
of modern physical science. *Gate.*

Oxford Book of Seventeenth Century Verse (1934). Ed. by H. J. C.
Grierson and G. Bullough. The standard collection: over 600
poems by over 100 poets, covering the length and breadth of
the century. *Oxford Univ. $5.*

PASCAL *Pensées.* Logic explaining faith to reason. See page. 187.

Penguin Book of French Verse: II (16th to 18th centuries). Ed. by
G. Brereton. The drama of France outshines the poetry in this
age, but the best is here, with English versions. *Pen.*

PEPYS, SAMUEL 1633–1703 ***Diary.*** The very human reformer of
the British Navy observes himself and others at work and play
in the London of Charles II. *Evman-h 3 vols., ML (abr.).*

RACINE. See CORNEILLE above.

Restoration Plays. Numerous handy and representative collections
are now available of these witty, courtly, cynical comedies of
manners. *Evman-h, ML, RivEd.*

SEVIGNE *Letters.* Graceful, witty, subtle. See page 168.

SPINOZA *Philosophy.* Geometrical metaphysics. See page 187.

WALTON, IZAAK 1593–1683 ***The Compleat Angler*** (1653). An
amiable retired shopkeeper's treatise on recreation, and a commentary on life and literature in delicious, serene speech.
Evman-h, ML, Nel.

_____ *Lives* (1678). Four Anglican churchmen seen as saints, in
"the most literary and the most readable today of the 17th-
century biographies." *WoC.*

B. Books About the 17th Century

BREDVOLD, LOUIS I. 1888– ***The Intellectual Milieu of John
Dryden*** (1934). How the interaction of skepticism, religion, and
the "new science" created intellectual turmoil in the last half
of the century. *AA.*

CATHER, WILLA 1876–1947 *Shadows on the Rock* (1931). French
settlers on the Quebec frontier strive to maintain in their villages the decorum of their homeland. *Knopf $3.95.*

CHUTE, MARCHETTE 1909– ***Two Gentle Men: The Lives of
George Herbert and Robert Herrick*** (1959). Caroline England,
gracefully evoked through the lives of two great lyric poets.
Dutton $5.

DEFOE, DANIEL 1660–1731 *A Journal of the Plague Year* (1722).
A vivid description of what London went through during the
horrible year of 1665. A tour de force of imaginative journalism.
Evman-h, ML.

DUMAS *The Three Musketeers.* The court of Louis XIII. See page
90.

GRIERSON, H. J. C. 1866– ***Cross Currents in 17th Century English
Literature*** (1929). The age-old oppositions of world, flesh, and
spirit in a complex milieu. *Torch.*

HALLER, WILLIAM 1885– ***The Rise of Puritanism*** (1938). From
humble beginnings to Cromwell's New Model Army, Puritanism
grew into a force to be reckoned with. *Torch.*

HAWTHORNE *The Scarlet Letter.* Sin and its aftermath in Puritan New England. See page 120.

HOLLAND, A. K. 1894– *Henry Purcell* (1932). In music, England shone in this century; Purcell was the brightest star. *Pen.*

JOHNSON, SAMUEL 1709–1784 *The Lives of the Poets* (1779–81). Independent criticism of the personalities and works of Milton, Cowley, and other 17th-century poets. Very good reading. *Evman-h 2 vols., Gate (abr.), SM, WoC.*

KOSSAK, ZOFIA 1890– *The Meek Shall Inherit* (1948). Novel about 17th-century Poland in military, social, and spiritual storm and stress. *Roy Publishers $3.*

LEWIS, W. H. 1895– *The Splendid Century: Life in the France of Louis XIV* (1953). The great and the lowly in French society during monarchy's finest hour. *Anch.*

MACAULAY, THOMAS B. 1800–1859 *The History of England* (1855). Life in England between 1685 and 1700, actualized by scholarship, imagination, and a sense of the dramatic. *Evman-h 4 vols.*

_____ *Essays.* Lively critical essays on Bacon, Milton, Bunyan, Sir William Temple, the Restoration dramatists. *Evman-h 2 vols.*

PRAZ, MARIO 1896– *The Flaming Heart* (1958). Learned and fascinating essays on metaphysical and baroque art in the 17th century. *Anch.*

SCOTT, SIR WALTER 1771–1832 *Old Mortality* (1816). Presbyterian revenge, resolution, and fortitude under Royalist persecution. *Macmillan $2.75, Evman-h, Nel, SM.*

STEEGMULLER, FRANCIS 1906– *The Grand Mademoiselle* (1956). The age of Louis XIV as seen through the activities of his cousin. *Farrar, Straus & Cudahy $3.75.*

TAWNEY, RICHARD H. 1880– *Religion and the Rise of Capitalism* (1926). The religion of the Reformation in its bearing on social and economic thought. *NAL.*

VAN LOON, HENDRIK W. 1882–1944 *R.V.R.: The Life and Times of Rembrandt* (1931). Imaginative reconstruction of a great man in a great time. *Black.*

WILLEY, BASIL 1897– *The Seventeenth Century Background* (1934). Critical essays examining religion and poetry against contemporary "climates of opinion." *Anch.*

WILSON, JOHN HAROLD 1900– *The Court Wits of the Restoration* (1948). Rochester, Buckingham, and Wycherley are among the gay rakes whose frequently scandalous doings are chronicled against the social framework of their times. *Princeton Univ. $4.*

6. The 18th Century

WILLIAM C. GREENE, *Massachusetts Institute of Technology*

The 18th century opened in Europe with the expensive grandeur of Louis XIV and came to a costly but ignoble end in Napoleon. While the continent was troubled, England staked out the outlines of her empire. The small state of Prussia began under Frederick to expand its power and to establish a paternal militarism. In America the abundance of land and the absence of an hereditary ruling class bred an independent spirit which rebelled against Britain.

It was a century in which trade began to be world-wide. But trade is seldom an activity of a noble class, and its growth meant the rise to wealth of city merchants, country squires, and occasionally of clerks, yeomen, and mechanics who broke out of their social subjection and pursued their fortunes. This shifting of weight between classes steadily transformed England. In France the nobility held primacy somewhat longer, scorning the English as a nation of shopkeepers.

Most thoughtful men of the 18th century believed that the world was rational. A century earlier scientists had seemed to establish the laws by which physical bodies acted and the mathematics by which their motions could be predicted. Might there not be moral, social, and political laws quite as inescapably true and quite as self-operating and as systematic as Newton's laws of mechanics? Could not Reason find the "right" answers to all problems?

Hence Reason replaced Faith as a guide for the intellectual leaders of the period. The philosophers from Berkeley through Hume and Kant to Condorcet, whatever their first premises, worked by Reason, and in its name the satirists such as Swift and Voltaire criticized its products. The religion of the reasonable man in the 18th century was the Deism simply expressed by Franklin in his *Autobiography,* advocated with passion by Tom Paine in his *Age of Reason,* and adhered to by many of the founding fathers in America.

In political theory the way of Reason moved through the axiom that society was an agreement by all men to the practice of check-and-balance republicanism, a program deriving from John Locke in the previous century and finding exponents in Rousseau, Jefferson, and Madison. The same habit of mind was carried into economic theory by Adam Smith, whose *Wealth of Nations* gave the free-traders a rational justification for their break with the state-controlled mercantilism that had dominated Europe since the Renaissance.

A reasonable century, for which Benjamin Franklin may be taken as the prototype, is not one in which extreme emotionalism or strong individualism is likely to be honored. The 18th century produced no fresh and memorable tragedy, and only toward its end any intense, moving poetry. Its plays still enjoyed today—those of Sheridan, Goldsmith, Beaumarchais, and Goldoni—evolved from the satiric comedies of manners of Molière and Congreve. Pope, the poetic model of the century in England, believed the heroic couplet to be the one orderly form of verse. Anything may be said in the couplet, but it will render chiefly epigram, and emotion dies in its formality, as may be seen when Robert Burns tried to "rise" from his dialect to "polite" verse.

Reason and decorum are likely to be critical, but to be critical in a clear style. The century poured out its clarity in essays such as those of the *Spectator,* in letters such as those of Lord Chesterfield, even in the conversation of Samuel Johnson, captured from loss by Boswell—and all in a prose balanced and comprehensible.

The great creative speech of the century, however, was the novel, presenting human life in action. As early as the 1720's, Defoe was writing fabricated "eyewitness" accounts of plague and shipwreck, Le Sage had turned the story of adventure into a to-be-continued-next-week series of pictures of backstairs life, and the Abbé Prévost published in 1731 the archetype of all French novels of fatal passion in *Manon Lescaut.*

Virtue overtook the novel, of course: in *Pamela* Samuel

Richardson showed girls how to be good by a long series of letters telling of a servant girl who "held out for marriage." This cant so disgusted a minor playwright named Henry Fielding that he wrote a burlesque of it in *Joseph Andrews,* about Pamela's brother who fled from the ardent advances of Lady Booby. To Fielding's surprise the figures turned alive as he shaped them; and when he went on to a larger scheme, *Tom Jones,* he produced one of the greatest of all novels. Soon the novel's capacities had been extended into philosophical fable by Voltaire in *Candide,* into comic extravaganza by Sterne in *Tristram Shandy,* and into "Gothic" horror by Horace Walpole in *The Castle of Otranto.*

But when Reason faces up to man, it decides that each man is significant to himself; if men are equal, so are their feelings. By the third quarter of the century, order and restraint were giving way to a freer expression of individual emotions. Robert Burns could then declare boldly from the depths of poverty that "a man's a man for a' that." Goethe's young Werther could value no law but his own amorous despair. Rousseau could get men to read his own egotisms and impulses. And the French Revolution could burst out into enraged murder of one's own countrymen. Burke, opposing the French Revolution, was an 18th-century gentleman trying to keep the 19th century from being born.

Yet when we speak of the 18th century we tend to neglect the romantic. We feel the 18th century to be Franklin and Jefferson, Pope and Voltaire. It was the century in which for the first time since Periclean Athens men really began to plan their futures and to depend confidently upon their own reason.

A. 18th Century Literature

ADDISON, JOSEPH 1672–1719 and SIR RICHARD STEELE 1672–1729 *The Spectator* (1711–2). Pleasantly witty and polished commentary on fashions and foibles of Queen Anne's London. *Cambridge Univ. $1.25, Houghton Mifflin $1.88, Macmillan $2, Oxford Univ. $1.05, CoE, Evman-h 4 vols., Gate, Rine, SM.*

The Age of Enlightenment (1956). Ed. by Isaiah Berlin. Generous selections from the major philosophers of the 18th century with helpful commentaries by the editor. *Houghton Mifflin $3, NAL.*

BEAUMARCHAIS, PIERRE CARON DE 1732–1799 *The Barber of Seville* (1775) and *The Marriage of Figaro* (1778). Comedies satirizing class privilege, best known now in the opera versions by Rossini and Mozart. *French 75¢.*

BERKELEY, GEORGE 1685–1753 *A Treatise Concerning the Principles of Human Knowledge* (1710). Platonic idealism reworked in the light of Newton's science. *Open Court $1.10.*

BLAKE *Poems.* From lyric simplicity to symbolic mysticism. See page 142.

BOSWELL, JAMES 1740–1795 *The Life of Samuel Johnson* (1791). The widely ranging opinions of one of England's favorite minds, recorded by a shrewd, devoted admirer in perhaps the greatest biography ever written. Complete: *Evman-h 2 vols., MLG, OxA.* Abridged: *ML, ModSL, Vik, Vik-h.*

_____ *London Journal* (1762–3). Ed. by Frederick Pottle. An intimate account of Boswell's start in London. *McGraw-Hill $6, NAL.*

BURKE, EDMUND 1729–1797 *Reflections on the French Revolution* (1790). Strong defense of British monarchy. *Evman-h, Gate, Lib.*

BURNS *Poems.* Master of memorable song. See page 142.

CASANOVA, GIOVANNI 1725–1798 *Memoirs.* Amatory and other adventures. *ML (abr.).*

CHESTERFIELD *Letters to His Son.* Practical advice for living in high society. See page 166.

Constitution of the United States and *Declaration of Independence.* See chapters on "History" and "Politics."

CREVECOEUR *Letters from an American Farmer.* See page 166.

DEFOE, DANIEL 1660–1731 *Robinson Crusoe* (1719). The original and immortal desert-island story. *Rand McNally $2.60, Random House $1, Winston $1, Evman-h, Gar, GtIl, ML, Nel, PB, WoC.*

_____ *Moll Flanders* (1722). One woman's life through many marriages and several crimes. *Macmillan $2.50, Evman-h, ML, PB, Rine, RivEd.*

_____ *A Journal of the Plague Year.* See page 62.

DIDEROT, DENIS 1713–1784 *Rameau's Nephew and Other Works.* Pieces satiric and serious by the compiler of the French encyclopedia who was, after Voltaire, the most versatile French writer of the century. *Anch.*

Federalist Papers (1787–8). Political essays by Alexander Hamilton, James Madison, and others, which influenced the acceptance of our Constitution and remain prime examples of political theory. *Macmillan $2.50, Evman-h, Lib (selections), ML.*

FIELDING, HENRY 1707–1754 *Joseph Andrews* (1742). Adventures of a chaste footman and a sturdy parson, told in mockery of sentimentalism. *Evman-h, ML, ModSL, Nort, Rine, WoC.*

_____ *Tom Jones* (1749). The long, zestful story of a lively hero from childhood to marriage, richly filled with characters and adventures; one of the greatest of realistic novels. *Evman-h 2 vols., ML, MLP.*

FRANKLIN, BENJAMIN 1706–1790 *Autobiography* (1790). A great American and the prototype of the pragmatic man explains his rise to fame and fortune. *Peter Pauper $4.50, Univ. of California $2.50, Evman-h, Harp, Lib, ML, PB, Rine.*

_____ *Autobiographical Writings* (1945). Ed. by Carl Van Doren. This collection of letters and essays includes the *Autobiography*, enriches it, and continues it up to Franklin's last known letter. *Viking $6.*

GAY, JOHN 1685–1732 *The Beggar's Opera* (1728). Burlesque of political society; thieves, highwaymen, and harlots sing false sentiments to the tunes of street ballads. In several 18th-century play anthologies: *Evman-h, ML, MLG.*

GIBBON *The Decline and Fall of the Roman Empire.* A classic of history. See page 36.

GOETHE, JOHANN WOLFGANG VON 1749–1832 *Faust.* Frequently exciting, always profound, philosophical drama. See page 143.

_____ *The Sorrows of Young Werther* (1773). The hero commits suicide because his love is unrequited; an extreme in the then new romantic mood. *Rine.*

_____ *Wilhelm Meister's Apprenticeship.* See page 91.

GOLDSMITH, OLIVER 1728–1774 *She Stoops to Conquer* (1773). One of the most actable of all plays; a comic masterpiece. *Oxford Univ. $1.15, CoNC, Evman-h, Nel, SM.*

_____ *The Vicar of Wakefield* (1766). The amusing tribulations of the most famous of gentle and gullible clergymen. *CoNC, EvmanNA, ML, Nel, PB, SM, WoC.*

GRAY, THOMAS 1716–1771 *Poems.* Phrases and lines from "Elegy in a Country Churchyard" are now part of our sentimental heritage. *Cambridge Univ. 50¢ & $1.25, CoE, Evman-h, OxA.*

JEFFERSON, THOMAS 1743–1826 *Autobiographical and Political Writings.* A founding father writes clearly and eloquently. Collections under various titles: *Beacon $2.75, Grosset $1, Cap, Lib, ML, NAL.*

JOHNSON, SAMUEL 1709–1784 *The Portable Johnson and Boswell* (1947). Selected writings by the literary dictator of his age and passages from Boswell's *Life. Vik, Vik-h.*

_____ *Prose and Poetry. Oxford Univ. $1.40, Rine.*

_____ *History of Rasselas* (1758). Johnson's major effort at fiction. *Oxford Univ. $1.90, Evman-h, Rine.*

_____ *Lives of the English Poets.* See page 63.

KANT, IMMANUEL 1724–1804 *Critique of Pure Reason* (1781–7). A difficult explanation of intellect as the formulator of knowledge. *Evman-h, ML.*

_____ *The Metaphysics of Morals* (1797). The basic argument for the Puritan and democratic code many people live by. *Regnery* 75¢, *Lib.*

LESSING, GOTTHOLD EPHRAIM 1729–1781 *Laocoön* (1766). A classic of esthetic theory. *Evman-h* (with *Minna von Barnhelm*), *Lib, Noon*

_____ *Minna von Barnhelm* (1767). An influential and natural comedy. *Cambridge Univ.* $1.25, *Evman-h, SM.*

MALTHUS, THOMAS ROBERT 1766–1834 *Essay on the Principles of Population* (1798). Classic study of the relationship between population growth and means of subsistence. *Evman-h* 2 vols.

PAINE, THOMAS 1737–1809 *Common Sense* (1776), a pamphlet that roused the American colonies to independence; *The Rights of Man* (1791), Paine's answer to Burke's criticism of the French Revolution; and *The Age of Reason* (1794, 1796), a defense of Deism—all bound with Howard Fast's biographical novel, *Citizen Tom Paine*. *MLG.*

POPE, ALEXANDER 1688–1744 *Poems.* Ideas, satire, occasionally emotion, in neat epigrammatic heroic couplets. *Houghton Mifflin* $4, *Oxford Univ.* $1.40, *St Martin's* $2.50, *Evman-h, ML, Nel, Rine.*

_____ *Essay on Man* (1733). Develops in skillful couplets the philosophy of Optimism: "Whatever is, is Right." In all collections cited above.

PRÉVOST, ANTOINE 1697–1763 *Manon Lescaut* (1731). The story of a young man fascinated by a courtesan who loves him, deceives him, but never gives him up; source of Massenet's opera *Manon*. *Cambridge Univ.* $1.50, *Evman-h, Pen.*

RICHARDSON, SAMUEL 1689–1761 *Pamela* (1740). In letters that reveal the "sentiments" of the age, a maidservant tells how she resisted her young master until he offered marriage. *Evman-h* 2 vols., *Nort.*

ROUSSEAU, JEAN JACQUES 1712–1778 *Confessions* (1782–9). Uninhibited self-revelation of a romantic egoist. *Heritage* $5, *Evman-h* 2 vols., *ML, PB, Pen.*

_____ *Emile* (1762). A didactic novel, an important source of progressive education theory. *Evman-h.*

_____ *The Social Contract* (1762). The influential French document for the Revolution. *Hafner* $1.80 & 90¢ (paper), *Regnery* $2.75, *EvmanNA, Gate.*

SHERIDAN, RICHARD BRINSLEY 1751–1816 *The Rivals* (1775) and *The School for Scandal* (1777). Two famous social comedies, noted for their wit, complicated but effective design, and memorable caricatures (notably Mrs. Malaprop). *CoNC, Drama, Evman-h, Nel, WoC.*

SMITH, ADAM 1723–1790 *The Wealth of Nations* (1776). The classic explanation of the economic value of individualism and of the division of labor. *Evman-h* 2 vols., *Gate* (abr.), *MLG.*

SMOLLETT, TOBIAS 1721–1771 *Humphry Clinker* (1771). Various adventures and pictures of the times on a coaching trip through England and Scotland. *Evman-h, ML, Nel, Nort, Rine, WoC.*

_____ *Roderick Random* (1748). Adventures on sea and land, famous for portraying the miserable lot of 18th-century seamen. *Evman-h, WoC.*

STERNE, LAURENCE 1713–1768 *Tristram Shandy* (1759–67). Comic domestic episodes, done in all sorts of styles—whimsical, digressive, extravagant. *Odyssey $3, Black, Evman-h, ML, PB, Rine, WoC.*

SWIFT, JONATHAN 1667–1745 *Gulliver's Travels* (1726). Imaginary journeys that amuse children but are really thoroughgoing satires of man's irrational inhumanity. *Crown $1.98, Dutton $2.75, Heritage $3, Oxford Univ. $1.70, Ronald $1.90, Evman-h, Gtll, Harp, ML, MLP, NAL, Nel, OxA, PB, Rine, RivEd, SM, Vik, Vik-h, WoC.*

_____ *The Portable Swift.* A good cross-section of Swift's writing. *Vik, Vik-h.*

VOLTAIRE, FRANÇOIS MARIE AROUET DE 1694–1778 *Candide* (1759). A short, funny, well-spiced adventure story, a masterly satire of Optimism, war, religion, governments, love, wealth, and a host of other things. *Holt $1.60, Ban, Evman-h, Liv, ML, NAL, Pen,* and in *The Portable Voltaire, Vik, Vik-h.*

WALPOLE, HORACE 1717–1797 *The Castle of Otranto* (1764). The first and most famous "Gothic" novel of horror and supernatural invention. In *18th-Century Shorter Novels, Evman-h.*

_____ *Letters.* See page 169.

B. Books About the 18th Century

BECKER, CARL LOTUS 1873–1945 *The Heavenly City of the Eighteenth-Century Philosophers* (1932). A lively but scholarly analysis of 18th-century thought. *Yale Univ. $3, Yale.*

CARLYLE, THOMAS 1795–1881 *The French Revolution* (1837). A monumental narrative, with unscholarly warmth, color, drama, yet essential truth. *Cambridge Univ. 80¢ (abr.), Evman-h 2 vols., MLG.*

CASSIRER, ERNST 1874–1945 *The Philosophy of the Enlightenment* (1955). A much-admired discussion of the thought of the Age of Reason. *Bea.*

DICKENS, CHARLES 1812–1870 *A Tale of Two Cities* (1859). Love and self-sacrifice set in a vivid picture of the French Revolution. *Grove $3.50, Macmillan $2.40, Oxford Univ. $3.50, CoNC, Evman-h, Gtll, Liv, ML, NAL, Nel, PB, SM 3 eds., WoC.*

FORESTER, CECIL SCOTT 1899– *Captain Horatio Hornblower* (1939). A three-decker yarn about a first-class sailing man in fights and frolics. *Little, Brown $5.*

ROBERTS, KENNETH 1885–1957 *Arundel* (1930), **Rabble in Arms** (1933), **Northwest Passage** (1937), **Oliver Wiswell** (1940). Scrupulously documented and vigorously told novels of military adventures and various classes of people during the American Revolution. *Doubleday $4, $4.50, $4.50, & $4.95, respectively.*

SCOTT, SIR WALTER 1771–1832 **Waverley** (1814). A romantic tale of the Jacobite rebellion of 1745. *Nel.*

STEVENSON Both *Kidnapped* and *Treasure Island* are stories of adventure in the 18th century. See page 107.

THACKERAY, WILLIAM MAKEPEACE 1811–1863 **Henry Esmond** (1852). Clear picture of Queen Anne's England, with Addison, Steele, and Swift as minor characters. *Evman-h, Gtll, Harp, ML, Nel, SM.*

7. The Orient

NORMAN C. STAGEBERG, *Iowa State Teachers College*

The emergence of Asia as one of the most significant forces in world affairs had been foretold long ago by some of our keenest American observers (Henry Adams for one). However, the actual arrival of this event found the American people unprepared. Who would have dared to prophesy a few years earlier that in 1950 the United States would be engaged in its fourth largest war in far-off Korea? Who would have had the temerity two decades ago to intimate that American political life would be vitally influenced by events occurring in India, China, or the Near East?

With great suddenness we have been precipitated into the very midst of Asiatic affairs. The mysterious Orient, which has hitherto held merely a romantic interest for Americans, must now be understood and dealt with. School children, high-school youth, and adult citizens are now confronted with the need of learning how to think about the entire East in new ways. New courses dealing with Eastern affairs have been introduced into school and university curricula. A steadily increasing flow toward the East of American observers (journalists, congressmen, businessmen, technicians, and others) is now to be noted.

We cannot all visit the Orient, but there is a way for all of us to enter upon an understanding of its life and cultures. For all who can read there is a rich and diverse Oriental literature, old and new, which invites us. Surprisingly enough, some of this Eastern literature has become so thoroughly a part of our own tradition that we scarcely give thought to its Oriental origins.

Most pervasive of Eastern influences in Western homes is the Bible. In books of the Old Testament we have a whole library of traditional literature of an ancient Oriental people, reflecting both attitudes and imageries which are characteristically Eastern, and the universal humanity which changes not from East to West: gloomy doubts of Job, joyous delight in the Song of Songs, radical propaganda as in Micah, visions of utopias as in Isaiah, romances of daring achievement like those of Joshua and David, picturesque love stories like those of Esther and Ruth, common-sense folk wisdom as in the Book of Proverbs, sophisticated pessimism of Ecclesiastes.

The ancient wisdom of India can be found in its literature. The *Bhagavad-Gita,* from the 2,000-year-old epic *Mahabharata,* teaches the necessity of good deeds "without regard to selfish benefit but for devotion to God." The simple yet subtle fables of the *Panchatantra* afford insights into human nature and have been the source of many stories retold by Aesop, Scheherazade, Boccaccio, and La Fontaine. The life and teachings of Buddha reveal to us the ethical and religious way of life of millions in the Orient.

To understand the aspirations of India today and to savor the quality of intelligence and devotion given to the cause of Indian independence, read first of all Louis Fischer's biography of Gandhi, and Pandit Nehru's *Toward Freedom,* a self-portrait of one of the great men of our age.

Islamic beliefs and the development of Mohammedanism must be understood to interpret the international scene in the Near East today. For such understanding, the basic religious book is the *Koran,* the Bible of 315 million believers; and one can learn of the rise of Islam in the short but scholarly accounts by Guillaume or by Gibb.

Americans have perhaps shown a greater interest in China than in any other Oriental nation, particularly since the rise of Communist China. This interest has, however, been primarily economic and religious—we have viewed China as a prospective market and as a vast field for missionary endeavor. Very few Americans have in the past considered Chinese culture as a reservoir of wisdom from which we too might learn. The heritage of China includes a time-tested moral philosophy which the West needs to understand just as urgently as China needs the conveniences of Western technology. The basis of this heritage is the enduring wisdom of the subtle mystic Lao-tzu and the practical moralist Confucius.

The Chinese sage—more than the Western intellectual —may seek spiritual truth along several avenues: Taoism, Confucianism, folk wisdom, Buddhism, Western science, and sometimes also Christianity or Mohammedanism— each of which he is likely to use for whatever values he finds therein. But, writes Lin Yutang, "If there is one book in the whole of Oriental literature which one should read above all others, it is Lao-tzu's *Books of Tao.*" "Tao" ("the way") lays emphasis upon the same moral paradox that Jesus taught: "Blessed are the meek, for they shall inherit the earth." "He that humbleth himself shall be exalted," Lao-tzu says, and enforces this most basic, yet most difficult, of moral principles, with practical illustrations in Oriental imagery.

When we turn to Confucius we come to one of the great world forces like Moses, Plato, Jesus, and Mohammed. The *Analects* has shaped the thoughts and actions of millions of men through many centuries. As Lin Yutang explains:

> Confucianism was primarily an historical school; all the Confucian classics are history. To the Chinese, that system of moral and social order, based on history, is contained in the one word "li," which has such a broad meaning that it is untranslatable. In the narrowest sense, it means "ritual," "propriety," and just "good manners"; in an historical sense, it means the rationalized system of feudal order; in a philosophical sense, it means an ideal social order with "everything in its place"; and in a personal sense, it means a pious, religious state of mind, very near to the word "faith."

For other classics of Chinese literature the most convenient introduction is through the selections in Lin Yutang's *Wisdom of China and India,* especially the democratic philosophy of Mencius (contemporary of Plato and Aristotle), the "magic fairylike" poetry of Li Po (8th century A.D.), and the fascinating autobiographical novel, *Six Chapters of a Floating Life* (about 1800).

A. General

KIRK, GEORGE E. *Short History of the Middle East* (4th ed. 1955). Compact factual account emphasizing present political and socio-economic problems. *Praeger $5 (hard) & $1.75 (paper).*

MULLER, HERBERT J. 1905– *Loom of History* (1958). Studies of old civilizations in Asia Minor, viewed from a humanistic position with "reverence and irony." *Harper $7.50.*

NORTHROP, F. S. C. 1893– *The Meeting of East and West* (1946). A pioneer comparative analysis of the dominant cultures on a world scale. *Macmillan $5.90.*

VINACKE, HAROLD M. 1893– *History of the Far East in Modern Times* (5th ed. 1950). Developments to the end of 1949. *Appleton-Century-Crofts $5.75.*

Wisdom of the East. A series that includes many classics of the Indian, Iranian, Arabic, Chinese, and Japanese literatures. *Grove $1.50–$2.50 ea.*

B. Arabia, Iran, and Palestine

ALBRIGHT, W. F. 1891– *The Archaeology of Palestine* (rev. ed. 1956). This well-illustrated summary of the last 20 years of Palestinian archeology reveals the unfolding of civilization in ancient Palestine; describes races, languages, cultures; and shows bearing of findings on the Bible. *Pen.*

Arabian Nights (8th to 15th century). Fascinating stories of genii and magicians, of golden palaces, and beautiful gardens, of wonderful voyages and adventures, of intrigue and enchantment. *Longmans, Green $3, Macmillan $2.75, Gar, GtIl, ML, Nel, Pen, Vik-h.*

ATIYAH, EDWARD 1903– *The Arabs* (1955). Survey of the Arabs' place in history up to 1955. *Pen.*

The Bible. Monumental in the history of religion and literature. Major versions available today: Rheims-Douay, King James, Revised Standard, and Ronald Knox. Innumerable editions.

DOUGHTY, CHARLES M. 1843–1926 *Travels in Arabia Deserta* (1888). An abridgment (1955) of a travel classic which takes the reader to desert camps to share the daily life and adventures of the Bedouins. *Anch.*

ELLIS, HARRY B. *Israel and the Middle East* (1957). Traces the inception and development of the Palestine problem. Valuable on post-Suez period. *Ronald $5.*

GIBB, HAMILTON A. R. 1895– *Mohammedanism* (2nd ed. 1953). Historical survey from Mohammed to the present, with the outlook for the future. *Oxford Univ. $1.20, NAL.*

GUILLAUME, ALFRED 1888– *Islam* (1954). Mohammed, the Koran, the evolution of Mohammedanism with its various schools of thought, and the place of Islam in the world today. *Pen.*

GURNEY, O. R. 1911– *The Hittites* (1952). The historical Hittites— their society, institutions, languages, races, literature, and art— as revealed by excavations and decipherment of ancient documents. *Pen o.p.*

Koran. The scriptures of Islam by Mohammed (570–632). The new translation, almost literal but highly readable, by Mohammed Marmaduke Pickthall is recommended. *NAL.* Other versions available in *Evman-h, Pen, WoC.*

MICHENER, JAMES A. 1907– *The Voice of Asia* (1951). Astute but sympathetic report on the restless Orient. *Random House $3.95.*

MORIER, JAMES 1780–1849 *The Adventures of Hajji Baba of Ispahan* (1824). Picaresque Persian tales, humorous in tone and genially satiric of human frailty. *ML, WoC.*

MORRIS, JAMES 1926– *Islam Inflamed: a Middle East Picture* (1957). The Near and Middle East countries since 1956; colorful, informative, entertaining. *Pantheon $5.*

OMAR KHAYYAM d. 1123? *The Rubaiyat.* Pleasant cynicism in quatrains filled with vivid Oriental images and symbols. The splendidly poetic translation by Edward Fitzgerald is available in countless editions.

SAADI 1184–1291 *Gulistan (The Rose Garden)* (1258). Charming moral anecdotes. *Transatlantic Arts o.p.*

ST. JOHN, ROBERT 1902– *Ben Gurion* (1959). Living Near East history through the life of one who helped make it. *Doubleday $3.95.*

SITWELL, SACHEVERELL 1897– *Arabesque and Honeycomb* (1957). Vivid descriptions of many cities and places in the Middle East, with stress on Islamic art. A rich book by a sensitive and scholarly observer. *Random House $6.*

SMITH, WILFRED CANTWELL 1916– *Islam in Modern History* (1957). A penetrating and thought-provoking study of Turkey, Pakistan, Muslim India, and the Arab states. *Princeton Univ. $6, NAL.*

WILSON, EDMUND 1895– *The Scrolls from the Dead Sea* (1955). An absorbing but strongly prejudiced report of the exciting discovery of the ancient Dead Sea Scrolls and of their implications for Biblical scholarship. *Oxford Univ. $3.25, Mer.* For a more balanced, scholarly study see Burrows, page 192.

C. India

Bhagavad-Gita (5th to 3rd century B.C.). The most popular book in Hindu religious literature. *Harper $2.50, NAL.*

BOWLES, CHESTER 1901– *Ambassador's Report* (1954). A readable, perceptive appraisal of India today, exhibiting a sensitive appreciation of its many unique problems. *Harper $5.*

CORBETT, JAMES E. 1875–1955 *Man Eaters of Kumaon* (1946). True, gripping stories of tiger hunting related straightforwardly by a master hunter. *Oxford Univ. $4.50.*

FISCHER, LOUIS 1896– *Gandhi: His Life and Message for the World* (1955). A great man portrayed fully and sympathetically by one who knew him well. *NAL.*

FORSTER *A Passage to India.* Penetrating novel of the misunderstanding between East and West in British India. See page 113.

GHOSE, SUDHIN N. *The Vermilion Boat* (1953). Autobiographical account of college years, describing the richness of Indian life with eloquence, color, and humor. *Macmillan $3.75.*

HERZOG, MAURICE 1919– *Annapurna* (1953). Informative, thrilling story of the ascent of Annapurna. *Dutton $5.*

HUMPHREYS, CHRISTMAS 1919– *Buddhism* (1951). Development and doctrines of the varied schools of Buddhism. *Pen.*

KIPLING, RUDYARD 1865–1936 *Kim* (1901). A vivid picture of India and her people is given in this exciting tale of secret-service activity. *Dell, ML.*

LIN YUTANG 1895– (ed.) *Wisdom of China and India* (1942). Selections from the *Upanishads,* the *Bhagavad-Gita,* the ancient epic *Ramayana,* the *Panchatranta,* Edwin Arnold's *The Light of Asia,* etc. *MLG.*

MASTERS, JOHN 1914– *Bhowani Junction* (1954). A lively novel about modern India in the throes of change and racial problems, with satiric portraits of the British. *Grosset $1.95, Viking $3.75.*

MORELAND, WILLIAM H. 1868–1938 and SIR ATUL C. CHATTERJEE 1874– *A Short History of India* (4th ed. 1957). Factual account of principal events against the social, religious, and political background. *Longmans, Green $6.*

NEHRU, JAWAHARLAL 1889– *Toward Freedom* (1941). The great leader of modern India recounts his struggle toward the dream of justice and freedom. *Day $7.50, Bea.*

Panchatantra (6th century). Animal fables that constitute a treatise on human nature and a text in "the wise conduct of life." *Univ. of Chicago $6.*

RAMA RAU, SANTHA 1923– *East of Home* (1950). The daughter of an Indian diplomat finds unusual travel adventure in Japan, China, Indochina, Siam, and Indonesia. *Harper $3.75.*

The Teachings of the Compassionate Buddha (1955). Ed. by E. A. Burtt. Wide-ranging selection of Buddhist texts, with helpful introductions and notes. *NAL.*

TRUMBULL, ROBERT 1912– *As I See India* (1956). A *New York Times* correspondent gives a personal report on contemporary life in India based on a 7-year sojourn. *Sloane $4.*

ZINKIN, TAYA *India Changes* (1958). Political and social changes in India since 1945, and the impact of these on the people. *Oxford Univ. $5.*

D. China and Japan

Four excellent works of Chinese fiction that are out of print but obtainable in libraries are *Shui Hu Chuan (All Men Are Brothers)*, trans. by Pearl Buck (rev. ed. 1937); *Chin Ku Chi Kuan (The Inconstancy of Madam Chuang)*, trans. by E. B. Howell (1924); Pu Sung-ling's *Stories from a Chinese Studio*, trans. by H. A. Giles (1880); and *Chin P'ing Mei*.

Anthology of Japanese Literature (1955). Ed. by Donald Keene. Poetry, plays, essays, and selections from novels up to mid-19th century, with useful notes. *Grove 2 vols. $6.50.*

BENEDICT, RUTH 1887–1948 *The Chrysanthemum and the Sword* (1946). A sociologist analyzes the contradictions of Japanese civilization. *Houghton Mifflin $4.50.*

BUCK, PEARL 1892– *The Good Earth* (1931). A moving novel of the Chinese peasant in daily living, famine, disaster, and affluence. *Grosset $1.49, Liv, ML, PB.*

CAMERON, JAMES 1911– *Mandarin Red* (1955). A sharp-eyed reporter travels 7,000 miles in Communist China in 1954 and writes informatively of his experiences. *Rinehart $3.50.*

CARTER, DAGNY *Four Thousand Years of China's Art* (rev. ed. 1951). Development of major and minor arts of China, with profuse and excellent illustrations. *Ronald $7.50.*

CONFUCIUS 551–478 B.C. *The Analects.* The thoughts of China's great ethical thinker, whose influence is still much alive. *Macmillan $3.50, ML, NAL, WoC.*

CREEL, HERRLEE G. 1905– *The Birth of China* (1936). An enthralling account of life during the two earliest periods of Chinese history, 1400–600 B.C., reconstructed from archeological, linguistic, and literary evidence. *Ungar $7.50.*

——————— *Chinese Thought from Confucius to Mao Tse-tung* (1953). Main outlines of Chinese thought developed in nontechnical language. *Univ. of Chicago $6, NAL.*

CRESSY, EARL H. 1883– *Daughters of Changing Japan* (1955). Life among the upper middle classes in Japan as seen through the eyes of ten young Japanese women and recounted by an eminent Orientalist. *Farrar, Straus & Cudahy $4.*

FITZGERALD, C. P. 1902– *China, A Short Cultural History* (3rd rev. ed. 1950). Chinese art and thought against the backdrop of history, richly illustrated. *Praeger $7.50.*

HENDERSON, HAROLD G. 1889– *Introduction to Haiku* (1958). Translation of about 375 haiku, the popular Japanese verse form, together with the original Japanese, literal translations, and historical discussion. *Anch.*

KANG, YOUNGHILL 1903– *The Grass Roof* (1931). Autobiographical novel reporting a sensitive young man's youth in Korea and his struggles in America. *Scribner $3.50.*

KEENE, DONALD 1922– *Japanese Literature* (1955). A brief history dealing with the novel, poem, play, language, and literary spirit. *Grove $2.50, Ever.*

KUO, PIN-CHIA 1908– *China: New Age and New Outlook* (1956). Interpretation of the Chinese Communist Revolution in terms of the past. Dispassionate, realistic, lucid. *Knopf $4.50.*

LAO-TZU 604–531 B.C. *The Way of Life.* The important and influential teachings of Taoism. *Day $1.50, ML.*

LATOURETTE, KENNETH S. 1884– *History of Modern China* (1954). A concise history with emphasis on the present century, leading to an understanding of contemporary China. *Pen.*

———— *The Chinese, Their History and Culture* (3rd ed. 1946). A full, authoritative, readable account. *Macmillan $8.75.*

LIANG YEN (MARGARET YANG BRIGGS) 1917– *Daughter of the Khans* (1955). Personal story of the daughter of a conservative Mongol family who breaks with tradition to make her way in a modern world. *Norton $3.75.*

LIN YUTANG 1895– (ed.) *Famous Chinese Short Stories* (1952). Tales from classical Chinese literature retold in an easy, storyteller tone. *Day $3.50, PB.*

———— *The Gay Genius; The Life and Times of Su Tungpo* (1947). Su Tungpo was a 12th-century poet, painter, statesman, politician, and wit. *Day $4.50.*

MALRAUX *Man's Fate.* A superb French political novel, with a leftist slant, dealing with the Shanghai insurrection of 1927, when Chiang Kai-shek turned against the Communists. See page 98.

Modern Japanese Literature, An Anthology (1956). Ed. by Donald Keene. Stories, poems, plays of modern Japan in readable translations. *Grove $4.75.*

MURASAKI, SHIKIBU 978–1015 *The Tale of Genji.* An absorbing novel about the culture of ancient Japan. *Houghton Mifflin 2 vols. $7.50, Anch.*

PAYNE, ROBERT 1911– *Mao Tse-tung* (1950). Objective, informative biography of the former library clerk and poet who now rules Communist China. *Schuman o.p.*

PERCHERON, MAURICE 1891– *Buddha and Buddhism* (1957). An interpretation for the Western reader of the central concepts of different kinds of Buddhism. Short, clear, copiously illustrated. *Harper $1.35.*

REISCHAUER, EDWIN O. 1910– *Japan, Past and Present* (rev. ed. 1953). Short and accurate political and social history, with a long section on postwar Japan. *Knopf $3.*

SHAW, LAU 1898– *Rickshaw Boy* (1945). Modern novel of a simple country boy and his troubled life as a rickshaw boy in Peking. *Harcourt, Brace o.p.*

SHOR, JEAN BOWIE *After You, Marco Polo* (1955). An engaging account of a trip following the route of Marco Polo from Venice to Peking. *McGraw-Hill $4.75.*

SONE, MONICA 1919– *Nisei Daughter* (1953). Warm, honest, gay biography of a young Japanese-American woman, dealing candidly with race prejudice in America. *Little, Brown $4.50.*

SUZUKI, D. T. 1870– *Zen Buddhism* (1956). History and doctrines of Zen described clearly and freshly. *Anch.*

TS'AO HSUEH CHIN 1717?–1764 *Dream of the Red Chamber.* A gigantic, complicated 18th-century novel dealing with a love affair and the decline of a noble family. A major work of literature. *Pantheon $7.50, Anch.*

WALEY, ARTHUR 1889– *Translations from the Chinese* (1941). Poignant and beautiful poems, skillfully phrased. *Knopf $7.50.*

WANG CHI-CHEN 1899– *Current Chinese Readings* (1944). Excellent stories in a realistic vein from 1918, beginning of the Chinese literary Renaissance. *Twayne $3.*

———— *Traditional Chinese Readings* (1944). Ancient stories, tinged with the supernatural, of both classical and popular types. *Twayne $3.*

WILLETTS, WILLIAM 1918– *Chinese Art* (1958). Straightforward, detailed, well-illustrated history of the development of the major and minor arts in China. *Braziller $5, Pen 2 vols.*

WU CH'ENG-EN 16th century *Monkey.* Delightful picaresque novel, translated by Arthur Waley. *Ever.*

YOSHIKAWA, EIJI 1892– *The Heiké Story* (1956). Long, complex novel, threaded with love stories, based on a 13th-century epic. Abridged for Western readers. *Knopf $4.95, Ever.*

8. Latin America

DONALD DEMAREST, *Centro Mexicano de Escritores*

Latin American writing has gone through three distinct stages. During its Colonial period, the writers—like the artists and architects—found their models in Mother Spain. During its Revolutionary period, which extended over two centuries, the literature of France—first France of the Encyclopedists, then of the Symbolists—was the vital influence. Only very recently has Latin American literature entered a renaissance; compounded of North American techniques and developing from indigenous roots, it promises to have the vitality of the plastic arts of the 30's.

The Indian has always been a key (and problematic) figure in Latin American letters. During the Colonial period he was either a quaint sort of Uncle Tom or an even more fantastic and romantic Natty Bumppo; during the various revolutionary cycles he was first a Rousseau-esque Noble Savage and afterwards a faceless symbol of the oppressed. For the new generation, however—especially in Mexico (where the new artistic movements generally originate)—he is the complex protagonist of an exceptionally split but also extraordinarily rich culture. For mestizo writers like Juan Rulfo, Rosario Castellanos, and Carlos Fuentes, the Indian epitomizes an ancient wisdom that the Toltecs and Maya once possessed long before the conquistadors arrived on the scene.

In their creative preoccupation with who they are and what they mean, young Latin American writers have a fruitful literary tradition to explore and return to. The pre-Columbian legends—preserved by priest-ethnologists of the caliber of Sahagún and Ximénez and (today) Angel Garibay, or by Europe-educated natives such as the Inca Garcilaso—have a stylistic and symbol-packed richness

81

resembling that of the Upanishads and the Old Testament. A work like *Chilam Balam,* compiled long after the people whose legends and history it preserves had vanished, ranges in style and theme from a Grimm (and Freudian) fairy tale through an Ecclesiastican curse on the conquerors to a Blakean myth of a New Jerusalem.

Even the Colonial period produced some works of lasting importance. An Alarcón, a Sor Juana Inés de la Cruz —even a Lizardi, whose picaresque novel, *The Itching Parrot* (effectively translated by Kay Boyle but now unfortunately out of print), was the first written and published in this hemisphere—deserve more attention from students of international literature than they have been given.

During the revolutionary cycles (which can be divided into the 19th-century wars of independence and the continuing struggles against native dictators), much of the major writing was done by intellectuals turned soldiers— from Hidalgo to Martí. Their manifestoes often took the form of poetry, novels, newspaper columns, and philosophical essays. To the latter phases of the revolutions we owe such vital novels as those by Alegría (Peru), Arciniegas (Colombia), Azuela (Mexico), De Cunha (Brazil), Gallegos (Venezuela), and Quiroga (Uruguay). Most such novels suffer, however, from being written too close to the scene: either as protest novels, or as combat diaries compiled by the light of the campfire on the eve of battle. In this genre the semifictionalized accounts of the Villa campaigns by Martín Luis Guzmán are classics. Though there is still no Latin American *War and Peace,* sons of guerrillas have composed battle scenes as convincing as Stephen Crane's.

The novelists and journalists fought and wrote. The poets tended to retreat to the ivory towers which Mallarmé and other Symbolists inhabited with great style. In Mexico the retreat took the form of the complex and opaque, death- and God-centered poetry of Villaurrutia and Gorostiza. Enlistment in the Spanish Civil War gave Octavio Paz (as he gave Neruda) a social focus for what had been private pyrotechnics.

Meanwhile, a special genre of Latin American writing —which echoes the bitter epigrams of *Chilam Balam* and borrows from such diverse sources as La Rochefoucauld and O. Henry—deserves attention. In the field of the very short story, prose poem, or essay (of from 100 to 1000 words) such Latin Americans as José Luis Borges (Argentina), Ramón Lopez Velarde, Julio Torri, Juan José Arreola (all of Mexico) have perfected a form as stylized as the Japanese haiku and as lethal as the scorpion. Combining a European elegance of style with Indian impassivity, these pieces might bring a hectic flush to the pale faces of the "sick" humorists now plying in the U.S.

The Latin American contribution to international literature has been sadly neglected—especially by the English-speaking world. That the scales are being currently brought into balance is due to several factors: new good translations of Latin American poetry by such distinguished English and American poets as Robert Graves, William Carlos Williams, Dudley Fitts, and John Ciardi; the slick magazines' intensive coverage of the tourist charms of our South and Central American neighbors; the emerging recognition of Latin America's archeological and architectural contributions; and the two Nobel Prizes awarded to Hispanic poets in past decades—to Gabriela Mistral (Chile) in 1945, and to the expatriate Spaniard Juan Ramón Jiménez in 1956.

The years 1958 and 1959 have seen an increasing attention to Latin American writing, resulting in the discovery and translation of the younger writers. In December 1958 *New World Writing #14* carried a Latin American section notable for its scope; in January 1959 *The Evergreen Review* (Vol. 2, #7) devoted most of its pages to new Mexican writing; and in February of the same year *The Texas Quarterly* (Vol. 2, #1) issued a 381-page Mexican literature collection.

Meanwhile, new translations of novels by Rulfo, Castellanos, and Fuentes as well as Irene Nicholson's creative version of pre-Columbian poetry have been scheduled for publication on both sides of the Atlantic. Through translation, Latin American writing is at last becoming known and respected in the English-speaking world.

A. Background Books

ARCINIEGAS, GERMAN (Colombia) 1900– *Caribbean: Sea of the New World* (1946). Weaves a rich tapestry of clashing empires, merging cultures, struggle and achievement. *Knopf $5.75.*

BRENNER, ANITA (U.S.A.) 1905– *The Wind That Swept Mexico* (1943). Compact history of the Mexican revolution which began in 1911. Richly illustrated. *Harper $5.*

CALDERON DE LA BARCA, FRANCES E. (England) 1804–1882 *Life in Mexico* (1931). Classic account by a 19th-century diplomat's wife; still largely accurate. *Evman-h.*

CASO, ALFONSO (Mexico) 1896– *The Aztecs: The People of the Sun* (1958). A classic of style and learning. *Univ. of Oklahoma $7.95.*

CHAPMAN, CHARLES E. (U.S.A.) 1880– *Colonial Hispanic America* (1933) and *Republican Hispanic America* (1937). A distinguished historical survey of our neighbors to the south. *Macmillan $6.25 ea.; 2 books in 1, $8.*

COVARRUBIAS, MIGUEL (Mexico) 1904–1957 *Mexico South* (1946). The Tehuantepec region fascinatingly described; archeology, history, social conditions, cultural arts, current problems. Abundantly, beautifully illustrated. *Knopf $12.50.*

———— *Indian Art of Mexico and Central America* (1957). Last and most brilliant work, definitive yet revolutionary. *Knopf $17.50.*

CROW, JOHN (U.S.A.) 1906– *Mexico Today* (1957). Extraordinarily balanced account of the contemporary situation—art, industry, politics, journalism, tourism. *Harper $5.*

DIAZ DEL CASTILLO, BERNAL (Spain) c. 1492–1581 *Discovery and Conquest of Mexico* (1632). Blunt, engaging chronicle by one of Cortés's conquistadors. *Farrar, Straus & Cudahy $6.50, Ever (abr.).*

FLORNOY, BERTRAND (France) *The World of the Inca* (1956). Authoritative, literate account of a colorful vanishing empire. *Vanguard $4.50, Anch.*

HERRING, HUBERT C. (U.S.A.) 1889– *History of Latin America* (1955). The kaleidoscopic interplay of varied cultures and forces upon an immense, rich continent. *Knopf $6.50.*

HITCHCOCK, HENRY-RUSSELL (U.S.A.) 1903– *Latin American Architecture Since 1945* (1955). Daring triumphs of modern design reflecting a new civilization that is taking shape. Handsomely illustrated. *Doubleday (Museum of Modern Art) $6.50.*

MADARIAGA, SALVADOR DE (Spain) 1886– *The Fall of the Spanish American Empire* (1947). Brilliant, provocative attack on "The Black Legend" of Spanish colonialism. *Macmillan $5.75.*

MORLEY, SYLVANUS G. (U.S.A.) 1883–1948 *The Ancient Maya* (rev. 1956). Classic account of the "Greeks" of Central America. *Stanford Univ. $8.50.*

MYERS, BERNARD S. (U.S.A.) 1908– *Mexican Painting in Our Time* (1956). Cogent, readable coverage of the Renaissance in Mexican art. *Oxford Univ. $15.*

OAKES, MAUD (U.S.A.) *Beyond the Windy Place* (1951). Adventures of an American girl studying Mayan survivals in Guatemalan highlands, pleasantly salted with dry humor. *Farrar, Straus & Cudahy o.p.*

PRESCOTT (U.S.A.) *Conquest of Mexico* and *Conquest of Peru.* Colorful classics of history. See page 50.

RENNIE, YSABEL R. (U.S.A.) 1918– *The Argentine Republic* (1945). History and social analysis; readable, provocative. *Macmillan o.p.*

RODMAN, SELDEN (U.S.A.) 1909– *Haiti, The Black Republic* (1954). Rounded, poetic view of a strange, complex country. *Devin-Adair $5.*

_____ *Mexican Journal* (1958). Richly informative survey of political and intellectual leaders, artists and architects, archeologists and shopkeepers, the ancient and modern. *Devin-Adair $6.50.*

B. Latin American Literature

ARCINIEGAS, GERMAN (Colombia) 1900– (ed.) *The Green Continent* (1944). Excellent anthology of writings by more than 30 Latin American historians, biographers, essayists, and novelists, showing how our southward neighbors think and feel. *Knopf $5.*

ASSIS, MACHADO DE (Brazil) 1839–1908 *Epitaph of a Small Winner* (1880). Ironic psychological novel about a 19th-century Brazilian George Apley. *Noon.*

AZUELA, MARIANO (Mexico) 1873–1951 *The Flies* (1918) and *The Bosses* (1917). Two pungent novelettes of the Mexican revolution by the author of *The Underdogs. Calif.*

CASTELLANOS, ROSARIO (Mexico) 1922– *Balún-Canán (The Nine Guardians)* (1957). Rich novel of contemporary descendants of Mayan Indians. *Vanguard $3.75.*

CRANFILL, THOMAS M. (U.S.A.) (ed.) *The Muse in Mexico* (1959). Outstanding anthology of contemporary Mexican art and literature. *Univ. of Texas $4.*

CUNHA, EUCLYDES DA (Brazil) 1866–1909 *Rebellion in the Backlands* (1902). The wild west of the Amazon Valley erupting in dramatic action. The epic narrative of Brazil's struggle from tropic jungle toward modern civilization. *Univ. of Chicago $6.50, Phoen.*

FITTS, DUDLEY (U.S.A.) 1903– (ed.) *An Anthology of Contemporary Latin-American Poetry* (1947). Over 700 pages giving both original Spanish (or Portuguese) and English renderings, supplemented by brief biographies. *New Directions $2.50.*

GALLEGOS, ROMULO (Venezuela) 1884– *Doña Bárbara* (1942). A symbolic novel about a femme fatale, developing the conflict between civilization and barbarism, by a former President of Venezuela. *Appleton-Century-Crofts $2.25.*

GALVAN, MANUEL DE JESUS (Dominican Republic) 1834–1911 *Enriquillo (The Cross and the Sword)* (1879). Tr. by Robert Graves. About life in the Caribbean during Spain's greatest moment (c. 1503–1533). *Univ. of Indiana $3.75.*

GUZMAN, MARTIN LUIS (Mexico) 1890– *The Eagle and the Serpent* (1930). The classic account of Pancho Villa. *Knopf o.p.*

MANACH, JORGE (Cuba) 1898– *Marti, Apostle of Freedom* (1950). Fascinating biography of the martyr of Cuban independence and forerunner of modernism. *Devin-Adair $4.50.*

MISTRAL, GABRIELA (Chile) 1889–1957 *Selected Poems* (1957). Tr. by Langston Hughes. Cross-section of verse by a Nobel Prize winner. *Univ. of Indiana $3.*

ONIS, HARRIET DE (U.S.A.) 1899– (tr. and ed.) *The Golden Land* (1948). A rich anthology of Latin American writings from the Spanish conquest to the present, chosen to show how native folklore has influenced literature. *Knopf $4.50.*

Popol Vuh: The Sacred Book of the Ancient Quiché Maya (1957). A marvelous myth put into English by Delia Goetz and Sylvanus G. Morley. *Univ. of Oklahoma $5.*

RULFO, JUAN (Mexico) 1918– *Pedro Paramo* (1957). Powerfully haunting novel about a ghost town in Jalisco; somewhat Faulknerian, but completely indigenous and unique. *Ever.*

SUBERCASSEAUX, BENJAMIN (Chile) 1902– *Jemmy Button* (1954). Curious, provocative historical novel about a Fuegian Indian subjected to British culture of the 1830's. *Macmillan $4.*

VERISSIMO, ERICO (Brazil) 1905– *Time and the Wind* (1949). A long novel of epic richness recounting the evolution of the state of Rio Grande do Sul. *Macmillan $4.95.*

LITERARY TYPES

---

9. The Novel

A. 19th Century Continental

ARTHUR WALDHORN, *City College of New York*

More good novels were written in Continental Europe in the 19th century than in any other place or period. It seems doubtful that this was mere happenstance. The arts flourish in peace, and there were no general wars after Napoleon's defeat in 1815. A novelist feeds on his time, and Continental Europe in the 19th century served varied and nourishing fare. Ferment in art, science, and politics leavened the age and infused the novel with new ideas and new points of view. For those with intellectual appetite, it was a zestful time to live and to write. No other place or period has produced so many good novels.

France and Russia showed the greatest activity. Out of the turmoil of French politics a new middle class was arising. Increasingly, careers were open to talent instead of to aristocratic privilege. The greatest French novelists were bourgeois—Balzac, Zola, Stendhal, Flaubert—and it was the rise of their class that they portrayed with varying degrees of disapproval. Where the French Romantics saw man as a passionate individual, nobler or baser than he consistently was, Balzac placed this individual in society, and in his novels the Romantic goals of an abstract liberty or an exalted love change to money and social ambition. His *Comédie Humaine* had the most comprehensive plan any novelist ever made, nothing less than to depict in a series of novels a whole nation, the France of his time, as it actually was. For Zola, actuality was scientific: "Study men like simple elements and note their reactions," he advised. His novels about the Rougon-Macquart families shocked France to the core although they never quite achieved the scientific objectivity he aimed for: a strong moral disapproval shows through. In his three chief novels Stendhal wrote the same story three times, that of a young man making his way in the world: in *The Red and the Black,* a poor young man in a real France; in *Lucien Leuwen,* a rich young man; but in the *Charterhouse of Parma* (sometimes called the greatest French novel), a young aristocrat fails to gain happiness in an imaginary Italian principality. The actions, operatic and extravagant, are moved by a hard-boiled modern psychology.

With Flaubert's *Madame Bovary,* the novel changed. Although he was called a realist in his time, it can now be seen that he not only fused the Realistic and Romantic ideas but he moved the novelist out of the book. The characters seem to think and act by themselves. His intense care for structure and the fall of the individual sentence gave novelists a new sense of the seriousness of their art; thus he is the bridge to Joyce and through him to the 20th century.

In Russia the situation was different. The Tsars, frightened by the democratic ideas that had spread from revolutionary France, tried to shut them out by suppressing freedom of assembly and imposing a strict censorship. It is possible that most Russian novels, although politically "correct," were a defiant response to these pressures. Tolstoy was a rich nobleman, an army officer, and had none but the artist's obligation to be a novelist at all, yet in *War and Peace, Anna Karenina,* and *Resurrection,* he tries to portray the permanent, essential Russia, regardless of the accidents of politics, and his vision is so profound that he gives us not merely Russians but very human beings. After a term in Siberia as a political offender, Dostoevski was tormented by the problems of Christian belief and the existence of evil. His lifelong aim was to write a huge work called *Life of a Great Sinner,* but he never did. However, his great novels, *The Brothers Karamazov, Crime and Punishment,* and *The Possessed,* may be fragments of this work. He owed much

THE NOVEL: 19TH CENTURY CONTINENTAL 89

to Dickens, but he treats his characters with a psychological penetration that often foreshadows Freud and makes Dickens seem at times naïve. Turgenev, like Tolstoy, was a rich nobleman; he was sent to jail for depicting serfs as human beings in his *Sportsman's Sketches*. In *Fathers and Sons* he examines with great clarity the impact of liberal ideas on two generations of Russians. Isolated though they were, these Russian novelists have a power and intensity that abolish national boundaries.

Other European countries had fewer great novelists, but fine novels were published nevertheless. Manzoni's *The Betrothed* and Verga's *The House by the Medlar Tree* were the best to come out of Italy. The charm of Alarcón's *The Three-Cornered Hat* and Pérez Galdós's *Doña Perfecta* makes one wish that Spain had been more prolific. Among German novels, *Wilhelm Meister*, although not Goethe's greatest work, is still a product of one of the most fertile minds of the age. Novels by Scandinavian, Polish, Hungarian, Belgian, Dutch, and Portuguese authors had merit but made little stir internationally.

In 1800 the novel had been a new thing, scarcely to be ranked with poetry or drama as serious literature. By 1900 the novel was clearly the most popular and most influential of all literary forms.

ALARCON, PEDRO ANTONIO (Spain) 1833–1891 *The Three-Cornered Hat* (1874). How the miller's wife fooled the mayor. Clever, witty, charming. *BES*.

BALZAC, HONORE DE (France) 1799–1850 *Cousine Bette* (1846). Frantic social ambition of minor bureaucrats and their wives. Some consider this Balzac's best. *ML*.

_____ *Eugénie Grandet* (1833). A realistic study of what bourgeois money-hunger will drive people to endure. Particularly vivid in its description of the resultant emotional sterility. *Holt $2.90, Ban, Evman-h, ML, Nel, Pen*.

_____ *Old Goriot* (1834). An old Parisian sacrifices everything for his worthless daughters. A French version of the King Lear theme. *Evman-h, GtIl, ML, MLCE, Pen, Pyr, Rine*.

Balzac combines sweeping imagination with minute observation. The two novels just above are part of his *Comédie Humaine*, which tries to record all French life from the fall of Napoleon to 1848. Its theme is the impact of bourgeois standards on morals and culture. Also recommended are *The Magic Skin* (1831) and *Séraphita* (1835).

CONSTANT, BENJAMIN (France) 1767–1830 *Adolphe* (1815). One of the earliest psychological novels, it draws autobiographically upon Constant's long and dramatic relationship with Mme. de Staël. *NAL.*

DAUDET, ALPHONSE (France) 1840–1897 *Sapho* (1884). Absorbing study of enslavement to love's passion by the most poetic of the Naturalists. *Avon.*

DOSTOEVSKI, FEDOR (Russia) 1821–1881 *The Brothers Karamazov* (1880). Dmitri Karamazov and his father are rivals for the love of Grushenka. Smerdyakov, an illegitimate son, murders the father. Dmitri is tried and convicted on circumstantial evidence. Out of this "plot" Dostoevski magically turns the book into a search for faith. His last and greatest work. *Grosset $2.49, Dell (abr.), Evman-h 2 vols., Harp, ML, MLCE, MLG, NAL, Pen 2 vols.*

———— *Crime and Punishment* (1866). A half-starved student murders two old women, one of them for money. One of the world's great detective stories as well as a trenchant portrayal of remorse for crime. *Cambridge Univ. $3, Macmillan $2.50, Ban, Dell, Evman-h, Harp, Liv, MLCE, MLP, Pen, UL, WoC.*

Also recommended: *Letters from the Underworld* (1864). *Evman-h.* A frightening book because of its intensity. Analysis of liberty and a criticism of modern civilization. *The Idiot* (1868–9). *Macmillan $2.50, Ban, Evman-h, MLG, Pen.* You realize slowly that Prince Muishkin, an eccentric epileptic, is a Christ figure. *The Possessed* (1873). *Macmillan $3.75, Evman-h 2 vols., ML, Pen.* A story of political radicals whom Dostoevski loathed.

DUMAS, ALEXANDRE (France) 1802–1870 *The Count of Monte Cristo* (1844). An exciting story of melodramatic revenge, romance, and adventure. *Ban (abr.), Evman-h 2 vols.*

French history is brilliantly dramatized in Dumas's novels. Among the best known are *The Three Musketeers, Twenty Years After,* and *The Vicomte de Bragelonne,* depicting French life under Louis XIII (17th century).

FLAUBERT, GUSTAVE (France) 1821–1880 *Madame Bovary* (1857). Emma Bovary expected to find in marriage the romance of which she had read and dreamed. Her husband and the town were dull. She took lovers, ran into debt, killed herself. A literary landmark often called the perfect novel. The Steegmuller translation (*MLCE*) is recommended. *Ban, Dell, Evman-h, Harp, Liv, ML, ModSL, Ox, PB, Pen, Rine, UL, WoC.*

———— *Salammbô* (1862). A model of the historical novel. A barbaric, colorful story of love and war in ancient Carthage. *Berk, Evman-h.*

———— *Sentimental Education* (1869). The disillusionment of a young Parisian through love. Many French critics call this Flaubert's best work. *Evman-h, New.*

FRANCE, ANATOLE (France) 1844–1924 *The Crime of Sylvestre Bonnard* (1881). Presented against a background of gentle humor, pathos, urbanity, Bonnard is one of the most lovable characters of French literature. *Dodd, Mead $2.75.*

_____ *Thaïs* (1890). Alexandria in the 1st century: a fanatical monk converts a courtesan to Christianity, only to fall from purity into sin. *GC o.p.* See also page 97.

GAUTIER, THEOPHILE (France) 1811–1872 *Mademoiselle de Maupin* (1835). A romantic, sensual love story by a fine poet. *Pyr.*

GOETHE, JOHANN WOLFGANG VON (Germany) 1749–1832 *Wilhelm Meister's Apprenticeship* (1795–6). The love affairs of a dilettante of vacillating temperament, while traveling with a theatrical troupe. *Page 2 vols. o.p.*

GOGOL, NIKOLAI (Russia) 1809–1852 *Dead Souls* (1842). Amusing yarn about a genial fraud trading in nonexistent serfs. By Russia's finest prose stylist. *Evman-h, Rine, WoC.*

_____ *The Overcoat* (1842). A curious tale of such influence that it prompted Dostoevski to say, "We all came out of Gogol's overcoat pocket." Included in *6 Great Modern Short Novels, Dell.*

GONCHAROV, IVAN (Russia) 1812–1891 *Oblomov* (1859). Oblomov, a rich landowner, is the laziest man in the world. The account of his getting up in the morning is one of the funniest, most touching passages in fiction. *Evman-h, Pen.*

HUGO, VICTOR (France) 1802–1885 *Les Misérables* (1862). Hugo was one of the founders of French Romanticism. Here, the characters of Jean Valjean, Javert, and Fantine are unforgettable. With overpowering pathos the French poor of the post-Napoleonic era are portrayed in this vast panorama. *Evman-h 2 vols., MLG, Nel.*

_____ *The Hunchback of Notre Dame* (1831). The strange love of a hunchback for a dancer. A great historical novel laid in the 15th century. *Grosset $1.95, Avon, Ban, CoNC, Evman-h, GtIl, ML, Nel.*

HUYSMANS, JORIS KARL (France) *Against the Grain* (1884). A caricature of the excesses of the symbolist movement. Ironically, the decadent tastes of the aristocratic hero are those of the author. *MLP, Pen* (titled *Against Nature*).

LOTI, PIERRE (France) 1850–1923 *An Iceland Fisherman* (1886). With descriptive brilliance and romantic sadness, Loti depicts the poverty of the Breton fishermen who go to fish off Iceland every year. *Evman-h.*

LOUYS (France) *Aphrodite.* Lush decadence of Greek Alexandria. See page 30.

MANZONI, ALESSANDRO (Italy) 1785–1873 *The Betrothed* (1826). Fascinating historical novel of 17th-century Italy. Robber barons, the plague, true love. *Dutton $5, Evman-h.*

MAUPASSANT, GUY DE (France) 1850–1893 *Bel-Ami* (1885). A scoundrel makes his way by his good looks. *Pantheon Books $1.25.*

_____ *A Woman's Life (Une Vie)* (1883). Realistic analysis of the frustrations of a woman in Normandy. *Vik-h.*

MERIMEE, PROSPER (France) 1803–1870 *Carmen* (1845). A gypsy girl enslaves and destroys a Spanish soldier. Famous in story, film, opera. *Evman-h.*

MURGER, HENRI (France) 1822–1861 *Vie de Bohème* (1848). Warm, vivid record of penniless artists, musicians, writers in Paris garrets—their loves, sufferings, gaieties, jealousies, triumphs. Source of the opera *La Bohème.* No edition in English.

NERVAL, GERARD DE (France) 1808–1855 *Sylvie* (1853). Affecting semiautobiographical narrative of adolescent love recollected in maturity. *Ever.* In *Selected Writings of Gérard de Nerval, Grove $3.75.*

PEREZ GALDOS, BENITO (Spain) 1843–1920 *Doña Perfecta* (1876). The finest of Galdós's several portraits of Spanish life. The scene is provincial, the time before the Carlist War, the treatment at once romantic and realistic. *BES.*

SIENKIEWICZ (Poland) *Quo Vadis?* See page 37.

STENDHAL (HENRI BEYLE) (France) 1783–1842 *The Charterhouse of Parma* (1839). Delightful, colorful novel of love and politics. *Anch, Black, Pen.*

_____ *The Red and the Black* (1830). The brilliant portrayal of the ambitious young Frenchman to whom France is a foreign country. *Ban, Black, ML, Pen.*

_____ *Lucien Leuwen* (1894). Probably the sharpest political novel ever written. Published in America as two novels: *The Green Huntsman, The Telegraph. New Directions $3.50 ea.*

SUE, EUGENE (France) 1804–1857 *The Wandering Jew* (1845). One of the great legends of literature. *MLG.*

TOLSTOY, LEO (Russia) 1828–1910 *War and Peace* (1866). Richly detailed chronicle of two noble families. The principal action is the invasion of Russia by Napoleon. The choice of many critics for the greatest novel ever written. *Grosset $2.98, Ban (abr.), Dell (abr.), Evman-h 3 vols., MLG, Pen 2 vols.*

_____ *Anna Karenina* (1877). An engrossing story of an adultery among the Russian nobility. Thomas Mann called it the greatest novel of society in the history of the world. *Evman-h 2 vols., Liv, ML, MLCE, MLG, Pen, WoC.*

_____ *Resurrection* (1900). A Russian prince seduces a peasant girl, realizes his responsibility for her, and joins her in Siberia. *WoC.*

Also recommended: *The Cossacks* (1862). *NAL.* A rich young officer is enchanted by life among the Cossacks. *The Kreutzer Sonata* (1889). *MLP, WoC.* Profoundly affecting problem novel about an unconventional attitude toward marriage.

TURGENEV, IVAN (Russia) 1818–1883 *Fathers and Sons* (1862). In Bazarov, Turgenev shows clearly the attitudes of mind that led to the October Revolution. *Evman-h, Harp, ML, MLCE, Noon, Rine.*

VERGA, GIOVANNI (Italy) 1840–1922 *The House by the Medlar Tree* (1890). Dramatically moving story of Sicilian peasants. *Anch.*

ZOLA, EMILE (France) 1840–1902 *Germinal* (1885). Very powerful account of an unsuccessful strike of coal miners, and the pathos of the children who toiled in the mines. *Evman-h, Pen.*

———— *Nana* (1880). The stunning vulgarity of the demimonde of the Second Empire. The life of a harlot described in Naturalistic detail. *Liv, ML, PB.*

Although there was a poet lurking beneath his pretended scienticism, Zola was the founder of the modern school of Naturalism. Recommended also are *L'Assommoir (The Dram-Shop)* (1877), a terrible warning on the evils of drink; and *La Terre* (1888), about the selfishness and brutality of peasant life. *Ever.*

B. 20th Century Continental Novels

ROBERT CLARKE WHITE, *Castleton Teachers College*

At the dawn of the 20th century, Europe was relatively sound and healthy, its writers comfortably detached. By 1920 the Continent had suffered a stroke; its writers were disturbed, restless, and deeply engaged in the fever of events. In 1939 came a second stroke, followed since by cold wars, hot police actions, dissolving empires, bad consciences, émigré writers, spiritual drift and anguish. Each nation, uniquely ill, has made its separate diagnoses and prescriptions for health.

Before examining the major national literatures, we should note the dominant types in modern European fiction: the *family novel*—Mann (Germany), Couperus (The Netherlands), Martin du Gard (France); the *peasant novel*—Hamsun (Norway), Lagerlöf (Sweden), Sillanpää (Finland), Nexø (Denmark), Silone and Vittorini (Italy); the *novel of contemporary history*—Malraux (France), Koestler (Hungary, Britain), Ehrenburg (Russia), Seghers (Germany); the *world-survey novel* or *novel-group*—Mann's *The Magic Mountain,* Romain Rolland's *Jean Christophe,* Jules Romains's *Men of Good Will.*

France, ever in the cultural van, regularly provides prototypal novels that develop and test all acts and isms. To treat her modish malady—a sick conscience—she has many doctors. François Mauriac offers the novel of Catholic faith; Gide, the honest if unorthodox search for selfhood and for right relations with man and God. The ironies of Anatole France can still bring refreshment. Sartre, Camus, and de Beauvoir, all existentialists, call for "personal responsibility" in a world that is itself godless and absurd. Malraux urges the tonic of action; Romains the balm of brotherhood (unanimism); Chevallier and Colette the satisfactions of physical sensation;

Proust and the Franco-Belgian Simenon the steadying sedatives of memory and Inspector Maigret.

Russian fiction flourished from about 1920 to 1932 when "Dr." Gorki's "social realism" pill cooled many a fine imaginative frenzy. Yet Sholokhov in Tolstoy's way and Leonov in Dostoevski's have transcended, while obeying, party-line directives. More recently, in *Not By Bread Alone* and in *Dr. Zhivago,* Dudintsev and Pasternak have transcended while "obeying" the restrictions of Soviet censors; and Nabokov (Russia, United States) has aroused attention and debate with his Moravia-like, sad sex comedy, *Lolita.*

Norway and Greece have won fresh laurels by the translation into English, in 1958, of *Four Stories* by Sigrid Undset and of *The Odyssey: A Modern Sequel* by Nikos Kazantzakis. Switzerland, in 1959, is represented by an audacious and philosophical writer of suspense stories, Friedrich Duerrenmatt (*The Pledge*).

Italian fiction, until the death of Mussolini, had concerned itself primarily with an intense regionalism, a microscopic report of provincial life. The more broadly conceived novels by D'Annunzio and Fogazzaro reached English-language readers in the first decade of the century, those of the paradoxical Pirandello in the second. Quite recently a spate of Italian novels (some written in Fascist days, some more recently) give notice, together with some excellent films and ever-glorious musical creations, that the genius of Italy is in ferment. The names of Ignazio Silone, Alberto Moravia, and Carlo Levi are perhaps currently the most considerable.

German storytellers produced significant fiction up to the brainwashings or flights-from-hell of Hitler's regime. Incidentally, "German" novels include some by Austrians, Swiss, and Czechs (such as Kafka). Prolifically translated but uneven in merit, German novels that have been available in English could be cited to the extent of several pages, yet few are still in print and still read. The late Thomas Mann—erudite literary artist, at home in all countries, diagnostician of the 20th-century ills of Germany, Europe, and the world, revealer of the human and divine in the characters of Joseph and his brethren— is a Goethe *redivivus.* Erich Remarque, classic analyst of

war and its aftermath; Feuchtwanger and Werfel, writers
of historical novels with meanings for today; and Wasser-
man, depicter of the searching soul in modern man—all
are novelists of stature. The sober, nightmare surrealism
of Kafka (a Czech); the excruciating vivisections of errant
Galahads by Arthur Koestler (Hungarian); the humanitarian dramas of Arnold Zweig (Austrian) belong, in the
language sense, in the roster of "German" novels. Czech
fiction will be long renowned for the prophetic scientific
fantasies, in novels as in plays, of Karel Cápek, as readable as they are wise.

The special features and saga-strength of Scandinavian
life (lived so far from Rome and Paris!) may be assim-
ilated, like blood transfusions, from the pages of Lagerlöf
and Hellstrom (Sweden), Bojer and Gulbranssen (Norway), Sillanpää and Hemmer (Finland), Nexø and Jen-
sen (Denmark), Gunnarsson and Laxness (Iceland).

Historical novels are sufficient in number and merit to
form a considerable modern library. Blending keen research, fresh insights into history and human nature, and
engrossing melodrama, the novels of Sholem Asch (Yid-
dish), Sigrid Undset (Norway), Annamarie Selinko (Austria), Zofia Kossak (Poland), and Mika Waltari (Finland)
are both scholarly and popular.

Such is today's world of European fiction: sick in
conscience, critical in mood, strong at heart, striving,
the blood singing, indomitable.

ANDREYEV, LEONID (Russia) 1871–1919 *Seven Who Were Hanged*
(1909). Revolutionary idealists pay the death penalty. *MLP.*

BACCHELLI, RICCARDO (Italy) 1891– *A Mill on the Po* (1950,
1954). A trilogy: three generations in the life of a flour-miller's
family. *Pantheon $4.95.*

BEAUVOIR, SIMONE DE (France) 1908– *The Mandarins* (1956).
A provocative satire of the manners and morals of postwar
French intellectuals by a leading existentialist. *World $6.*

BOJER, JOHAN (Norway) 1872–1959 *The Great Hunger* (1918).
An engineer goes from rags to riches to rags but wins spiritual
victory in material defeat. *Grosset o.p.*

BUNIN, IVAN (Russia) 1870–1953 *The Village* (1923). Unflattering
depiction of two brothers, materialist and mystic-idealist,
against the background of tragic Tsarist village life. *Knopf o.p.*

CAMUS, ALFRED (France) 1913– *The Plague* (1948). When plague
hits Oran, North Africa, Tarrou, an existentialist hero, accepts

the hard fact and battles the plague to victory—and death. *Knopf $3.95.*

CAPEK, KAREL (Czechoslovakia) 1890–1938 *War with the Newts* (1937). The newts take over! Science fiction, excellent as humor, social commentary, and story. *Ban.*

COUPERUS, LOUIS MARIE ANNE (Holland) 1863–1923 *The Book of Small Souls* (1923). Lives of tradition-bound Hollanders delineated with the eye of a sociologist, the art of a novelist. *Dodd, Mead o.p.*

D'ANNUNZIO, GABRIELE (Italy) 1863–1938 *The Flame of Life* (1900). Passionate glorification of passion; based on his liaison with the famous actress Eleanora Duse. *Page o.p.*

DUERRENMATT, FRIEDRICH (Switzerland) 1922– *The Pledge* (1959). Thought-arousing *récit,* sparely written, of a police-force captain whose logic is defeated by reality. *Knopf $3, NAL.*

EHRENBURG, ILYA (Russia) 1891– *The Storm* (1949). Story of Russia and France during World War II. Biased—but a sample of the "novel of contemporary history." *Gaer o.p.*

FOGAZZARO, ANTONIO (Italy) 1842–1911 *The Saint* (1907). Story of Piero Maironi, a near-sinner who becomes a near-saint. This novel became "the gospel, even platform" of Italian Christian Democrats. *Putnam o.p.*

FRANCE, ANATOLE (France) 1844–1924 *Penguin Island* (1908). Satirical fantasy pinpricking the history of Western civilization (particularly that of France) in terms of an island populated by penguins. *Ban, ML.*

——————— *Revolt of the Angels* (1914). A guardian angel, off duty, investigates and denounces the God of the theologians and organizes a revolt of the fallen angels of Paris. *Heritage $5, Evman-h.* See also page 90.

Also recommended: *The Crime of Sylvestre Bonnard* (1881), *Dodd, Mead $2.75; The Red Lily* (1894), *Pyr; The Rotisserie of the Queen Pédauque* (1893), *Evman-h.*

GIDE, ANDRE (France) 1869–1951 *The Counterfeiters* (1927). Ironic analysis of troubled youth. *Knopf $4.*

GULBRANSSEN, TRYGVE (Norway) 1894– *Beyond Sing the Woods* (1936). Literally getting out of the woods and ahead in the world of romance and bourgeois business. *Putnam $4.*

HAMSUN, KNUT (Norway) 1859–1952 *Growth of the Soil* (1921). While neighbors fret, a Norwegian farm couple grow in nature-wise serenity. *Knopf $4.75.*

HASEK, JAROSLAV (Czechoslovakia) 1883–1923 *The Good Soldier Schweik* (1923). What fools we privates be—not to mention brass hats, army doctors, military police, young lieutenants, and war itself. *NAL o.p.*

KAFKA, FRANZ (Germany) 1883–1924 *The Trial* (1937). Weird, haunting story of man's loneliness in an accusing, incomprehensible world controlled by implacable, irresponsible authorities. *Knopf $4.50.*

KAPEK See CAPEK above.

KAZANTZAKIS, NIKOS (Greece) 1885–1957 *Freedom or Death* (1955). An impassioned novel of one Captain Michales, but even more of sensual, spiritual, freedom-loving Crete and Cretans. Exotically fresh in style and pattern. *Simon & Schuster $4.50.*

_____ *The Odyssey: A Modern Sequel* (1958). Modern man's search for his soul adumbrated in a poetic epic-novel. To be compared with Joyce's *Ulysses. Simon & Schuster $10.*

KOESTLER, ARTHUR (Hungary, now England) 1905– *The Age of Longing* (1951). Ghastly forecast of what Frenchmen and Americans in France might be like awaiting conquest from the East. *Macmillan $3.75.*

_____ *Darkness at Noon* (1941). Penetrating, memorable dramatization making clear the ideological and psychological factors in a Communist purge trial. *Macmillan $4.75, ML, NAL.*

_____ *The Gladiators.* See page 36.

KOSSAK, ZOFIA (Poland) *Blessed Are the Meek.* St. Francis of Assisi. See page 43.

LAGERKVIST, PAR (Sweden) 1891– *Barabbas* (1951). The 1951 Nobel Prize winner gives a powerful character study of the man released to the mob instead of Christ. *Random House $2.75, MLP.*

_____ *The Sibyl* (1956). Companion piece to *Barabbas.* Christian and pagan religious concepts are handled in paradox and parable. *Random House $3.*

LAGERLOF, SELMA (Sweden) 1858–1940 *The Story of Gösta Berling* (1891). An unfrocked priest, after a career of love-errantry, marries and dedicates himself to a life of service. Excels in humor, characterization, and dramatically significant Swedish backgrounds. *Heineman $5.*

MALRAUX, ANDRE (France) 1895– *Man's Fate* (1933). An examination of men's political obsessions in terms of the Shanghai insurrection of 1927, when Chiang Kai-shek turned against the Communists. *ML.*

MANN, THOMAS (Germany) 1875–1955 *Buddenbrooks* (1924). Detailed saga of a decadent middle-class family in northern Germany. Often considered Mann's masterpiece. *Knopf $5.*

_____ *The Confessions of Felix Krull, Confidence Man* (1955). Comic novel with an irresistible scoundrel hero. *Knopf $4.95, NAL.*

_____ *The Joseph Tetralogy* (1924–44). Recreates ancient Egypt and the Biblical saga of Joseph. *Knopf $7.50.*

_____ *The Magic Mountain* (1924). A provocative novel picturing a mountaintop sanitarium as a symbol of mankind in a pathologic universe. *Knopf $4.50.*

MARTIN DU GARD, ROGER (France) 1881– *The World of the Thibaults* (1922–36). A series of novels searching with Tolstoyan vitality the moral forces at work in our complex world. Two volumes in print: *The Postman* and *The Thibaults*, *Viking*, *$3 ea.*

MAURIAC, FRANÇOIS (France) 1885– Leading Catholic novelist of France, whose forte is the psychology of faith and sin; as brooding a moralist as Hawthorne. Representative novels include *The Desert of Love* (1949), *Farrar, Straus & Cudahy $3.75; Flesh and Blood* (1955), *Farrar, Straus & Cudahy $3.50;* and *Thérèse* (1928), *Farrar, Straus & Cudahy $3.50, Anch.*

MEREJKOWSKI (Russia) *The Romance of Leonardo da Vinci.* See page 50.

MORAVIA, ALBERTO (Italy) 1907– *Conjugal Love* (1951). Desire, inspiration, desperation, and acceptance in marriage. *Farrar, Straus & Cudahy $2.75, NAL.*

_____ *The Time of Indifference* (1953). An Italian version of the tyranny of sex. *Farrar, Straus & Cudahy $3.50, NAL.*

_____ *Two Adolescents* (1944, 1948). Two short novels, each dealing with a young boy's discovery of adult sexual emotions. *Farrar, Straus & Cudahy $2.75, NAL.*

NABOKOV, VLADIMIR (Russia, now United States). See page 130.

NEXO, MARTIN ANDERSON (Denmark) 1869–1954 *Pelle, the Conqueror* (1906–11). This Communist author's own experiences are mirrored in the life of a boy, typifying the rise of the Danish working class. *Peter Smith $6.*

PASTERNAK, BORIS (Russia) 1890– *Dr. Zhivago* (1958). Yuri Zhivago, orphaned at ten, later an upper-class doctor, poet, husband, lover, philosopher, struggles successfully, despite upheavals and regimentation in his beloved Russia, to preserve his humanity and spiritual independence. *Pantheon $5.*

PIRANDELLO, LUIGI (Italy) 1867–1936 *The Late Mattia Pascal* (1905). A man who incautiously sheds his identity is unable to resume it at will. *Dutton o.p.*

PROUST, MARCEL (France) 1871–1922 *Remembrance of Things Past* (1928). In seven novels Proust exhibits the many-fibered texture of French society. The protagonist is the hypersensitive author; the method, largely reverie. *Random House 2 vols. $15, ML 7 vols. Swann's Way* (1918) is the best known single volume.

REMARQUE, ERICH MARIA (Germany) 1897– *All Quiet on the Western Front* (1929). Perhaps the best-known World War I novel; the war as a typical German soldier saw it. *Little, Brown $4, Crest.*

ROLLAND, ROMAIN (France) 1866–1944 *Jean Christophe* (1912). A musical genius battles poverty, attains success, and finally wins peace in death. *Dell (abr.), MLG.*

ROMAINS, JULES (France) 1885– *Men of Good Will.* A many-volume prose epic of France from 1900 to 1933. Outstanding single volumes are *Verdun* (1939), a powerful evocation of the 1917 crisis—*Knopf o.p.;* and *Seventh of October* (1946), the final volume picturing tensions and strains as of 1933—*Knopf $4.*

Russian Reader, The Portable (1947). Ed. by Bernard G. Guerney. Novelettes by Andreyev and Chekhov, short stories, etc. *Vik-h.*

SAGAN, FRANÇOISE (*pseud.*) (France) 1935– *Bonjour Tristesse* (1955). Deft, ironic, surprisingly sophisticated analysis by an adolescent of the tragicomedy of love. *Dutton $2.50, Dell.*

SARTRE, JEAN PAUL (France) 1905– *Troubled Sleep* (1951). Third and most interesting of an existentialist tetralogy of Sartre novels: the revolutionizing impact of the events of June, 1940, and the psychology of defeat. Earlier books: *Age of Reason* and *Reprieve. Knopf $3.95 ea.*

SCHNITZLER, ARTHUR (Austria) 1862–1931 *Ten Little Novels* (1929). A skeptical doctor's slant on ten Viennese women in love. *Simon & Schuster o.p.*

SEGHERS, ANNA (Germany) 1900– *The Seventh Cross* (1942). Fortunes of seven escapees from a German concentration camp. *Little, Brown o.p.*

SENDER, RAMON (Spain) 1902– *The King and the Queen* (1948). Remarkable love story (possibly an allegory of modern Spain), suggesting a comparison with *Lady Chatterley's Lover* by D. H. Lawrence. *Vanguard $3.*

SHOLOKHOV, MIKHAIL (Russia) 1905– *And Quiet Flows the Don* (1934) and *The Don Flows Home to the Sea* (1941). Two parts of a novel published in one volume as *The Silent Don* (1942). Epic in scope, it is a massive yet lyrical portrait of Russian life from late Tsarist days through World War I and the revolution. *NAL 2 vols.*

SILLANPAA, FRANS EEMIL (Finland) 1888– *Meek Heritage* (1919). Civil war between Finnish Whites and Reds; the tragedy of elemental man. *Knopf o.p.*

SILONE, IGNAZIO (Italy) 1900– *Bread and Wine* (1936). Uncensored picture of Italy under the Fascists, and of the underground resistance. *NAL.*

SIMENON, GEORGES (Belgium) 1903– *The Snow Was Black* (1950). Known mostly for his realistic detective stories, Simenon plumbs depths in this frank portrayal of a despicable underworld youth who defies the German military police and dies. *NAL.*

UNDSET (Norway) *Kristin Lavransdatter.* The Middle Ages in Scandinavia. See page 45.

VITTORINI, ELIO (Italy) 1908– *In Sicily* (1949). An affirmative Italian story of mother and son; a modern parable of fine earthy quality. *New Directions $2.50.*

WALTARI, MIKA T. (Finland) 1908– *The Egyptian* (1949). Novelized history, dramatic and authentic, of the times of youthful Pharaoh Akhnaton. *Putnam $4, PB.*

WERFEL, FRANZ (Austria) 1890–1945 *The Forty Days of Musa Dagh* (1934). Saga of seven Armenian villages resisting the Turks in 1915. *ML o.p.*

ZWEIG, ARNOLD (Germany) 1887– *The Case of Sergeant Grischa* (1928). Unjust condemnation of one simple, good-natured peasant soldier exemplifies the essential cruelty and injustice of war. *Viking o.p.*

Additional Recommended European Novels in Paperbounds

ALAIN-FOURNIER, HENRI *The Wanderer. Anch.*

ASCH, SHOLEM *The Prophet. PB.*

BRECHT, BERTOLT *Threepenny Novel. Ever.*

CAMUS, ALFRED *The Rebel. Vin.*

―――――― *The Stranger. Vin.*

CHEVALLIER, GABRIEL *The Wicked Village. Dell.*

COLETTE *Gigi. NAL.*

FEUCHTWANGER, LION *Raquel. NAL.*

GIDE, ANDRE *The Immoralist. Vin.*

GUARESCHI, GIOVANNI *Don Camillo and His Flock. PB.*

HESSE, HERMANN *Siddhartha. New.*

LEVI, CARLO *Christ Stopped at Eboli. UL.*

MALRAUX, ANDRE *The Conquerors. Bea.*

NABOKOV, VLADIMIR *Laughter in the Dark. Berk.*

RADIGUET, RAYMOND *Count D'Orgel. Ever.*

REMARQUE, ERICH *Arch of Triumph. NAL.*

SVEVO, ITALO *The Confessions of Zeno. Vin.*

WERFEL, FRANZ *The Song of Bernadette. Comp, PB.*

YOURCENAR, MARGUERITE *Hadrian's Memoirs. Anch.* See page 37.

C. 19th Century British Novels

EDWARD S. LE COMTE, Columbia University

In *The Progress of Romance* (1785), Clara Reeve stated that "the Novel is a picture of real life and manners and of the times in which it is written." By her implied distinction, of the two figures who loom largest in the second decade of the 19th century in England, Jane Austen wrote novels, Sir Walter Scott, romances. Writing admiringly to Miss Austen, Scott called himself the author of "Big Bow-wow stories." Scott meant his historical romances, which legions of readers have found unsurpassed for adventure and descriptions of natural scenes—all full of the joy of living and the glory of the past. Emerson said that Scott gave him a feeling of longevity, a sense of the oneness of the pageant of humanity. If you would live 700 years of English history—from the 12th century through the 18th—you can do so by reading a selection of Scott's romances, beginning with the stories of Richard the Lion-Hearted and Robin Hood in *Ivanhoe* and ending with the humble Scottish cottagers of Scott's own youth in *The Heart of Midlothian*.

While Scott wove large and colorful tapestries, Jane Austen stitched in petit point the minute details of the small world she knew. She herself said she created on "a little piece of ivory of two inches wide" on which she worked "with a brush too fine to get any large effect." But what she may have lacked in breadth she gained in depth of perception—in her delicate, witty delineation of people and manners. We find her deft reporting of homely details as absorbing as our own plotless lives.

The age of the machine had arrived in England, and the first steps in reform legislation had been taken by the time Charles Dickens began to write in the 1830's. The experiences of his own boyhood (imaginatively projected into *David Copperfield*) and his sympathy for the poverty-ridden class produced melodramatic novels animated by social awareness. Humanitarian Dickens dramatized the abuses of factory, school, church, and the courts. Possibly the best-remembered portrayal of a "have-not" in a cruelly heedless society is Oliver Twist in the workhouse. The Dickens gallery of original portraits is tremendous in its scope. Perennial favorites are those touched with his characteristic humor—Pickwick, Micawber, Barkis, Sarah Gamp. In comic character and situation, Dickens is a master.

More than a century ago, in 1847 and 1848, Thackeray wrote a novel never absent from "best book" lists: *Vanity Fair,* in which we get to know the world's most designing female, Becky Sharp; her hapless husband; sweet, patient Amelia; and dashing but faithless George Osborne—and we never forget them.

Although Thackeray may not have been deeply moved by the social changes of 19th-century England, they presented him with models for snob, climber, rogue, hypocrite, a parade in which he also poses for us the sweet but vapid, the dull, the spoiled. But Thackeray, satirist and moralist, does not preach; consequently, he entertains superbly. For his own life story read *Pendennis,* with its autobiographical reflection of the life of a favored young man of the 19th century.

A new psychological study of man, a highly intellectualized probing of motives, conduct, and emotions, is blended in the novels of George Eliot (Mary Ann Evans), with understanding, sympathy, and humor. Her genre novels of English country folk, *Adam Bede* and *The Mill on the Floss,* have never lost their appeal. *Middlemarch* exhibits her powers on a grand scale.

Another challenging writer, one who calls upon his readers for concentration and patience, is George Meredith. In penetrating studies of late Victorian society he employs devastating ridicule to punish those who offend. His two most frequently read novels, written twenty-six years apart, are *The Ordeal of Richard Feverel* and *Diana of the Crossways.*

Toward the close of the century which began with Scott, who nearly always provided happy endings, came Thomas Hardy, in whom deterministic melancholy reached the depths of the Greek tragedies. The futility of human struggle against unpredictable nature and chance pervades his somber novels, of which *Tess of the D'Urbervilles* and *The Return of the Native* have been most esteemed for their structural precision and bitter ironic force.

To name these seven novelists as representing the main streams of imaginative writing in Victoria's century is not to deny the importance of such a novelist as Trollope, with his lively and intimate pictures of a cathedral town, or such individual masterpieces as *Jane Eyre, Wuthering Heights, The Cloister and the Hearth, Dr. Jekyll and Mr. Hyde,* and *Esther Waters.*

AUSTEN, JANE 1775–1817 *Emma* (1816). Story of a girl who tries to regulate the love affairs of others without success, yet who, despite her meddling, endears herself to the reader. *Ban, CoNC, Evman-h, Nel, RivEd, SM, WoC.*

———— *Pride and Prejudice* (1813). Concerned mainly with the conflict between the prejudice of a young lady and the well-founded, though misinterpreted, pride of the aristocratic hero. A masterpiece of gentle humor. *CoNC, Dell, EvmanNA, GtIl, Harp, ML, MLCE, ModSL, Nel, PB, Rine, RivEd, SM, UL, WoC.*

———— *Sense and Sensibility* (1811). A striking contrast of two sisters—one the prototype of common sense, the other of romantic "sensibility"—with simple domestic scenes of rural England forthrightly portrayed and flavored with pleasing humor. *CoNC, Dell, Evman-h, GtIl, ML, MLCE, Nel, SM, WoC.*

———— *Complete Novels.* Above three plus *Mansfield Park* (1814), *Northanger Abbey* (1818), and *Persuasion* (1818). *MLG.*

BLACKMORE, R. D. 1825–1900 *Lorna Doone* (1869). An historical romance blending revenge, love, and adventure. *CoNC, Evman-h, GtIl, Nel, PB, WoC.*

BRONTE, CHARLOTTE 1816–1855 *Jane Eyre* (1847). Modern realism and wildest melodrama in a story that four generations of readers have found fascinating. *CoNC, Evman-h, GtIl, Harp, ML, MLCE, NAL, Nel, PB, Pen, Rine, RivEd, WoC.*

BRONTE, EMILY 1818–1848 *Wuthering Heights* (1847). A tale of psychological horror deriving from the morbid passions of an ill-treated and vindictive waif. *CoNC, Evman-h, GtIl, Harp, ML, MLCE, NAL, Nel, PB, Pen, Rine, RivEd, WoC.*

BULWER-LYTTON *Last Days of Pompeii.* See page 36.

BUTLER, SAMUEL 1835–1902 *Erewhon* (1872). A satire upon shams in education, religion, social customs, and ethics. As sharply pointed as Aristophanes, as modern as today's headlines. *Evman-h, ML, Nel, Pen.*

———— *The Way of All Flesh* (1903). A semi-autobiographical account of an artist in rebellion against Victorian convention and parental authority. *Evman-h, GtIl, Harp, ML, MLCE, PB, Pen, Rine, WoC.*

CARROLL, LEWIS (*pseud.*) 1832–1898 **Alice in Wonderland** (1865). A masterpiece of inimitable fantasy and deft satire. *Grosset $3.50, Heritage $3. Macmillan $2, Peter Pauper $2.50, Evman-h, ML, Nel, Nort, PB, SM.*

COLLINS, WILKIE 1824–1889 **The Moonstone** (1868). Mystery thriller about a priceless diamond stolen from a Hindu shrine. *Evman-h, GtIl, MLG, Nel, Pyr, WoC.*

CONRAD, JOSEPH 1857–1924 **Almayer's Folly** (1895). Story of a lone white man in Malaya destroyed by a dream of gold. *CoNC.*

———— **The Nigger of the Narcissus** (1897). Extraordinary delineation of a common man of the sea. *Doubleday $2.50, Harp, Vik-h.*

DICKENS, CHARLES 1812–1870 **Bleak House** (1853). A long-drawn-out lawsuit blights the innocent young and brings in its train murder, madness, shame, poverty, in one of the biggest—in every sense—of Dickens's novels. *CoNC, Evman-h, GtIl, Nel, RivEd, SM, WoC.*

———— **David Copperfield** (1850). Dickens's own favorite, perhaps because it reflects the author's own youth. *Grosset $2.49, St Martin's $2.75, CoNC, Dell (abr.), Evman-h, GtIl, ML, MLCE, Nel, PB, RivEd.*

———— **Oliver Twist** (1838). The underworld of early 19th-century London portrayed by a reformer. *Macmillan $2.52, CoNC, Evman-h, GtIl, Nel, PB, SM, WoC.*

———— **Pickwick Papers** (1837). Not exactly a novel, but rather a series of loosely connected incidents. Extravagantly funny, rich in memorable characters. *CoNC, Evman-h, GtIl, ML, Nel, SM.*

———— **A Tale of Two Cities.** Drama of the French Revolution. See page 70.

Other novels of popular appeal (none of Dickens's fifteen books lack it) are **Great Expectations** (1861), a mocking narrative of absurd waiting for legacies (*CoNC, EvmanNA, GtIl, Nel, PB, Rine, WoC*); **Nicholas Nickleby** (1839), an exposure of bad conditions in private schools (*CoNC, Evman-h, GtIl, Nel, SM*); **Martin Chuzzlewit** (1844), in which some crudities of American life are sharply satirized (*CoNC, Evman-h, GtIl, Nel, SM*); **Our Mutual Friend** (1865), warmly human story of disguise and inheritance and young love (*CoNC, Evman-h, GtIl, Nel, Nort, SM*); and **Hard Times** (1854) (*Evman-h, Harp, Nel, Rine*).

DU MAURIER, GEORGE 1834–1896 **Peter Ibbetson** (1891). A story of true love realized only in dreams. *ML o.p.*

ELIOT, GEORGE (MARY ANN EVANS) 1819–1880 **Adam Bede** (1859). The simple charm of the English countryside pervades this story. *CoNC, Evman-h, GtIl, MLG, Nel, PB, Rine.*

_____ *Middlemarch* (1872). A novel of great cumulative power dealing with two unhappy marriages in a provincial community that becomes as familiar to us as our own home town. *Evman-h 2 vols., RivEd, WoC.*

_____ *The Mill on the Floss* (1860). Revelation of youthful perplexities in the person of Maggie Tulliver—sensitive, impulsive, strong-willed, misunderstood, destined to sorrow. *Evman-h, MLG, Nel, PB, WoC.*

_____ *Romola.* An adventurer in Renaissance Florence. See page 49.

_____ *Silas Marner* (1861). Sentimental story of a victim of deceit restored to happiness through the love of a child. *Cambridge Univ. $1.25, Houghton Mifflin $1.48, Macmillan $2, Evman-h, GtIl, MLG, NAL, Nel, PB, WoC.*

GASKELL, ELIZABETH 1810–1865 *Cranford* (1853). Delightful picture of quaint characters and customs in a quiet village. *Evman-h, Nel, WoC.*

HARDY, THOMAS 1840–1928 *Far from the Madding Crowd* (1874). The drab existence of country people is made vivid and vital. *Evman-h, Harp, Rine, RivEd, SM.*

_____ *Jude the Obscure* (1896). A tragic, powerful study of ambition thwarted by weak will and poor environment. *Dell, Harp, ML, SM.*

_____ *The Mayor of Casterbridge* (1886). The worldly rise and fall of a man who, while drunk, sold his wife to a stranger. *Harp, ML, MLCE, PB, Rine, SM.*

_____ *The Return of the Native* (1878). A story of joy, sorrow, and tragedy told against the somber background of Egdon Heath. *Macmillan $3, GtIl, Harp, ML, ModSL, NAL, PB, Rine, SM.*

_____ *Tess of the D'Urbervilles* (1891). The poignant tragedy of a betrayed woman. *Harp, ML, MLCE, Nort, PB, RivEd, SM.*

Also recommended: *Under the Greenwood Tree* (1872), *SM;* and *The Woodlanders* (1887), *Harp, SM.*

JAMES, HENRY. See page 120.

KINGSLEY *Westward Ho!* The Spanish Armada and later. See page 55.

MARRYAT, FREDERICK 1792–1848 *Mr. Midshipman Easy* (1836). Lively, amusing yarn about a youngster who learns that democratic equality is out of place in His Majesty's Navy. *Evman-h, Nel.*

MEREDITH, GEORGE 1828–1909 *The Egoist* (1879). A novel satirizing man's inherent selfishness. *ML, Nort, RivEd, WoC.*

_____ *The Ordeal of Richard Feverel* (1859). The hero bitterly resents the smug inhumanity of his father's educational system. *Evman-h, ML, MLCE.*

MOORE, GEORGE 1852–1933 *Esther Waters* (1894). The misfortunes and brief happiness of a servant girl portrayed sympathetically by a follower of Zola's Naturalism. *Black, Evman-h, Nort.*

_____ *Héloïse and Abélard.* A tragic true love story. See page 44.

READE *The Cloister and the Hearth.* 15th century. See page 44.

SCOTT, SIR WALTER 1771–1832 *The Heart of Midlothian* (1818). This authentic novel of the cruelty of Scots law, rich in homely characterization and emotional intensity, centers about the struggle of Jeanie Deans to save her erring sister without sacrificing her own word of honor. *Macmillan $1.50, Evman-h, Nel, Rine.*

Among the ever-popular historical novels by Scott are *Ivanhoe* and *Quentin Durward,* dealing with the Middle Ages (see page 44); *The Abbot, Kenilworth,* and *The Monastery,* about Elizabethan England (see page 56); *Old Mortality* and *Waverley,* concerning the 17th and 18th centuries (see pages 63 and 71).

SHELLEY, MARY WOLLSTONECRAFT 1797–1851 *Frankenstein* (1818). A man-made monster destroys all whom his master loves. *Evman-h, Pyr.*

STEVENSON, ROBERT LOUIS 1850–1894 *Kidnapped* (1886). A young Scot's romantic adventures on sea and land. *Rand McNally $2.60, Scribner $3.95, Evman-h, GtIl, NAL, Nel, PB, WoC.*

_____ *The Master of Ballantrae* (1889). A feud between brothers begins in Scotland, comes to an eerie end in the wilderness of America. *Evman-h, Nel, Rine, WoC.*

_____ *The Strange Case of Dr. Jekyll and Mr. Hyde* (1886). Psychological study of the struggle between right and wrong within the soul. *Coward-McCann $3, CoNC, Evman-h, Nel, PB.*

_____ *Treasure Island* (1883). A delightful yarn of buried gold, pirates, mutiny, and a brave cabin boy. *Dutton $2.75, Grosset $1.75, Houghton Mifflin $1.88, Rand McNally $2.60, Scribner $3.95, CoNC, Evman-h, Gar, GtIl, Nel, PB, WoC.*

STOKER, BRAM 1847–1912 *Dracula* (1897). A blood-curdling narrative about the king of vampires and the beautiful women he horribly transforms. *ML, Perm.*

THACKERAY, WILLIAM MAKEPEACE 1811–1863 *Henry Esmond.* Queen Anne's reign brought to life. See page 71.

_____ *Pendennis* (1848–50). A typical young man displays typical faults and mistakes, the chief of which is selfishness. *Evman-h 2 vols.*

_____ *Vanity Fair* (1847–8). Essentially an unsparing portrayal of a designing female, who succeeds very nicely until retribution sets in. Fascinating, selfish Becky Sharp contrasts with sweet, simple Amelia Sedley, whose brother and husband are but two of the men Becky attracts. *CoNC, Evman-h, GtIl, Harp, MLCE, MLP, Nel, PB, Rine.*

TROLLOPE, ANTHONY 1815–1882 *Barchester Towers* (1857). Animates with zest and humor the small-town, middle-class life of Victorian England, making interesting the intrigues and gossip of petty church officialdom. *Ban, Evman-h, ML, MLCE, Nel, Pen, Rine, WoC.*

_____ *The Warden* (1855). A brash young reformer stirs up trouble and raises delicate questions of conscience in a hitherto outwardly quiet ecclesiastical town. *Evman-h, ML, MLCE, Nel, WoC.*

Also recommended: ***Doctor Thorne*** (1858), *Evman-h, Nel, RivEd, WoC;* and ***The Last Chronicle of Barset*** (1866-7), *Evman-h, Nel, Nort, WoC.*

WILDE, OSCAR 1854-1900 ***The Picture of Dorian Gray*** (1891). Dorian is doomed to keep the unsullied exterior splendor of youth while the gradual deterioration of his portrait reveals his accumulating internal depravity. *CoNC, Dell, Liv, ML, Pen, Vik, Vik-h.*

D. 20th Century British Novels

ARTHUR ZEIGER, The City College of New York

In the decade preceding World War I some very impressive British novels were written: John Galsworthy's *The Man of Property* (1906), first volume of *The Forsyte Saga;* Arnold Bennett's *The Old Wives' Tale* (1908); H. G. Wells's *Tono-Bungay* (1909). Produced by perceptive novelists who respected truth and their craft, these are serious and substantial works.

Yet the younger novelists found them unsatisfying. Galsworthy had conceived his Philistine saga ironically, but in execution the iron melted. The author became the novelist member of the Forsyte family, esteeming them—and their solid possessions—almost as much as they did. Sentiment blurred his vision, and the Forsytes seem never wholly in focus.

Bennett built compacter, perhaps more durable, structures. In his best, most deeply felt novel, he placed two sisters against a drab industrial background—Bursley, one of the "five towns" of Staffordshire. He pictured their unlovely, joyless lives in immense and accurate detail, so that one knows all *about* them—but never quite knows them, never feels their life as they felt it. Like other naturalistic novels, *The Old Wives' Tale* impresses by its massed data, not by the immediacy with which it enables us to know the characters it describes.

H. G. Wells had formidable novelistic equipment; curiosity, intelligence, social conscience, fertility of invention, and an incapacity for dullness. Yet, proudly regarding himself as a journalist and deprecating the artist's role, he willfully sacrificed form to social reform. His people seem frequently to illustrate a thesis rather than to live even a fictitious life.

Admitting the virtues of Wells, Bennett, Galsworthy, and their industrious school, Virginia Woolf, the most articulate spokesman for the opposition, denounced their resolute externality, their documentary materialistic

bias, their refusal to immerse in the stream of consciousness. *To the Lighthouse* (1927) illuminates her strictures.
The author enters the consciousness of her characters,
reproduces sensitively the quality and content of their
feeling, and herself intrudes only obliquely. From the
subtle, lambent prose, one deduces not only the characters and their relationships but also the environment
itself. An admirable stylistic achievement, *To the Lighthouse* becomes at times impalpable and rarefied as the
shadow of a flame. One admires, but longs for plot and
incident, for more solidity, more substance.

Virginia Woolf did not of course inaugurate the sub-
jective novel: she acknowledges two great ancestors,
Henry James and James Joyce. James's involute sen-
tences, which at first block the reader's progress and
obscure the dramatic structure of his fiction by their
dislocated clauses, fragmented phrases, displaced ad-
verbs, piled-up punctuation, and wrenched rhythms,
seem ultimately right; for they capture the delicate, fleet-
ing, apparently ineluctable nuance of feeling. Joyce's
mythic ordering of the flux of contemporary experience,
his dedication to the word, his comic vision, and above
all his power of rendering the inward life of his characters, make *Ulysses* a triumph of the introvertive method.

Because of the compelling examples of Joyce, James,
and (to a lesser extent) Virginia Woolf, many novelists
since have progressively shunned external reality, prefer-
ring instead to record—intensively, almost raptly—the
feelings and thoughts it induces. The unhappy fact, however, is that the reality itself often attenuates or disinte-
grates. As practiced by most contemporary English writers
—for example, Philip Toynbee (whose *Tea with Mrs.
Goodman* [1947] explores the "events" occurring at a tea)
—the novel has lost force and breadth (and readability)
and gained technique. Writers in our decade generally
have turned their backs on the elements that vitalize
technique.

But charting the development of the 20th century thus
broadly, one inevitably distorts. A number of writers
refuse to submit to facile classification. Two whom Virginia Woolf associated herself with in the revolt against
the realistic and naturalistic novel, E. M. Forster and

D. H. Lawrence, escape the perils incident to both the extrovertive and introvertive novel. Each novelist has a central, governing theme. Forster, beautifully, lucidly, penetrates the moral situation of our time, the difficulties we have "connecting" with one another, establishing truly human attitudes. Lawrence, in passionate, thrusting prose, probes the vital relationship between men and women, their failures to achieve fulfillment, the deepest longings of their subterranean beings.

And there are writers so sharply individual that only an arbitrary critic will name them within a paragraph. Perhaps most eccentric, Ivy Compton-Burnett has written her characteristic novel since the 20's (though not until recently has her reputation approached her performance): through the witty, stylized conversation of her country-house characters, the reader comes to learn of monstrous doings afoot—the urbanity enhancing the melodrama. Henry Green writes in a lower, more modulated key. Though his novels, too, unfold through conversation, it is accurately reproduced conversation that brilliantly reveals his characters, the world surrounding them, the atmosphere they inhabit.

Other names arise to undermine generalizations concerning the progressive inwardness of the novel during this century. Aldous Huxley, Evelyn Waugh, and George Orwell have attained notable success in satire, a genre which, requiring a definite credo, finds the climate of our divided age inhospitable. Nevertheless, Huxley, Waugh, and Orwell, men firmly grounded in belief (the first in Vedanta, the second in Roman Catholicism, the last in socialism), have withstood the forces impelling to unbelief.

Finally, traditional novelists—novelists who have never abjured plot, chronology, climax, never renounced the world outside us from which presumably our impressions derive—have flourished. Somerset Maugham, an astute craftsman, produced clever and extremely readable novels, though hardly anyone would claim that they were searching or powerful creations, enlarging our apprehension or increasing our sensibility. Christopher Isherwood has not realized the promise of his Berlin novels—penetrating, moving, prophetic evocations of pre-Hitler Germany; but *The Last of Mr. Norris* and *Goodbye to Berlin* stand, perhaps the best "social" fiction in the last half-century. Graham Greene freights his well-made novels of suspense with theological insight—unlikely matter, but far from capsizing, it imparts gravity and dimension to them. Joyce Cary, nearly alone among his contemporaries, has dedicated his splendid novelistic abilities—a marvelous creative vigor, a warm and sympathetic insight into human imperfections, a flexible and resilient style—to celebrating the enduring, vaulting spirit of man.

Though C. P. Snow and Lawrence Durrell have written the best novels of the decade, the 1950's have been dominated by the Angry Young Men—writers like Kingsley Amis, Iris Murdoch, John Wain, J. P. Donleavy, and John Braine. "Angry" seems an inadequate characterization for most of them: far more often they are beaten, bored, disaffected, or disassociated. No member of the group (whether he has voluntarily enlisted or has been dragooned by the critics) has yet published a great novel. And, in spite of their various excellences, the novels generally bear too marked a resemblance to one another. Nevertheless, the members are young (most of them under forty), talented, and energetic. Almost certainly some of them will, ultimately, write novels that show us not only the shape and direction but also the meaning of our age.

AMIS, KINGSLEY 1923– *Lucky Jim* (1954). A funny, at times cruel, story of a young, inept instructor on probation at an English college, his difficulties and fortunes in love. *Comp.*

BECKETT, SAMUEL 1906– *Molloy* (1955), *Malone Dies* (1956), *The Unnamable* (1958). A trilogy mainly focusing on crippled, mutilated beings who have passed beyond despair. Static, desolate, enigmatic, the novels are curiously fascinating, sometimes poetic, sometimes funny, sometimes blank. *Ever 3 vols.*

BEERBOHM, MAX 1872–1956 *Zuleika Dobson* (1911). Undergraduate Oxford is disrupted by the maddening beauty of Zuleika in this deft comic fantasy. *ML.*

BENNETT, ARNOLD 1867–1931 *The Old Wives' Tale* (1908). Slowly, almost imperceptibly, the grimy Midlands town presses life from Sophia and Constance Baines. *Harp, ML.*

BOWEN, ELIZABETH 1899– *The Death of the Heart* (1939). A deeply moving tragedy of adolescence, brought about by adult cruelty and insensitivity. *Knopf $3.95, Vin.*

BRAINE, JOHN 1922– *Room at the Top* (1957). A brilliant chronicle of the fortunes—and ultimate misfortune—of a young man who knows all prices but no values. *NAL.*

CARY, JOYCE 1888–1957 *The Horse's Mouth* (1950). Last of a trilogy including *Herself Surprised* (1948) and *To Be a Pilgrim* (1949). Exuberant history of Gulley Jimson, visionary painter and outrageous person, told by himself. (In the other volumes, Sarah, his lady love, and Wilcher, his lawyer rival, tell their complementary stories.) *Harper $3.50, $3.50, & $3;* first named in *UL.*

COMPTON-BURNETT, IVY 1892– *Bullivant and the Lambs* (1948). A comedy of manners, couched in anti-Naturalistic epigrammatic dialogue, involving a stingy father, his sinister children, and Bullivant, the butler, who never loses control. *Knopf o.p.*

CONRAD, JOSEPH 1857–1924 *Heart of Darkness* (1902). Reveals the heart's darkness, deeper than Africa's. *NAL.*

———— *Lord Jim* (1900). The hero suffers dishonor through cowardice; he atones, endures heroic defeat, and gains redemption. *Doubleday $3.50, Ban, Harp, ML, Nel, Rine, RivEd.*

———— *Nostromo* (1904). An intricately structured political novel, recounting in full detail the genesis and course of a South American revolution and pointing up the corrupting power of silver. *ML.*

DONLEAVY, J. P. 1926– *The Ginger Man* (1958). A rambunctious, often very funny story about one of the new rogues—a displaced American student in Dublin, earnestly avoiding study, work, and duty, eagerly courting several varieties of mischief. *Mc-Dowell-Obelensky $3.95, Berk.*

DOUGLAS, NORMAN 1868–1952 *South Wind* (1917). Amusing, cynical symposium on conventional morality. The setting is a Mediterranean island whose shifting winds effect shifts in moral values among the visitors. *British Book Centre $2.75, Ban, ML, UL.*

DURRELL, LAWRENCE 1912– *Justine* (1957), *Balthazar* (1958), *Mountolive* (1959). Stunning baroque "sibling novels" of cosmopolitan Alexandria (the fourth, completing the tetralogy, to be published in 1960): the "truth" about the beautiful, shimmering, exotic heroine seen from shifting perspectives. *Dutton $3.50 ea.*

FORSTER, E. M. 1879– *The Longest Journey* (1907). A sensitive young man regularly accepts illusion for reality, an error that leads to a destroying marriage and ultimate destruction. *Knopf $4.*

———— *A Passage to India* (1924). Focusing on a dramatic situation, this philosophical novel explores the tensions between Englishmen and Indians—and, symbolically, other, more basic tensions as well. *HarB.*

GALSWORTHY, JOHN 1867–1933 *The Forsyte Saga* (1906–21). A trilogy affectionately centering on a large, wealthy, middle-class family from 1886 to 1920, and tracing the effect on them of property and the possessive instinct. *Scribner $6.50, ModSA.*

GREEN, HENRY 1905– *Loving* (1945). A comic-pathetic realistic novel, set against a romantic Irish background: the story concerns the love of Edith, a housemaid, for Raunce, a butler. *Viking $3, Anch.*

GREENE, GRAHAM 1904– *Brighton Rock* (1938). One of Greene's "entertainments," involving pursuit, gang warfare, and murder; encompassed by terror—and informed with theological doctrine. *Viking $3.50, Comp.*

_____ *The Heart of the Matter* (1948). A "theological thriller," but equally a tale of frustrated goodness and thwarted love. *Viking $3.50.*

HUDSON, W. H. 1841–1922 *Green Mansions* (1904). Romantic tale, set in the tropical forests of South America, recounting the ill-starred love of Rima, the "bird-girl," and the narrator, Mr. Abel. *Heritage $5, Ban, Gtll, Harp, ML, UL.*

HUGHES, RICHARD 1900– *The Innocent Voyage* (1929). (Also published as *A High Wind in Jamaica*.) A revealing study of the separate world of childhood: a group of children, captured by pirates, undergo a violent voyage into experience. *ML o.p.*

HUXLEY, ALDOUS 1894– *Brave New World* (1932). Satire on the mechanized, dehumanized world of the future; the time is 632 A.F. (After Ford). *Ban, Harp, ML.*

_____ *Point Counter Point* (1928). Through "parallel contrapuntal plots," Huxley atomizes the upper-class world in pursuit of "pleasure"—its sensuality, debauchery, parasitism, and purposelessness. *Avon, Harp, ML.*

_____ *The World of Aldous Huxley* (1947). Ed. by C. J. Rolo. Includes *Antic Hay*, extracts from other important novels, and various shorter works. *Harper $4, UL.*

ISHERWOOD, CHRISTOPHER 1904– *The Berlin Stories* (1946). Two short novels that hauntingly evoke Berlin in the five years before Hitler—its degeneration, futility, ominous brutality. *New Directions $3.50.*

JOYCE, JAMES 1882–1941 *Portrait of the Artist as a Young Man* (1916). A semiautobiographical "novel of initiation": the young artist strives to gain his freedom—from religion, country, family—to practice his art untrammeled. *Comp.* Included in *The Portable James Joyce, Vik-h.*

_____ *Ulysses* (1922). Ostensibly the record of a single day filtered through the consciousness of Leopold Bloom and Stephen Dedalus; but more than that, a great comic-epic poem, a paradigm of modern man's search for values. *Random House $4.75, MLG.*

KIPLING *Kim.* Vivid portrait of India. See page 77.

LAWRENCE, D. H. 1885–1930 *Lady Chatterley's Lover* (1958). Long censored because of the author's unreticent description of the processes of passionate love, the novel seems a bit old-fashioned today in spite of the plain language. *Grove $6, Dell, NAL, PB, Pyr.*

_____ *The Rainbow* (1915). An analysis (sometimes concrete, sometimes mystical) of the nature of sexuality, divisive and unifying—and ultimately insufficient. *Avon, ML.*

_____ *Sons and Lovers* (1913). A semi-autobiographical novel. powerfully dramatizing the sexually inhibiting force of excessive mother-love. *Comp, Harp, ML, NAL.*

_____ *Women in Love* (1921). A loose sequel to *The Rainbow*, demonstrating a nearly perfect love relationship (Ursula and Birkin's) and several disastrously imperfect ones. *ML.*

MAUGHAM, W. SOMERSET 1874– *The Moon and Sixpence* (1919). This *roman à clef* (the prototype of the hero is Paul Gauguin, the French impressionist painter) tells of an artist whose only morality is in his art. *Ban, ML.*

_____ *Of Human Bondage* (1915). An engrossing "educational novel," based on the author's life: the hero comes to the realization of his individual identity through suffering, defeat, and tragic love. *Doubleday $4.50, ML, MLP, PB (abr.).*

O'FLAHERTY, LIAM 1897– *The Informer* (1926). Dublin during "the Trouble" is the scene: what passed through the mind of a man who betrayed his best friend to the English enemy. *O.p.*

ORWELL, GEORGE 1903–1950 *The Animal Farm* (1946). Brilliant satirical allegory on dictatorship, especially on its penchant for devouring its own. *Harcourt, Brace $2.95, NAL.*

_____ *Down and Out in London and Paris* (1933). A low-pitched but horrifying autobiographical narrative of abysmal poverty in Paris and London. *Berk.*

_____ *1984* (1949). A nightmare projection of a future police state ruled by "Big Brother," where "War is Peace" and all values are transvalued. *Harcourt, Brace $4, NAL.*

PATON, ALAN (South Africa) 1903– *Cry, the Beloved Country* (1948). The race question in South Africa poignantly depicted in this intense, sometimes lyric, novel. *Scribner $3.50, ModSA.*

PRIESTLEY, J. B. 1894– *The Good Companions* (1929). Long, diverting, picaresque tale involving a troupe of wandering English players. *Harper $4.95.*

SHUTE, NEVIL 1899– *Round the Bend* (1951). Provocative blend of aviation pioneering, interplay of East and West, and a suggested gospel of good work. *Morrow $3.75.*

SNOW, C. P. 1905– *The Conscience of the Rich* (1958). Warmly and perceptively, Snow draws the portraits of the Marches, a family of great Jewish financiers. *Scribner $3.95.*

_____ *The Masters* (1951). Absorbing neo-realistic account of the election of a new Master to a Cambridge college. *Macmillan $3.75, Anch.*

These two novels are part of a continuing sequence—*Strangers and Brothers* (1940–)—a rich and complex panorama of modern society at the sources of power. Three other volumes have had

American publication: *The New Men, Homecoming* (both *Scribner $3.95*), and *Time of Hope* (*Macmillan $3.75*). Others are scheduled for publication soon. Though each novel is autonomous, Lewis Eliot, the narrator, links the series.

WAUGH, EVELYN 1903– *Brideshead Revisited* (1946). A muted satirist in this novel written from a Catholic stance, Waugh presents dissipation, boredom, and an insurmountable hopelessness as the only alternative to faith and works. *Grosset $1.49, Little, Brown $3.95, Dell.*

_____ *A Handful of Dust* (1934). A satire of the contemporary wasteland: The career of Last, the man of good will, ends in tragic-absurd fashion, as captive reader to a Dickens-loving lunatic. *Dell, NewC.*

WEBB, MARY 1883–1927 *Precious Bane* (1926). Somber, poetic novel of the Shropshire country, in the tradition of Hardy. *Dutton $3.50, ML.*

WELLS, H. G. 1866–1946 *Tono-Bungay* (1908). Vigorous history of the rise and fall of the promoters of a patent-medicine fraud, with perceptive sidelights on the evils commercialism breeds. *ML.*

WOOLF, VIRGINIA 1882–1941 *Orlando* (1939). The hero turns heroine in this pseudo-biography, which is also a survey of England's history and literature since Elizabethan times. *NAL.*

_____ *To the Lighthouse* (1927). From shifting centers of consciousness, this beautifully textured symbolic novel shows rather than describes Mrs. Ramsay and her widening effect (even after she has died) on the lives that touch hers. *HarB.*

E. 19th Century American Novels

EDWARD FOSTER, *Georgia Institute of Technology*

In the culturally mature Europe and England of the 19th century the novelist flourished. In the young America he was still just coming of age. Though hundreds of American novels were produced, few attained greatness. The first American who could be called a professional novelist was Charles Brockden Brown, whose tales of terror, while patterned on the Gothic romances endemic in England, used native American scenery. Throughout the 19th century many American novelists deliberately aimed to show that American settings were as fruitful for romance as the ivy-covered towers of England. The many novels of James Fenimore Cooper glorified the American frontier landscape and celebrated the panorama of our history. William Gilmore Simms treated the South much as Cooper had romanticized the North and West.

New England, which contributed a major portion of the nonfictional literature of America before 1860, produced relatively few novels—perhaps because the inherited Puritan sense of moral earnestness inhibited the use of a form still considered frivolous by many. One New Englander of this period, however, ranks with major novelists. Nathaniel Hawthorne, of Massachusetts, turned his Puritan preoccupation with evil to good account in a series of studies of the depths of human nature. His humane understanding, his ingenious, intricate symbolism, and his clear prose combine to illuminate the complexities of the troubled soul.

His friend Herman Melville was a New Yorker who served a hard apprenticeship as a seaman on a Liverpool packet, a South Seas whaler, and a United States Navy frigate; between voyages, he lived short periods with South Sea cannibals. He returned to land to write furiously, drawing upon his travels for background and on his spiritual adventures with books and ideas for substance. With *Moby Dick* he reached a peak of drama and rebellion. Then he fell silent for years until just before his death he wrote in *Billy Budd* a more serene final testament.

The Civil War affected profoundly the course of the American novel. In the face of the hard fact of war, the romantic impulse surrendered gradually to a new spirit of realism. Throughout the land writers enriched their fiction with local color. The old literary domination of the East declined, and a broader national literature emerged.

Out of this movement, but superbly transcending it, came Mark Twain. As newspaperman, Mississippi River pilot, prospector, and humorous lecturer he gained first-hand acquaintance with the people and their folk humor. Perhaps no other American writer has been held in so high esteem by general readers, other writers, and critics alike. Behind his apparently artless stories is literary craftsmanship of a high order and often scorn of injustice and corruption masquerading under the banner of democracy.

Notorious scandals in high office and ruthless accumulation of wealth by individuals and corporations in the 1870's and 1880's produced an inevitable literary protest. The end of the century witnessed a flood of utopian novels that challenged the evils of contemporary American life, notably Bellamy's *Looking Backward*. Some of the later work of William Dean Howells is of this type, but his principal contributions were a shelf of competent realistic novels about characters still recognizable to Americans.

Henry James, a New Yorker who spent much of his life in Europe, brought to the novel a conscious, deliberate artistry and a concern for subtle, delicate shades of meaning. More popular with students of the novel than with general readers, his works set a high standard of craftsmanship that was to make the American novel international in its influence.

At the end of the century, out of agrarian hardships and industrial bitterness, and influenced in part by the example of Zola, there developed a harsher realism. The naturalistic fiction of Stephen Crane, Frank Norris, Theodore Dreiser, and other realists who began to appear in the 1890's has left a marked impression on the 20th-century American novel.

ALCOTT, LOUISA MAY 1832–1888 *Little Women* (1868). Mrs. March and her irresistible daughters "carry on" while father fights in the Civil War. Though love of life permeates this novel of New England family life, it is never sticky because the author is witty and sensible. *Dutton $2.75, Little, Brown $3, Dell, Evman-h, Gar, Nel, Pen.*

BELLAMY, EDWARD 1850–1898 *Looking Backward* (1888). One of the most popular utopian romances in English: a vision of our nation in the year 2000, showing how planning and nationalization of industry can create prosperity of both body and spirit. *Houghton Mifflin $3, ML, MLCE.*

BIRD, ROBERT MONTGOMERY 1806–1854 *Nick of the Woods* (1837). Vivid and often realistic account of a Kentucky frontier "Indian hater." *American Book o.p.*

COOPER, JAMES FENIMORE 1789–1851 *The Deerslayer* (1841). The initiation of Natty Bumppo (also called Deerslayer and Leatherstocking), the hero of Cooper's 5-volume epic of the frontier. Natty kills his first Indian, serves his friend Chingachgook, rejects love, moves toward the integrity that will mark his whole career as frontiersman. *GtIl, Harp.*

———— *The Last of the Mohicans* (1826). The most intense of the Leatherstocking series, featuring a breathless chase. Natty reaches resourceful maturity. *CoE, GtIl, EvmanNA, Nel, PB, Rine.*

———— *The Pathfinder* (1840). Combines adventure in the forest and on water in the Lake Ontario country. *GtIl, ML, Nel.*

———— *The Pioneers* (1823). Stressing social conditions in the New York State frontier. Though Natty in middle age is keen and crafty, he can maintain integrity only by retiring into the forest. *GtIl, Rine.*

———— *The Prairie* (1827). In the Great Plains beyond the Mississippi, Leatherstocking lives and meditates his last adventures. *Evman-h, Rine.*

Also recommended: *The Spy* (1821), espionage during the Revolution, *GtIl;* and *The Pilot* (1823), about John Paul Jones, *GtIl.*

CRANE, STEPHEN 1871–1900 *Maggie: A Girl of the Streets* (1893). Seduced and then abandoned, Maggie kills herself. A grim and partly objective study of life in a New York slum. In *Selected Prose and Poetry, Rine.*

_____ *The Red Badge of Courage* (1895). In this Civil War story without glory, Crane explores the fear, shame, disgust, and courage of a young Union soldier. The imagery is crisp and accurate. *Grosset $1.49, CoE, GtIl, Harp, Liv, ML, MLCE, NAL, PB, Rine.*

DEFOREST, JOHN WILLIAM 1826–1906 *Miss Ravenal's Conversion from Secession to Loyalty* (1867). A surprisingly realistic novel of manners, delineating characters neither "good" nor "bad" and projecting a well-balanced view of the Civil War. *Rine.*

HAWTHORNE, NATHANIEL 1804–1864 *The Blithedale Romance* (1852). A partially autobiographical novel, growing out of the author's participation in the Brook Farm experiment in socialism. *MLG, Nort.*

_____ *The House of the Seven Gables* (1851). A novel about sinister hereditary influences within an old New England family, sunnier than Hawthorne's other works despite its grim subject. *Houghton Mifflin $2.04, Macmillan $2.20, Evman-h, GtIl, MLG, PB, Rine.*

_____ *The Marble Faun* (1860). In Italy several characters live through an experience of old evil projected into the present. *MLG, PB.*

_____ *The Scarlet Letter* (1850). The aftermath of adultery for the wife, her lover, their child, and the husband. The characters are studied deeply, the style is symbolic, and there is no clear commitment to either moral liberalism or the rigorous Calvinistic code. *Hendricks $2.50, Macmillan $2.80, Ronald $1.50, Evman-h, GtIl, Harp, Liv, ML, NAL, MLG, Nel, PB, Rine, RivLib, Vik, Vik-h.*

HOWELLS, WILLIAM DEAN 1837–1920 *A Modern Instance* (1882). A realistic study of average people, a young newspaperman and his wife, and their marital difficulties. *Rine.*

_____ *The Rise of Silas Lapham* (1885). Deftly, Howells contrasts the worth of the newly rich Laphams with the sterility of an old aristocratic Boston family. Much less dated than one might think. *Houghton Mifflin $2.04, Harp, ML, RivEd, WoC.*

JAMES, HENRY 1843–1916 *The Ambassadors* (1903). James's richest novel contrasting the European and American traditions. Slowly, slowly, the American Strether feels his way into the liberal European code and learns that he must not break Newsome's liaison with Madame Vionnet. *Harp, NAL, RivEd.*

_____ *The American* (1877). Wealthy, capable, candid Christopher Newman came to Paris to "live" and to get a wife who will be "the best article on the market." This early novel, relatively direct in style, is a good introduction to James. *Rine.*

_____ *Daisy Miller* (1878). The heroine is a buoyant American girl whose actions shock her European associates. *Dell.*

_____ *The Golden Bowl* (1905). When the husband loves his wife's father's wife, the stage is set for messy domestic tragedy. The wife, one of James's great women, solves the problem beautifully. *Grove $6.50, Ever.*

_____ *The Portrait of a Lady* (1881). Isabel Archer, the feminine counterpart of Christopher Newman *(The American)*, hopes to find in Europe the best of life and men. Another probing contrast of American and European types and codes. *ML, RivEd, WoC.*

_____ *The Turn of the Screw* (1898). A psychological ghost story. *Dell, ML.*

_____ *The Wings of the Dove* (1902). Milly Theale, a young American doomed to early death, is determined to crowd all fine experiences into her short life. *Dell, ML.*

MELVILLE, HERMAN 1819–1891 *Billy Budd, Foretopman* (1891, pub. 1924). Goaded beyond endurance, Budd kills his persecutor and is punished. This Job-like questioning of justice is Melville's last and most haunting sea story. *Black, Evman, MLG, Vik-h.* Also in *Four Great American Novels, Holt $4;* and *Six Great Modern Short Novels, Dell.*

_____ *Moby Dick* (1851). As simple tale, a gusty account of a whaling voyage, packed with the lore of Leviathan and with the doings of a wild and brilliantly characterized crew. As allegory, a probing into the nature of evil and into the spiritual torments of a man who set himself against it. *Farrar, Straus & Cudahy $3.50, Grosset $1.49, $1.95, CoNC, Dell, EvmanNA, Harp, ML, MLCE, MLG, NAL, PB, RivEd, Rine, S&S, WoC.*

_____ *Omoo* (1847). Well-developed episodes and twenty characters sharply realized as Melville recounts his Tahiti adventures. *Dodd, Mead $3.95, Farrar, Straus & Cudahy $3.50, Hendricks $4.50, Grove $3.95, Ever.*

_____ *Typee* (1846). A fictionized account of Melville's stay in the Marquesan Islands. Chiefly descriptive of the natives' simple and lovely way of life. *Dodd, Mead $3.95, Farrar, Straus & Cudahy $3.50, Grosset $1.98, Avon, Ban, Evman, Evman-h, WoC.*

NORRIS, FRANK 1870–1902 *McTeague* (1899). A realistic study of the disintegration of character, ending in murder. *Rine.*

_____ *The Octopus* (1901). Farmers vs. monopoly. See page 130.

STOWE, HARRIET BEECHER 1811–1896 *Uncle Tom's Cabin* (1852). Powerful antislavery propaganda in sentimental fiction. *Coward-McCann $3, Evman-h, GtIl, ML, Nel, RivLib.*

TWAIN, MARK (SAMUEL LANGHORNE CLEMENS) 1835–1910 *The Adventures of Huckleberry Finn* (1885). Huck wants to be "free and satisfied." With Nigger Jim, his father-brother-friend, he travels down the Mississippi on a raft. Drama, humor, satiric social criticism, and all that Twain felt most deeply about boys and men are tossed into this grand story. *Dutton $2.75, Heritage $4.50, CoNC, Evman-h, Gar, GtIl, Harp, MLG, NAL, Nel, PB, Rine, RivEd, Vik, Vik-h.*

_____ *The Adventures of Tom Sawyer* (1876). This book for young and old pictures boys' life in little lazy Hannibal, Missouri, contrasting their superficial cussedness with their inner decency. *Dutton $2.75, Heritage $4.50, CoNC, Evman-h, Harp, MLG, NAL, Nel, PB, Pen.*

_____ *A Connecticut Yankee in King Arthur's Court* (1889). A modern American finds himself among the Knights of the Round Table and discovers that Yankee ingenuity is more than a match for medieval magic and superstition. *Grosset $1.49, Harper $3.50, Harp, ML, PB.*

_____ *Pudd'nhead Wilson* (1894). A nonconformist too wise for his backwoods community, Wilson solves several mysteries. Partly a triumph of bitter humor, partly a daring treatment of miscegenation. *Grove $3.50, Harper $3.50, Ban, Ever.*

WESTCOTT, EDWARD NOYES 1846–1898 *David Harum* (1898). About a shrewd but warmhearted horsetrader. *Ban.*

F. 20th Century American Novels

JOHN WILLIAM WARD, *Princeton University*

Two figures dominate the American novel at the beginning of the century: Henry James and Theodore Dreiser. The two are important in quite different ways. Dreiser, happily for literary historians, wrote his first novel, *Sister Carrie,* exactly in 1900 to inaugurate the century. Though James wrote several novels in the 19th century, he belongs to the 20th not only because his best work comes after 1900 but because he has been the single largest influence on novel-writing in our time.

James's importance lies in the high sense of craftsmanship he brought to the art of fiction; after him no American writer could produce a careless novel without being self-conscious of the fact. Dreiser's influence, on the other hand, lies not in his art (his style is artless at best) but in his attitude. Dreiser was a naturalist; that is, he believed that man is controlled by forces outside himself. In such a universe morality is impossible, of course, and thus Dreiser marks a sharp break with the 19th century. He marks also a gain for the novelist. Dreiser destroyed the genteel tradition which denied the artist access to certain significant areas of human experience. Sex, for Dreiser, was not immoral; it merely dramatized the forces that act on man. So at the very outset of the 20th century we have two titans, important in their own right as well as for representing two tendencies in writing. James, a consummate craftsman, intent on reducing the chaos of experience to understandable form, and Dreiser, nearly impervious to the demands of style, intent on capturing life through sheer energy. Most contemporary fiction oscillates between these poles.

Apart from the "muckraking" of Upton Sinclair and the social fiction of Ernest Poole, there is a curious hiatus in the history of the American novel from about 1909 to 1920 (1909 because in that year appeared Gertrude Stein's experimental and intriguing *Three Lives,* which still seems too modern for many of us). These were the

years of the great poetic renaissance in America, but the
years of few good novels. Our two greatest women novelists, Edith Wharton and Willa Cather, were active, but
their best novels (*Age of Innocence* and *A Lost Lady*
respectively) were to come in the 20's.

After 1920 the American novel flourished. Two writers
stand out, Ernest Hemingway and William Faulkner,
but it is only against their great talent that other talents
seem less. Both take somber views of the modern world;
Hemingway finds meaning only in man's capacity for
courage in face of inevitable physical defeat, while
Faulkner, with his cult of primitivism, is even more pessimistic about the direction of a commercial, industrial,
dehumanized civilization. Both also extend the contrast
between James and Dreiser. Hemingway, with his spare
objectivity and rigorously disciplined prose, stands at the
opposite extreme from Faulkner and his lush rhetoric
and labyrinthine plots. Hemingway's first novel, *The
Sun Also Rises,* is still his best. *Absalom! Absalom!* is
Faulkner at his finest, but Faulkner's fiction is so densely
interwoven that a most useful introduction is Malcolm
Cowley's *Portable Faulkner,* which selects and arranges
the richness.

On the side of Hemingway and what has been called
the "novel of selected incident," one might range F. Scott
Fitzgerald, the moral historian of the 20's, Wharton,
Cather, and E. E. Cummings, the poet who wrote one of
the best books about World War I, *The Enormous Room.*
On Faulkner's side, where energy is constantly erupting
through the form of the novel, one could count Thomas
Wolfe, whose sprawling autobiographical novels are the
despair of critics and the delight of readers everywhere.
But to insist on a sharp contrast would do violence to
the mixture of art and energy one finds in each of these
writers; more significantly, it might cause us to miss
such important novelists as Sherwood Anderson and
Sinclair Lewis. Lewis, the social historian of Main Street,
U.S.A., will be important to anyone who tries to understand the 20's. Anderson, who discovered haunting beauty
in the gnarled and grotesque lives of midland America,
will impress anyone who tries to understand people.

The 30's, naturally enough, were years of increasing

social concern for writers. Naturalism, with its emphasis on man victimized by forces beyond his control, had an obvious appeal, and the concern for esthetic form lessened under the impact of social disaster. Now that the novelists who pleaded a cause to the exclusion of other obligations have been forgotten, three writers have shown that their appeal was more than immediate: John Dos Passos, John Steinbeck, and James T. Farrell. Farrell has expressed his admiration for Dreiser, and his sagas of the Chicago Irish manifest the same sympathy for the downtrodden and the same large scope of the older writer. Dos Passos' famous trilogy, *U.S.A.*, a significant experiment in novel form, is a biting criticism of American life from a leftist point of view. Steinbeck writes two kinds of books: protests against social injustice (*Grapes of Wrath, In Dubious Battle*) and happy pictures of the carefree life (*Cannery Row*), but both share a rejection of moral absolutes and celebrate man's capacity to live and survive.

World War II forced a pause in fiction writing (the best novels about the war and afterward are by Mailer, Jones, and Burns), and we are still too close to do justice to the diverse talent that has appeared since. Two writers, certainly, rank with the best: James Gould Cozzens and Robert Penn Warren. Cozzens, actually, has been turning out good novels since the 20's, but it was only with *Guard of Honor,* which won a Pulitzer Prize, that he began to receive the attention he merits. Cozzens projects a mature and measured view of a world in which a man's job is to do the best he can. Warren's theme, as in *All the King's Men,* is man's capacity for self-deception and inevitable involvement in corruption. Warren has a verbal talent matched only by Faulkner in the modern novel. Warren and Faulkner remind us of the dominance of the Southern school in contemporary fiction; Carson McCullers and Katherine Anne Porter also find in the traditions of the South a rich perspective for the writing of fiction. The North has hardly lost the literary battle, of course. Chicago alone has given us Nelson Algren, who has successfully combined a naturalistic vision with a poetic style, and Saul Bellow, whose *Adventures of Augie March* is one of the most important books of the last decade.

There seems to be a tendency in the American novel once more toward the big, inclusive novel. But this time not at a sacrifice of verbal texture or formal structure. The best modern writers try to encompass the energy of modern life without failing their responsibilities to their craft. The novel is so rich today that a brief summary must fail in completeness. But four writers have each produced a novel so good that they deserve attention: William Styron, J. D. Salinger, Ralph Ellison, and Bernard Malamud. Finally, generalizations like these—attempts to name the big books and the ranking authors —are useful only so far as they get the reader at the books themselves. Reading each novel for its own special delight is what counts.

ALGREN, NELSON 1909– *The Man with the Golden Arm* (1949). Grisly, antic, ribald saga of the Chicago underworld. *Doubleday $3, PB.*

ANDERSON, SHERWOOD 1876–1941 *Winesburg, Ohio* (1919). Frustrations behind the façade of small-town life. *Comp, ML, NAL, Vik and Vik-h (selections).*

BAKER, DOROTHY 1907– *Young Man with a Horn* (1938). Based on the life of Bix Beiderbecke, this is a successful fictional interpretation of jazz and jazzmen. *Houghton Mifflin $2.75.*

BALDWIN, JAMES 1924– *Go Tell It on the Mountain* (1953). The first novel by a skillful Negro writer, suggesting the solace of religion for his race. *Knopf o.p.*

BELLOW, SAUL 1915– *The Adventures of Augie March* (1953). A gay picaresque tale of an undefeatable 20th-century adventurer. *Viking $4.50.*

BROMFIELD, LOUIS 1896–1956 *The Green Bay Tree* (1924). An intriguing plot, fine characterization, and scathing denunciation of modern political, business, and social ethics. In *Bromfield Galaxy* (1957) with *Early Autumn* and *A Good Woman. Harper $3.95.*

BUCK, PEARL *The Good Earth.* See page 78.

BURNETT, WILLIAM R. 1899– *Iron Man* (1930). Sharply etched account of a prizefighter's rise and fall; excellent "hard-boiled" realism. *O.p.*

BURNS, JOHN HORNE 1916–1953 *The Gallery* (1947). A fine novel about G.I.'s in Italy during World War II. *Harper $3.75.*

CABELL, JAMES BRANCH 1879–1958 *Jurgen* (1919). Delightful satire on contemporary folkways clothed in the pattern of romantic legend. *ML.*

CAIN, JAMES M. 1892– *The Postman Always Rings Twice* (1934). Amoral, tough novel of a hobo's love for a sandwichstand-owner's wife. *PB.*

CALDWELL, ERSKINE 1903—*God's Little Acre* (1933). A violent tragicomedy of the new South, in the language of its dirt farmers and mill hands. *Grosset $2.50, ML, NAL.*

_____ *Tobacco Road* (1932). Poor whites on the poor earth. The burlesque masks deep bitterness, pity, and sympathy. *Grosset $2.50, ML, NAL.*

CATHER, WILLA 1876–1947 *My Ántonia* (1918). Nebraska girlhood of a Bohemian immigrant. *Houghton Mifflin $3.50.*

_____ *A Lost Lady* (1923). Clean-cut story of the old and new generations of empire builders in Nebraska, plus a fascinating, if immoral, lady. *Knopf $3.*

_____ *Shadows on the Rock.* See page 62.

CLARK, WALTER VAN TILBURG 1909– *The Ox-Bow Incident* (1940). An exciting novel of Western justice; an unusually sharp analysis of the mass mind in mob action. *Grosset $1.49, Liv, MLP, NAL.*

COZZENS, JAMES GOULD 1903– *Guard of Honor* (1948). What happened during three action-packed days in an air-training camp during World War II. *Harcourt, Brace $4.75.*

_____ *The Just and the Unjust* (1942). How a murder trial affects and is affected by the life of a small-town county seat. *HarB.*

CUMMINGS, E. E. 1894– *The Enormous Room* (1922). A witty and ironic assertion of the indestructibility of the private self; perhaps the best novel drawn from the experiences of World War I. *ML.*

DOS PASSOS, JOHN 1896– *U.S.A.* (1937). This trilogy comprises *The 42nd Parallel* (1930), *Nineteen-Nineteen* (1932), and *The Big Money* (1936), constituting a cross section of American life from 1900 through the boom of the 20's. *Houghton Mifflin $3.50 ea. vol., MLG.*

DREISER, THEODORE 1871–1945 *An American Tragedy* (1925). Clyde Griffith is condemned to the electric chair. Dreiser arraigns the social system that made Griffith what he was. *World $4.50, Dell, MLG.*

_____ *The Financier* (1912). Ponderous but impressive biography of a successful business pirate. *World $3.*

_____ *Jennie Gerhardt* (1911). Pictures an innocent and courageous victim of malicious destiny. *World $3.*

_____ *Sister Carrie* (1900). Aided by her lovers, a woman rises from poverty to spectacular stage fame. *World $3, Ban, Dell, ML, Rine, RivEd.*

ELLISON, RALPH 1914– *The Invisible Man* (1952). The story of a Negro's attempt to discover his identity; a parable for the isolation of all modern men. *Random House $3.95, NAL.*

FARRELL, JAMES T. 1904– *Studs Lonigan* (1935). Trilogy recording the career of a poor boy who aspired to be a "big shot" but died in wretchedness. *Vanguard $6, MLG, NAL.*

_____ *A World I Never Made* (1936). A blunt, forceful story of a low-class Irish family. *O.p.*

FAULKNER, WILLIAM 1897– *Absalom! Absalom!* (1936). The curse of slavery thwarts the ambitious dream of a Southern aristocrat. *ML.*

_____ *As I Lay Dying* (1930). A family of poor whites transports the body of their mother to the distant cemetery that she had chosen as the place of her burial. *ML, MLP.*

_____ *The Portable Faulkner* (1946). Ed. by Malcolm Cowley. Memorable short stories of decadence in the deep South and organized selections from novels of the American Balzac. *Vik-h.*

_____ *The Sound and the Fury* (1929). The decay of an aristocratic Southern family as seen by those involved. *ML, MLP, NAL.*

FERBER, EDNA 1887– *Show Boat* (1926). Romantic novel of the old Mississippi and showboat life. *Doubleday $3.95, Grosset $1.98.*

FISHER, DOROTHY CANFIELD 1879–1959 *The Deepening Stream* (1930). Despite parental discord in her girlhood home, the heroine achieves a happy marriage. *O.p.*

FITZGERALD, F. SCOTT 1896–1940 *The Great Gatsby* (1925). Satire of wealthy Long Island society in the jazz-bewitched 1920's. *Scribner $2.95, ModSA, Scrib.*

_____ *Tender Is the Night* (1934). One of Fitzgerald's most perceptive novels about the "lost generation." *Scribner $3.95, ModSA, Scrib.*

GLASGOW, ELLEN 1874–1945 *Vein of Iron* (1935). Grave, symphonic beauty marks this novel about the courage of a modern Virginian true to the hard traditions of her Scottish forebears. *HarB.*

GOODRICH, MARCUS 1897– *Delilah* (1941). One of the most powerful American sea stories since *Moby Dick. Rinehart $4.*

GRUBB, DAVIS, 1919– *Night of the Hunter* (1953). The relentless pursuit of two children by a murderous religious fanatic becomes more than just a hair-raising story. *O.p.*

GUTHRIE, A. B., JR. 1901– *The Big Sky* (1947). Remarkable novel of fur-trade days along the Missouri and in the Rocky Mountain country a century ago—swift, vivid, extraordinarily alive. *Houghton Mifflin $4.50, PB.*

HEGGEN, THOMAS O. 1919–1949 *Mister Roberts* (1946). The hilarious account of the boredom and frustrations of life on a cargo ship during World War II. *Houghton Mifflin $3.50, PB.*

HEMINGWAY, ERNEST 1899– *A Farewell to Arms* (1929). A deep, fierce, true love story of World War I—bitter, blunt, yet finely courageous. *ModSA.*

_____ *For Whom the Bell Tolls* (1940). A story of love and danger seen against the backdrop of the Spanish Civil War. *ModSA, Scrib.*

_____ *The Sun Also Rises* (1926). On one level, a novel about the "lost generation" of Americans after World War I in Paris and Spain; on a more abiding level, the hero's futile search for a way to live in a crippling and hostile world. *Scribner $3.50, Scrib.*

HERSEY, JOHN 1914– *A Bell for Adano* (1944). Mature, moving commentary on the strengths and weaknesses of American Army administration in conquered Italy. *Knopf $3.95.*

_____ *The Wall* (1950). The liquidation of the Warsaw ghetto by the Germans, as felt by the Jews being liquidated. *Knopf $5.95.*

JAMES, HENRY. See page 120.

JONES, JAMES 1921– *From Here to Eternity* (1951). Pulls no punches in detailing Army life in Hawaii just before Pearl Harbor. *Scribner $4.95, NAL.*

KEROUAC, JACK 1922– *On the Road* (1957). Typical of the fiction of the "beat generation" with its frenetic search for experience and sensation. *Viking $3.95, NAL.*

LEWIS, SINCLAIR 1885–1951 *Arrowsmith* (1925). An idealistic American physician struggles against the materialists who seek to dominate his life. Perhaps Lewis's masterpiece. *HarB.*

_____ *Babbitt* (1922). Caustic portrayal of an American go-getter. *HarB.*

_____ *Main Street* (1920). The crusade of a doctor's wife against the narrow-minded inertia of a small town. *HarB.*

LONDON, JACK 1876–1916 *Martin Eden* (1909). Partly autobiographical narrative of a battle against adverse economic and social environment. *Macmillan $3.75, Dell, Rine.*

_____ *The Sea Wolf* (1904). The most brutal, most exciting of London's "red-blooded" romances. *Grosset $1.98, Macmillan $3.75.*

McCULLERS, CARSON 1917– *The Heart Is a Lonely Hunter* (1940). Pitiful people in a Southern town confide their miserable secrets to a mute. *Ban.*

_____ *The Ballad of the Sad Café* (1951). Omnibus volume including six poignant short stories, the tragic novelette of the title, and three somber novels, including the above. *Houghton Mifflin $5.*

MAILER, NORMAN 1923– *The Naked and the Dead* (1948). An authentic report on how G.I.'s on South Pacific islands thought, talked, lived, and died. *Grosset $2.49, Rinehart $4.50, NAL.*

MALAMUD, BERNARD 1914– *The Assistant* (1957). Excellent first novel of a promising talent; a petty hoodlum seeks expiation and self-acceptance. *Farrar, Straus & Cudahy $3.50, NAL.*

MARQUAND, JOHN P. 1893– *H. M. Pulham, Esquire* (1941). The wryly humorous autobiography that H. M. Pulham might have written for his 25th Harvard reunion. *Little, Brown $4, Ban.*

_____ *The Late George Apley* (1937). Subtly satiric study of a Boston Brahmin. *ML, PB, UL.*

MITCHELL, MARGARET 1900–1949 *Gone with the Wind* (1936). Extended picture of the South before, during, and after the Civil War. *Macmillan $3.95, Gar, Perm.*

MORRIS, WRIGHT 1910– *Love Among the Cannibals* (1957). Hilarious fun, searing irony, caustic wit focused on two Hollywood writers and their "chicks" at Acapulco. *NAL.*

NABOKOV, VLADIMIR 1899– *Lolita* (1958). A brilliantly styled comedy of horrors on the theme of a middle-aged man's obsession with a young girl; compels serious laughter. *Putnam $5.*

NORRIS, FRANK 1870–1902 *The Octopus* (1901). Saga of a fight by California farmers against railroad domination, and of the triumphs of nature over the schemes of men. *Doubleday $3.95, Ban, RivEd, Saga.*

O'HARA, JOHN 1905– *Appointment in Samarra* (1934). A sharp, satirical novel of the country-club set. *Random House $3, ML, NAL.*

POOLE, ERNEST 1880–1950 *The Harbor* (1915). New York harbor overshadows even the strongly limned strikers and capitalists of this dramatic novel. *Saga.*

PORTER, KATHERINE ANNE 1894– *Pale Horse, Pale Rider* (1939). Three sensitively told short novels: *Old Mortality,* about scandals, passions, meannesses, tragedies in a Southern family; *Noon Wine,* about cow-farming and man-shooting in Texas; and the title story, about a newspaper girl whose soldier-lover dies of flu just before the 1918 armistice. *Harcourt, Brace $3, ML.*

RAND, AYN *The Fountainhead* (1943). An architect resembling the late Frank Lloyd Wright combats the adverse forces of conventional ideas and an unconventional woman. *Bobbs-Merrill $6.50, NAL.*

RAWLINGS, MARJORIE KINNAN 1896–1953 *The Yearling* (1938). Appealing novel of backwoods life in Florida; a deeply sympathetic portrait of a lonely boy. *Scribner $4.50.*

RICHTER, CONRAD 1890– *The Sea of Grass* (1937). Land butchery, human tragedy, and inner steadfastness in a short novel of the early Southwest. *Knopf $3.*

ROBERTS, KENNETH *Arundel, Northwest Passage, Rabble in Arms.* Factual realism about New England and New York before and during the Revolution. See page 71.

SALINGER, JEROME DAVID 1919– *The Catcher in the Rye* (1951). An hilarious and touching story of a latter-day Huck Finn who dreads the compromises of adult life. *Grosset $1.49, Little, Brown $4, ML, NAL.*

SAROYAN, WILLIAM 1908– *The Human Comedy* (1943). In this warm, sentimental novel, Marcus Macauley, though killed in the war, lives on in the hearts of those who love him. *Harcourt, Brace $2.12.*

SHAW, IRWIN 1913– *The Young Lions* (1948). The hate and the horror, the brutality and the glory, the lust and the heroism of World War II, European theater. *ML, NAL.*

SINCLAIR, UPTON 1878– *The Jungle* (1906). Graphic picture of the maze of chicanery, crime, and vice in the Chicago stock-yard district of a half-century ago. *Harp.*

SMITH, BETTY 1904– *A Tree Grows in Brooklyn* (1943). The poor Irish in Brooklyn get more out of life than do Farrell's poor Irish in Chicago. *Harper $4.50.*

SMITH, LILLIAN 1897– *Strange Fruit* (1944). A courageous novel of the Deep South—its hidden fears and prejudices—and of doomed interracial love. *Harcourt, Brace $3, NAL.*

STEIN, GERTRUDE 1874–1946 *Three Lives* (1909). One of the most important books in modern American literature. The story of three women (each can be read separately; try *Melanctha* first) told in a style that created a style. *MLP, NewC.*

STEINBECK, JOHN 1902– *The Grapes of Wrath* (1939). The suffering and despair of poor farmers tractored off their land in Oklahoma and exploited in California. *Comp, Harp, Liv, ML.*

———— *In Dubious Battle* (1936). The story of a strike in the fruit groves of California. Probably Steinbeck's best novel. *ML.*

STYRON, WILLIAM 1925– *Lie Down in Darkness* (1951). A superb first novel about the disintegration of a Virginia family; by the best recent talent in the American novel. *Bobbs-Merrill $3.50, Comp, NAL.* Read also his short novel *The Long March. MLP.*

TARKINGTON, BOOTH 1869–1946 *Alice Adams* (1921). Veracious picture of 22-year-old Alice and her problems. *Grosset $1.79.*

WARREN, ROBERT PENN 1905– *All the King's Men* (1946). Pulitzer Prize-winning portrait of a demagogue, presumably based on the life of Huey Long. *Harcourt, Brace $4, Ban, ML.*

WHARTON, EDITH 1862–1937 *The Age of Innocence* (1920). Social conventions of the 1870's strangle a sincere love. *ML.*

———— *Ethan Frome* (1911). This brief history of frustration is like a sleety wind from a New England forest. *Scribner $3, Scrib.*

———— *The House of Mirth* (1905). Tragedy in high society. *ModSA.*

WILDER, THORNTON 1897– *The Bridge of San Luis Rey* (1927). Entangled lives converging to a tragic destiny in Peru 400 years ago. *Grosset $1.49.*

WISTER, OWEN 1860–1938 *The Virginian* (1902). The best of Westerns, about a bold young cowboy and a girl from the East. *Grosset $2.49, Macmillan $4.50, PB.*

WOLFE, THOMAS 1900–1938 *Look Homeward, Angel* (1929). The turbulent youth of Eugene Gant in a small Southern town. *MLG, ModSA, Scrib.*

———— *You Can't Go Home Again* (1940). The last and most mature of Wolfe's autobiographical narratives, focused on the collapse of the false values of the 1920's. *Harp, UL.*

WOUK, HERMAN 1915– *The Caine Mutiny* (1951). Clean, deft narrative of the Pacific wanderings of a mine-sweeper with a neurotic for commander and a 90-day wonder as hero. *Doubleday $3.95*.

WRIGHT, RICHARD 1908– *Native Son* (1940). The violent life and death of Bigger Thomas, Chicago Negro; successful mixture of melodrama, striking character creation, and social criticism. *Grosset $1.49, Harp, NAL*.

Additional Recommended Novels in Paperbound

BOWLES, PAUL *The Sheltering Sky. NAL.*

BOYLE, KAY *Three Short Novels. Bea.*

BURDICK, EUGENE *The Ninth Wave. Dell.*

CAPOTE, TRUMAN *Other Voices, Other Rooms. MLP, NAL.*

CHEEVER, JOHN *The Wapshot Chronicle. Ban.*

DeVRIES, PETER *Comfort Me with Apples. NAL.*

_____ *The Tunnel of Love. NAL.*

FOOTE, SHELBY *Shiloh. NAL.*

LOWRY, MALCOLM *Under the Volcano. Vin.*

McCARTHY, MARY *The Company She Keeps. Dell.*

MARCH, WILLIAM *Company K. NAL, Saga.*

MORRIS, WRIGHT *The Field of Vision. NAL.*

SCHULBERG, BUDD *What Makes Sammy Run? Ban.*

_____ *The Disenchanted. Ban.*

TRILLING, LIONEL *The Middle of the Journey. Anch.*

WEST, NATHANAEL *The Day of the Locust. Ban, NewC.*

_____ *Miss Lonelyhearts. NewC.*

10. The Short Story

WILLIAM PEDEN, *University of Missouri*

The short story is probably the oldest and yet at the same time one of the newest of recognized literary forms. Although tales and narrative sketches appear in all ancient literatures, including the Bible, the short story as a consciously artistic literary type is essentially an American product of the early 19th century. Some critics claim that Washington Irving's pictorial narrative sketches are the first *modern* short stories. Others bestow the term upon some of Hawthorne's tales, like "Rappacini's Daughter," which are built around a single intense or bizarre situation. Still others maintain that only in Edgar Allan Poe's best work do we find the conscious striving for unity which makes the short story so different from the loosely strung together narrative sketch.

Such historical distinctions, however, are of little value to the lay reader. What is important is the fact that Irving, Hawthorne, and Poe were gifted storytellers who took their work seriously—as entertainment, as art, and as significant commentary on the problems of man's existence. Such authors brought originality and vigor to the short story and prepared the way for the many readers who have found the short story to be one of the most satisfying of all literary forms.

The short story has always been strongly influenced by the artistic, moral, and ideological climate of the world in which it is written. One group or generation of storytellers may emphasize plot; another will be primarily concerned with character revelation or social commentary; still another will present a plotless "slice of life." Literary fashions tend to change as radically and often with as little apparent reason as do those in wearing apparel; what today is considered a "good" short story may be dismissed as "old hat" by tomorrow. The superior story, however, survives these changes: it can delight, inform, or disturb the reader regardless of time or place, in spite of politics or prejudice. The superior story becomes part of the reader's vicarious experience. It lingers in his mind—often more real than actuality itself, because the writer through the magic of the creative imagination has transformed some specific aspect of experience into universally significant art.

Since World War II, with signs of decadence and fatigue apparent in some of the more traditional literary forms, the short story continues to grow in vigor, variety, and significance. What an Elizabethan poet affectionately termed a "tale which holdeth children from play, and old men from the chimney-corner" might prove to be the major literary contribution of the 20th century.

Volumes listed in other sections containing short narratives include the Bible, *Panchatantra*, AESOP's *Fables*, OVID's *Metamorphoses*, *Arabian Nights*, CHAUCER's *Canterbury Tales*, BOCCACCIO's *Decameron*, CERVANTES' *Don Quixote*, ADDISON and STEELE's *Spectator*. There are countless useful anthologies of short stories old and new; FRED L. PATTEE's *The Development of the American Short Story* is an informative survey from Irving to O. Henry.

ANDERSON *Winesburg, Ohio*. Masterly stories of frustrated lives in a drab town. See page 126.

BABEL, ISAAC 1894–? *Collected Stories* (1955). Stories of civil war and of Russian life before and after the Revolution by a Russian master believed to have died in a concentration camp. *Criterion $5*.

BENET, STEPHEN VINCENT 1898–1943 *The Stephen Vincent Benét Pocket Book* (1946). Colorful, romantic stories of America's past. *PB*.

BIERCE, AMBROSE 1842–1914? *In the Midst of Life* (1898). Sardonic sketches of soldiers and civilians in the terrifying world of our Civil War and after. *ML o.p.*

BRADBURY, RAY 1920– *The Golden Apples of the Sun* (1953). A first-rate collection of tales of fantasy and science fiction. *Doubleday $3, Ban.*

CALDWELL, ERSKINE 1903– *Short Stories*. Stories of ribald humor, social protest, and poignant tragedy by the author of *Tobacco Road. NAL, PB.*

CAPOTE, TRUMAN 1924– *A Tree of Night* (1950). Eight nebulous, haunting stories. *NAL.*

CHEEVER, JOHN 1912– *The Enormous Radio* (1953). Postwar suburbia viewed by a witty, sophisticated, and compassionate satirist. *Berk.*

CHEKHOV, ANTON 1860–1904 *Short Stories.* Skeptical commentaries on Russian life and character. Chekhov's indirect, implicational narrative method has profoundly influenced 20th-century fiction. *Macmillan $3.50, Oxford Univ. $3, Pitman $1.25, Anch, Avon, Cap, Evman-h, ML, UL, Vik, Vik-h.*

COLETTE 1873–1955 *My Mother's House* and *Sido* (1953). Reminiscences of childhood by one of the most celebrated French writers of this century. *Farrar, Straus & Cudahy $3.50.*

COPPARD, A. E. 1878–1957 *Collected Tales* (1948). Delightful stories by an English master, ranging from naturalism to fantasy and symbolism. *Knopf $5.75.*

CRANE, STEPHEN 1871–1900 *Stories and Tales.* Long narratives by a pioneer of realism in America. *Harp, Rine, Vin.*

Famous Chinese Short Stories (1952). Retold by Lin Yutang. A good introduction to the rich field of Chinese short fiction. *Day $3.50, PB.*

FARRELL, JAMES T. 1904– *Short Stories* (1946). A representative collection of stories of urban 20th-century America by the author of *Studs Lonigan. Vanguard $5, NAL.*

FAULKNER, WILLIAM 1897– *Collected Stories* (1950). 42 stories of World War I, of barnstorming pilots, of tensions and frustrations in an impoverished Southern county. *Random House $4.75.*

FITZGERALD, F. SCOTT 1896–1940 *The Short Stories of F. Scott Fitzgerald* (1951). 28 gay and tragic stories by the sad young spokesman for the Jazz Age. *Scribner $4.95.*

44 Irish Short Stories (1955). Excellent anthology: from Yeats and Joyce to O'Connor, O'Faolain, and McLaverty. *Devin-Adair $5.*

French Stories and Tales (1956). Representative collection from Balzac and Flaubert to Gide. *Knopf $4.50, PB.*

Great American Short Stories (1959). From Poe to the present. *Dell.*

Great English Short Stories (1959). Representative collection. *Dell.*

Great German Short Novels and Stories (1933). Fifteen stories and short novels, including GOETHE's *Sorrows of Werther* and MANN's *Death in Venice. ML.* Also *German Stories and Tales, Knopf $4.50, PB.*

Great Russian Short Stories (1959). A good representative collection. *Dell.*

HAWTHORNE, NATHANIEL 1804–1864 *Selected Tales.* Deeply symbolic and carefully wrought studies of sin and retribution, and romantic tales of colonial New England. *Evman-h, MLG, Nel, Rine, Vik, Vik-h, Vin.*

HEMINGWAY, ERNEST 1898– *Short Stories* (1942). Contains the best short fiction of one of the most significant, controversial, and influential writers of this generation. *Scribner $2.75.*

HENRY, O. (WILLIAM SIDNEY PORTER) 1862–1910 *Short Stories.* Clever stories of humor and pathos by a master of surprise endings. *Doubleday $2, Odyssey $2, ML, PB.*

IRVING, WASHINGTON 1783–1859 *Sketches.* Warmly colored, romanticized sketches, tales, and essays, such as "Rip Van Winkle" and "Legend of Sleepy Hollow." *GtIl, ML.*

JACKSON, SHIRLEY 1920– *The Lottery* (1949). Terrifying vignettes of the tensions underlying contemporary life. *Farrar, Straus & Cudahy $3.*

JAMES, HENRY 1843–1916 *Short Stories and Novelles.* Intricate analyses of conflicting personalities and their psychological and emotional reactions by a consummate craftsman. *MLG, Rine, Vik, Vik-h.*

JOYCE, JAMES 1882–1941 *Dubliners* (1914). Sensitive, perceptive stories by a leading exponent of stream of consciousness and symbolism. *Comp, ML, Vik-h (The Portable James Joyce).*

KAFKA, FRANZ 1883–1924 *Short Stories.* Searching, strikingly original commentaries on modern life presented in terms of grotesque imagery and fantastic symbols. *Schocken $3.50, ML.*

KIPLING, RUDYARD 1865–1936 *Selected Stories.* Representative collections of a celebrated British teller of tales. *Doubleday $3.95 & $7.50, Ban.*

LAGERKVIST, PAR 1891– *The Eternal Smile and Other Stories* (1954). Representative cross section demonstrating fictional power and philosophic thought of the Norwegian Nobel Prize winner. *Random House $4.50.*

LARDNER, RING 1885–1933 *Short Stories.* Satirical stories—sometimes humorous, often bitter—debunking hypocrisy in American life. *Scribner $4.50, Ban, Vik-h.*

LAWRENCE, DAVID HERBERT 1885–1930 *Stories.* A much discussed and widely influential craftsman and thinker. *Avon, Gar, Vik, Vik-h.*

The Local Colorists (1959). Ed. by Claude M. Simpson. Excellent collection of 23 local color stories, representative of the vogue in the U.S.A. *Harper $2.95.*

LONDON, JACK 1876–1919 *Jack London's Tales of Adventure* (1956). Stories of action, violence, and atmosphere, ranging from the Far North to the South Seas. *Doubleday $4.95.*

MANN, THOMAS 1875–1955 *Stories of Three Decades* (1936). Masterful short novels on subjects ranging from the adolescent to the artist. "Tonio Kröger" and "Death in Venice" are among the finest. *Vin.*

MANSFIELD, KATHERINE 1888–1923 *Short Stories.* Penetrating character studies of English folk in the Chekhov manner, and impressionistic portraits of situations. *Knopf $6, Liv, Vin.*

MARCH, WILLIAM 1893–1954 *Trial Balance* (1945). The major work of an underrated writer: paradox, serious commentary, farce. *Harcourt, Brace o.p.*

MAUGHAM, W. SOMERSET 1874– *Short Stories.* Dramatic stories by a popular raconteur, mostly dealing with strange people and faraway places. *Avon, ML, Perm.*

MAUPASSANT, GUY DE 1850–1893 *Short Stories.* Deft craftsmanship; brilliant, often ironic, always realistic impressions of French life. *Doubleday $5.95, Evman-h, ML, PB, Pyroy, Vik-h.*

MELVILLE, HERMAN 1819–1891 *Stories.* Impressive, usually provocative stories by the author of *Moby Dick. MLG, Rine, Vik-h.*

O'CONNOR, FRANK 1903– *Stories* (1952). Humor, insight, and satire characterize these representative stories by a leading Irish writer-critic. *Knopf $4.50, Vin.*

O'FAOLAIN, SEAN 1900– *The Man Who Invented Sin* (1948). 15 narratives of contemporary Ireland selected by the author as his most characteristic. *Devin-Adair $2.75.*

PARKER, DOROTHY 1893– *Stories.* Sophisticated sketches of American life in the Jazz Age. *ML, Vik, Vik-h.*

POE, EDGAR ALLAN 1809–1849 *Tales.* Memorable stories of atmosphere, horror, ratiocination by a master of short fiction. *CoNC, Evman-h, GtIl, ML, MLG, Nel, PB, Pen, Rine, RivEd, Vik, Vik-h, WoC.*

PORTER, KATHERINE ANNE 1894– *Short Stories.* Beautifully wrought and subtle stories of varied moods, themes, and settings. *HarB, Harv, ML.*

PRITCHETT, V. S. 1900– *The Sailor, Sense of Humour, and Other Stories* (1956). Mostly about the "double lives" of middle-class Britishers tormented by changing social forces. *Knopf $5.*

Rinehart Book of Short Stories. Good collection of major works by modern masters. *Rine.*

Russian Short Stories. Two good collections are *Treasury of Great Russian Short Stories,* Macmillan *$7.50;* and *Best Russian Stories, ML.*

SAKI (H. H. MUNRO) 1879–1916 *Complete Short Stories* (1930). Facetious manners and affectations of English society; stories of fantasy and surprise. *ML.*

SALINGER, J. D. 1919– *Nine Stories* (1953). Subtle, often moving defense of childhood and the childlike mind through revealing histories of people slightly off center. *Little, Brown $3.50, NAL.*

SAROYAN, WILLIAM 1908– *Forty-Eight Stories.* Brash, ingenuous, highly individualistic stories with a warmly sentimental flavor. *Avon.*

SHAW, IRWIN 1913– *Mixed Company* (1950). Talented, versatile exponent of the socially conscious story. *Random House $3.95.*

Spanish Stories and Tales. A representative collection. *PB.*

STAFFORD, JEAN 1915– *Children Are Bored on Sunday* (1953). Disturbing pictures of neuroses in contemporary society by a discriminating craftsman. *Random House $3.*

STEELE, WILBUR DANIEL 1886– *The Best Stories of Wilbur Daniel Steele* (1946). Ingeniously plotted stories of suspense, melodrama, and mystery, with psychological undertones. *Doubleday o.p.*

STEINBECK, JOHN 1902– *Stories.* Powerful short fiction by a leading contemporary. *Ban, Vik, Vik-h.*

THOMAS, DYLAN 1914–1953 *Adventures in the Skin Trade* (1955). Individualistic short stories, sketches, and tone poems; melodrama, fantasy, humor, and surrealism. *New Directions $3.50, NAL.*

TWAIN, MARK (SAMUEL L. CLEMENS) 1835–1910 *Short Stories.* Generous selections from the shorter works of America's greatest humorist. *Ban, Dell.*

UPDIKE, JOHN 1932– *The Same Door* (1959). "Still lives—with people," in the *New Yorker* manner, by a skillful young writer. *Knopf $3.75.*

VERGA, GIOVANNI 1840–1922 *Little Novels of Sicily* (1883). Stories reconstructing Sicilian life in the 1860's by a comparatively little known but highly significant artist. *Ever.*

WELTY, EUDORA 1909– *Selected Stories.* Sensitive, beautifully wrought stories of contemporary Mississippi. *Dell, Harv, ML.*

WOLFE, THOMAS 1900–1938 *The Hills Beyond* (1955). Semiautobiographical stories reminiscent of his novels. *Harper $4.50.*

11. Poetry

ROBERT C. POOLEY, *University of Wisconsin*

Poetry so often probes the imponderable elements of human experience that, like them, it is almost incapable of exact definition. Everyone, hearing such words as "soul" or "spirit," knows what area of man's life is meant, though scarcely ever will two people agree on exact definitions. Poetry, too, is experience in words that can be shared by all without precise definition. Nevertheless, what poets have said about poetry furnishes clues to gaining the greatest reward from reading it. The man who closes his ears to poetry shuts out a realm of riches in human understanding, in personal insight, in awakened sensitivity. The effort required to understand and enjoy poetry pays as rich returns as any form of human endeavor.

Even though poetry eludes exact definitions, an examination of what it is and what it does opens the way to understanding and appreciation. To start with one aspect, many poets agree that poetry is the expression of the best, the finest, and the most significant in all human knowledge. Shelley puts it, "Poetry is the record of the best and happiest moments of the happiest and best minds," and Matthew Arnold parallels him closely with, "Poetry is simply the most beautiful, impressive, and widely effective mode of saying things." All who have "travelled in the realms of gold" agree that poetry is the essence of man's unceasing effort to discover, retain, and express in imperishable form that which surpasses the ordinary, the best that life reveals, the most profound and meaningful —sometimes the painful and ugly, along with the happy and beautiful.

The technical aspects of poetry are occasionally mistaken by the uninitiated for poetry itself, as one at times judges a person by his clothes only rather than by his whole character. Rhythm, rhyme, repetition, meter, imagery—devices of form which enhance poetry—are not in themselves the substance of poetry, though in the analysis of a true poem it is not possible to isolate form and substance from each other. Poetry is life itself—tied inseparably to the words which shape it. Robert P. Tristram Coffin says, "Poetry is no marginal decoration, no luxury, no froth or fringe or frame on life. It is the solid center. . . . The poet is not a dreamer. . . . The poet is the man who is trying to see things as they are for the first time." As the rough diamond becomes a gem of beauty by cutting and polishing, so is the substance of poetry set glowing by its form. But there must be a diamond to start with.

If the reading of poetry offers difficulties, there are valid reasons. The appreciation of excellence, like excellence itself, requires sustained effort. One characteristic of poetry is compression. Emerson says, "Poetry teaches the enormous force of a few words." A poem must often be lived with patiently for the wholeness of its treasure to be released. Furthermore, poets suggest rather than state the truths they would manifest. When an ancient poet wrote, "The Lord is my shepherd," he suggested in an extended metaphor a relationship which has enriched the lives of countless thousands of persons. Had he attempted to define his idea explicitly, his words would have been forgotten before the end of his life. Most important to realize is that while some poetry seems universal in its appeal, much poetry is more particular. Coleridge cautions, "A poem is not necessarily obscure because it does not aim to be popular. It is enough if a work be perspicuous to those for whom it is written." If, therefore, a particular poem seems to say nothing on first reading, there is no cause for despair; the effort to understand often rewards with enlightenment. In other cases, the poem must be laid aside for a time of richer experience, greater knowledge, for "How can we reason but from what we know?"

A. Guides and Anthologies

Standard

BROOKS, CLEANTH 1906– and ROBERT PENN WARREN 1905– (eds.) *Understanding Poetry* (1950). An anthology of English and American poetry with subtle critical interpretations. *Holt $6.*

CIARDI, JOHN 1914– (ed.) *Mid-Century American Poets* (1950). Principles of poetry by the poetry editor of the *Saturday Review,* with generous selections from each of the fifteen contributors. *Twayne $5.*

CREEKMORE, HUBERT 1907– (ed.) *A Little Treasury of World Poetry* (1952). Poetry in translation from the great poets of the world, ancient and modern. *Scribner $4.25.*

FRIAR, KIMON and JOHN MALCOLM BRINNIN 1916– (eds.) *Modern Poetry: British and American* (1951). Selection of poetry of our times with brilliant introduction and frequently useful explications. *Appleton-Century-Crofts $3.25.*

MATTHIESSEN, F. O. 1902–1950 (ed.) *The Oxford Book of American Verse* (1950). A standard anthology of high literary merit with a fine introduction. *Oxford Univ. $7.*

PALGRAVE, FRANCIS 1824–1897 (ed.) *The Golden Treasury* (1864). Probably the best known of all anthologies of English poetry. *Houghton Mifflin $2.04, Macmillan $2.95, Oxford Univ. $1.40, Evman-h, ML, NAL, Nel.*

ROSENTHAL, M. L. 1917– and A. J. M. SMITH 1902– *Exploring Poetry* (1955). A stimulating introduction to poetry through the analysis of many particular poems. *Macmillan $4.50.*

UNTERMEYER, LOUIS 1885– (ed.) *Modern American Poetry; Modern British Poetry* (1950). The union of two earlier anthologies into one volume; a widely used and highly regarded collection with good introductions. *Harcourt, Brace $6.*

Paperbound

ELLIOTT, GEORGE 1918– (ed.) *Fifteen Modern American Poets* (1956). *Rine.*

HARRISON, G. B. 1894– (ed.) *A Book of English Poetry. Pen.*

HUMPHRIES, ROLFE 1894– (ed.) *New Poems by American Poets* (1953). *Bal.*

IVES, BURL 1909– (ed.) *The Burl Ives Song Book. Bal.*

ROBERTS, DENYS KILHAM (ed.) *The Centuries' Poetry. Pen 4 vols.*

SPEARE, M. E. (ed.) *Pocket Book of Verse. PB.*

142 GOOD READING

SWALLOW, ALAN 1915– (ed.) *Rinehart Book of Verse. Rine.*

UNTERMEYER, LOUIS 1885– (ed.) *An Anthology of Narrative Verse. PB.*

WHICHER, GEORGE F. 1889–1954 (ed.) *Poetry of the New England Renaissance* (1950). *Rine.*

WILLIAMS, OSCAR 1900– (ed.) *Silver Treasury of Light Verse* (1956). *NAL.*

B. Poets to 1900

For poetry of the Classical Era, the Middle Ages, the Renaissance, and other special periods, see Chapters 1 through 8.

ARNOLD, MATTHEW 1822–1888 *Poems.* A north light shines through this thoughtful, carefully wrought poetry. *Evman-h, ModSL, OxA, Pen, Rine, Vik, Vik-h.*

BAUDELAIRE, CHARLES PIERRE 1821–1867 *Flowers of Evil* (1857). Original French and translations by Geoffrey Wagner. The macabre and morbid handled with consummate artistry. *New (abr.).*

BLAKE, WILLIAM 1757–1827 *Poems.* The innocence of simplicity and the madness of genius. *Macmillan $2, CoE, Dell, Evman-h, MLG, OxA, Vik, Vik-h, WoC.*

BRYANT, WILLIAM CULLEN 1794–1878 *Thanatopsis and Other Poems.* One of America's first great nature poets. *Houghton Mifflin 80¢.*

BROWNING, ELIZABETH BARRETT 1806–1861 *Sonnets from the Portuguese.* An intellectual yet intensely human poet. *Crowell $1.50, Doubleday $2.95, Harper $2.50, McKay $1, CoE.*

BROWNING, ROBERT 1812–1889 *Selected Poems.* Rare strength, tough intellectual fiber, and vitality; famous for his dramatic monologues. *Cambridge Univ. $1, Macmillan $1.75, Oxford Univ. $1.40, Evman-h 4 vols., ML, MLCE, MLG, ModSL, Nel, OxA, Pen, Rine, RivEd, RivLib, WoC.*

BURNS, ROBERT 1759–1796 *Poems.* This Scottish farmer sang his loves, hopes, and sorrows into the hearts of many men. *CoE, CoNC, Evman-h, Nel, OxA, Pen, WoC.*

BYRON, GEORGE GORDON 1788–1824 *Poems.* The eternal rebel, in his weakness and strength, self-portrayed. *Oxford Univ. $1.40, CoNC, Evman-h 3 vols., ML, MLCE, OxA, Pen, Rine, WoC.*

CHAUCER His pilgrims living in a tumultuous world of sunshine and shadow make the later Middle Ages as real as today. See page 41.

COLERIDGE, SAMUEL TAYLOR 1772–1834 *Poems.* Haunting poetry of beauty and terror shaped by one of the most fertile imaginations in English literature. *Oxford Univ. $1.40, Dell, Evman-h, ML, MLCE, Nel, OxA, Rine, Vik, Vik-h.*

DANTE The greatest poet of the Middle Ages. See page 41.

POETRY 143

DICKINSON, EMILY 1830–1886 *Poems.* The humbly domestic and the cosmic unite to form lyrics of explosive brilliance and startling loveliness. *Harper $4.50, Little, Brown $4.75, Anch, Dell.*

DONNE Metaphysical wit and passion. See page 53.

DRYDEN Satire, wit—often lyric passion. See page 60.

EMERSON, RALPH WALDO 1803–1882 *Poems.* Probing insight, expansive vision, "meter-making arguments." *Dell, NAL, Rine, RivEd, Vik, Vik-h.*

GOETHE, JOHANN WOLFGANG VON 1749–1832 *Faust* (1808, 1832). The dramatic expression of a modern man seeking restlessly for the solution to the problem: What is the purpose of life? Recommended translation: C. F. MacIntyre's in *New.* Others: *Evman-h, Lib, ML, MLCE, Ox, Pen, Rine, WL, WoC.*

HEINE, HEINRICH 1797–1856 *Poems.* A poignant voice of lyric depth and power. *Heritage $5, Evman-h.*

HERRICK "Carvings on cherry stones." See page 60.

HOLMES, OLIVER WENDELL 1809–1894 *Complete Poetical Works.* Witty, polished verse, often composed for particular occasions; enjoyable rather than profound. *Houghton Mifflin $5.50.*

HOMER *The Iliad* and *The Odyssey.* The world's most famous epic poetry. See page 27.

HOPKINS, GERARD MANLEY 1844–1899 *Poems.* An intense, turbulent poet and metrical innovator. *Macmillan $1.50, Oxford Univ. $5, Pen.*

HOUSMAN, ALFRED EDWARD 1859–1936 *A Shropshire Lad* (1896). Cool but lovely lyrics catching the passions and disillusionments of youth. *Avon, CoE, Liv.*

KEATS, JOHN 1795–1821 *Poems.* The amazing achievements of a spirit that wrote against time, reaching heights of poetry "as final as Shakespeare." *CoNC, Evman-h, ML, MLCE, MLG, ModSL, Nel, OxA, Pen, Rine, RivEd, WoC.*

LANGLAND *Piers Plowman.* Medieval social protest. See page 42.

LANIER, SIDNEY 1842–1881 *Selected Poems.* Rich musical verse, clear and graceful, frequently on Southern themes. *Scribner $3.50.*

LONGFELLOW, HENRY W. 1807–1882 *Poems.* A cultivated gentleman and a skillful teller of tales in verse. *Heritage $5, Houghton Mifflin $4, Evman-h, ML.*

LOWELL, JAMES RUSSELL 1819–1891 *Poems.* Imitative in much verse, but distinctly original and American in the famous *Biglow Papers. American Book $1.75, Houghton Mifflin $5.50, Odyssey $2.50.*

MARVELL *Poems.* A great 17th-century lyricist intensely aware of "time's winged chariot hurrying near." See page 61.

MILTON *Poems.* The poetic voice of Puritan England, a voice of great range and power. See page 61.

OMAR KHAYYAM *The Rubaiyat.* Lyrical hedonism and skepticism. See page 76.

POE, EDGAR ALLAN 1809–1849 *Poems.* A divided artist in a fantastic world of his own creation. *Dell, Evman-h, ML, MLCE, MLG, OxA, PB, Rine, Vik, Vik-h.*

POPE *Poems.* Biting satirist, poetical essayist, fashioner of much-quoted couplets. See page 69.

RIMBAUD, JEAN ARTHUR 1854–1891 *The Illuminations* (1886). Violent originality, subtle imagery, mysticism. *New.*

SHAKESPEARE, WILLIAM 1564–1616 *Sonnets* (1609). The clear accents of genius, mirroring life with a lyrical beauty and significance that touches us all. For editions see page 54.

SHELLEY, PERCY BYSSHE 1792–1822 *Poems.* The cloud-treader brought to earth the music of the spheres. *Oxford Univ. $1.40, CoE, CoNC, Evman-h 2 vols., ML, MLCE, MLG, Nel, OxA, Pen, Rine, WoC.*

SPENSER See page 54.

SWINBURNE, ALGERNON CHARLES 1837–1909 *Poems.* Sumptuous, sensuous master of intricate melody. *Evman-h, WoC.*

TENNYSON, ALFRED 1809–1892 *Poems.* The poetic voice of Victorian England whose singing greatness is often undervalued. *Oxford Univ. $1.40, CoE, CoNC, Evman-h 2 vols., MLCE, MLG, Nel, OxA, Rine, RivEd, SM, WoC.*

THOMPSON, FRANCIS 1859–1907 *Poems.* The creator of *The Hound of Heaven* is far from a one-poem author. *ML, Nel, OxA.*

VERGIL The epic poet of Augustan Rome. See page 35.

VILLON The singing vagabond of old Paris. See page 43.

WHITMAN, WALT 1819–1892 *Leaves of Grass* (1855). The major poet of 19th-century America chants his own individuality and celebrates democratic man. *Evman-h, Gar, Harp, ML, MLCE, MLG, NAL, PB, Rine, RivEd, Vik, Vik-h.*

WHITTIER, JOHN GREENLEAF 1807–1892 *Poems.* The brave Quaker poet of New England sang simply of the beauty of nature and the duty of man. *American Book $1.75, Houghton Mifflin $4, Macmillan $2.36, CoE.*

WILDE, OSCAR 1854–1900 *Poems.* Varying from the lovely description of *The Nightingale and the Rose* to the poignant intensity of *The Ballad of Reading Gaol. Evman-h, ML, Vik, Vik-h.*

WORDSWORTH, WILLIAM 1770–1850 *Poems.* The serene and sympathetic expression of an interpretive spirit which made the unnoticed common beautifully uncommon. *Macmillan $1.75, CoE, Dell, Evman-h 3 vols., GT, ML, MLCE, ModSL, Nel, OxA, Pen, Rine, SM, WoC.*

C. Modern Poets

AIKEN, CONRAD 1889– *Collected Poems* (1953). A musical poet with a special interest in psychoanalysis. *Oxford Univ. $10.50.*

AUDEN, W. H. 1907– *Collected Poetry* (1945). A poet's reactions to the crosscurrents of thought and the changing aspects of a restless period. *Random House $4.75.*

BENET, STEPHEN VINCENT 1898–1943 *John Brown's Body* (1928). A vigorous epic of the Civil War. *Rinehart $2.50.*

CULLEN, COUNTEE 1903–1946 *On These I Stand* (1947). Integrity of purpose, honesty of expression, by an outstanding Negro. *Harper $3.*

CUMMINGS, E. E. 1894– *Collected Poems* (1954). Deep poetic insight expressed powerfully in unorthodox forms and manners. *Harcourt, Brace $5.*

DE LA MARE, WALTER 1873–1956 *Rhymes and Verses* (1941). The magic and mystery of life in haunting melody. *Holt $4.*

ELIOT, T. S. 1888– *Complete Poems and Plays* (1952). One of the most original and influential of modern poets and verse dramatists, independent in thought and form. *Harcourt, Brace $4.50.*

——— *The Waste Land and Other Poems. Harv.*

FROST, ROBERT 1875– *Poems.* From his New England countryside Frost views quietly, thoughtfully, lyrically the meaning of human experience. *Holt $4.50, ML, PB.*

HOUSMAN Hauntingly beautiful verse. See page 143.

LINDSAY, VACHEL 1879–1931 *Collected Poems* (1925). A minstrel who beat out the rhythms of America as he felt them. *Macmillan $6.75.*

LOMAX, JOHN AVERY 1867–1948 and **ALAN LOMAX** 1915– (eds.) *Cowboy Songs and Other Frontier Ballads* (rev. ed. 1938). The outstanding collection of Western folk poetry. *Macmillan $7.95.*

MACLEISH, ARCHIBALD 1892– *Collected Poems* (1952). A deeply patriotic critic and prophet of American democracy. *Houghton Mifflin $5.*

MACNEICE, LOUIS 1907– *Holes in the Sky: Poems 1944–1947* (1948). A liberal classicist uses effectively the symbols of 20th-century British life. *Random House $2.50.*

MASEFIELD, JOHN 1878– *Selected Poems* (1950). A teller of tales in rhythmic verse, he delights many who love a life of action. *Macmillan $2.*

MILLAY, EDNA ST. VINCENT 1892–1950 *Collected Sonnets* (1941). One who sings sweetly and powerfully, in traditional verse forms, of the richness of life. *Harper $5.*

MOORE, MARIANNE 1887– *Collected Poems* (1951). Fresh and musical verse in the modern manner by a Pulitzer Prize winner. *Macmillan $3.50.*

NASH, OGDEN 1902– *Poems.* Clever, witty, sometimes preposterous. *ML, PB.*

PARKER, DOROTHY 1893– *Poems.* A sophisticated and often cynical wit. *ML, Vik, Vik-h.*

POUND, EZRA 1885– *Selected Poems.* An expatriated American poet who has profoundly influenced Eliot, MacLeish, and many younger poets. *New, NewC.*

RANSOM, JOHN CROWE 1882– *Poems and Essays.* An intellectual poet finds the modern industrial age something less than satisfying. *Vin.*

ROBINSON, EDWIN ARLINGTON 1869–1935 *Collected Poems* (1937). Serious lyrics, powerful narratives, unforgettable characters in blank verse and other metrical forms. *Macmillan $9.50.*

SANDBURG, CARL 1878– *Complete Poems* (1950). The life work of one of the most American of Americans. *Harcourt, Brace $7.50. Selected Poems: Harcourt, Brace $4.*

SPENDER, STEPHEN 1909– *Collected Poems* (1955). Lyrics of social significance in the language and imagery of today. *Random House $4.*

STEVENS, WALLACE 1879–1955 *Collected Poems of Wallace Stevens* (1954). Intricate counterpoint of reality and imagination, with a diapason of exquisite melody. *Knopf $7.50.*

———— *Poems by Wallace Stevens* (1959). *Vin.*

THOMAS, DYLAN 1914–1953 *Collected Poems* (1953). The most powerful as well as the most sensational of this generation's poets. *New Directions $3.75.*

WYLIE, ELINOR 1887–1928 *Collected Poems* (1932). Delicate, witty, and thought-provoking verse. *Knopf $5.75.*

YEATS, WILLIAM BUTLER 1865–1939 *Collected Poems* (1951). The leading poet of the Irish Renaissance, a singer of rare lyric power. *Macmillan $6.*

D. Poetry on Records

(Note: All recordings are 33 rpm LP's unless otherwise noted.)

Poets Reading from Their Own Work

AIKEN, CONRAD 1889– Wistful reading of the colloquial but contemplative *Blues of Ruby Matrix* and *A Letter from Li Po* (*Caedmon*).

AUDEN, W. H. 1907– An intelligent interpretation that captures both the wit and seriousness of his poetry. The record contains also readings by Richard Eberhart and Mark Van Doren (*Library of Congress*).

BENET, STEPHEN VINCENT 1898–1943 Contains "Portrait of a Southern Lady" and "Ballad of William Sycamore" (*National Council of Teachers of English, 78 rpm*).

COFFIN, ROBERT P. TRISTRAM 1892–1955 Includes "The Secret Heart," with an explanation of its origin; "The Fog"; "The Lantern in the Snow" (*National Council of Teachers of English, 78 rpm*).

CUMMINGS, E. E. 1894– His eccentricities of voice help compensate for the missing vagaries of punctuation and typography (*Library of Congress, Caedmon, National Council of Teachers of English [78 rpm]*).

ELIOT, T. S. 1888– A cultivated voice, sometimes ironic, sometimes sepulchral—always effective. "The Waste Land," "Ash Wednesday," "Sweeney Among the Nightingales," etc. (*Library of Congress*); "Prufrock," "Portrait of a Lady," "Preludes," etc. (*Caedmon*).

FROST, ROBERT 1874– Brings an authentic New England accent to "Mending Wall," "Birches," "Death of the Hired Man," many others (*Caedmon, Library of Congress, National Council of Teachers of English*).

NASH, OGDEN 1902– A selection of old favorites and some less-known poems read in a sprightly style (*Caedmon*).

Pleasure Dome. An anthology of poets reading from their own works: Cummings, Eliot, Moore, Nash, Williams, etc. (*Columbia*).

SANDBURG, CARL 1878– Our most famous midwestern "minne-singer" enthralls listeners with his earnest humanity in *The People, Yes* and *Sandburg Reads Sandburg* (*Decca*).

THOMAS, DYLAN 1914–1953 Beyond the notable quality of his poetry and prose, Thomas's extraordinary vocal range and histrionic talent make all three of his recordings inimitable (*Caedmon*).

Readings from the Classics

Beowulf. Selections read in Old English, with a brief lecture of explanation, by the late Professor Harry Morgan Ayres of Columbia University (*National Council of Teachers of English*).

CHAUCER, GEOFFREY 1340–1400 *The Canterbury Tales.* The BBC dramatization of the "Prologue" and five tales in Nevil Coghill's skillful modernization (*Spoken Word, 4 LP*); Professor Harry Morgan Ayres discusses Middle English pronunciation and reads the opening lines of the "Prologue" as well as parts of "The Nun's Priest's Tale" (*National Council of Teachers of English, 78 rpm*).

DANTE ALIGHIERI 1265–1321 *The Divine Comedy.* John Ciardi reads, in a rather funereal voice, from his translation of *Inferno* (*Folkways*).

DICKINSON, EMILY 1830–1886 Austin Warren, critic and scholar, communicates with deep feeling her sharply drawn imagery (*Idiom*).

Early English Ballads. "The Three Ravens," "Lord Randall," "Chevy Chase" and many other ballads read by Kathleen Read (*Folkways*).

Elizabethan Verse and Its Music. W. H. Auden's lisp spoils occasional lines, but the musical settings of these English madrigals and lute songs are wholly charming as sung by the New York Pro Musica Antiqua *(Columbia).*

SHAKESPEARE, WILLIAM 1564–1616 *Sixteen Sonnets.* David Allen's voice and interpretation are almost perfect. The harp background might well have been dispensed with *(Poetry).*

WHITMAN, WALT 1819–1892 *Leaves of Grass.* David Allen brings his supple voice and poetic intelligence to superior readings of "When Lilacs Last in the Dooryard Bloomed," "I Hear America Singing," "Song of Myself," and others *(Poetry).*

Recorded Anthologies of Poetry

Anthology of Negro Poets in the U.S.A. Arna Bontemps reads gracefully from a 200-year span of Negro poetry ranging in mood from innocence to anger, and in manner from bold simplicity to subtle, complex imagery and rhythm *(Folkways).*

Caedmon Treasury of Modern Poets. Contains one or more poems of each of the following poets, read by the poet himself: Yeats, Eliot, Frost, Cummings, Auden, Moore, E. Sitwell, Thomas, MacLeish, Williams, Aiken, MacNeice, Stevens, Spender, Ransom, Bishop, Empson, Wilbur, Stein, Eberhart, and Graves *(Caedmon).*

Great Poems of the English Language. 29 poems, including many popular favorites, read effectively by David Allen *(Poetry).*

Hearing Poetry. Poems from Chaucer to Browning, introduced by Mark Van Doren and read with varying effectiveness by Hurd Hatfield, Frank Silvera, and Jo Van Fleet *(Caedmon).*

No Single Thing Abides. Standard classics, such as Gray's "Elegy" and Shelley's "Ozymandias," read by David Allen *(Poetry).*

Palgrave's Golden Treasury. Several readers interpret representative selections from this famous anthology *(Caedmon).*

Seventeenth Century Poetry. Sir Cedric Hardwicke and Robert Newton read feelingly from the poetry of Herbert, Lovelace, Vaughan, Marvell, and other 17th-century lyricists *(Caedmon).*

12. Drama

J. SHERWOOD WEBER, *Pratt Institute*

To be completely rewarding, reading a play requires considerable exercise of the imagination. Because a play is properly a story presented on a stage by actors before an audience, the printed version of a play is only part of a complete art form. In production the director, the actors, the scenic designer, the costumer, the lighter, even the audience collaborate with the playwright to make his bare words emphatically meaningful. Yet any good play retains much of its dramatic power even when read.

When only read, however, a play is a condensed, closely packed literary form; it has none of the novel's careful summaries and detailed explanations of character motivation. The reader must supply through his creative visualization what theatrical production normally adds to the playwright's words. Only during a second reading (or a third) will analogies, symbols, meanings become clear—elements that would cause only few puzzled brows if the same play were seen in the theater.

Because a play must immediately excite an audience or fail in production, the drama is a thoroughly social art. It must speak movingly to large groups of people, or quickly perish. It must have action, conflict, theme—all emanating from the bedrock of all art, our common humanity.

On this bedrock of what is common to all of us men have built many different structures, ranging from the huge, formal open-air amphitheater of the Greeks through the intimate, flexible apron stage of the Elizabethans to the detached picture-frame or versatile "center" stages of today. It has developed many forms, running from slapstick farce to austere tragedy. It has employed the sister arts of music, the dance, architecture, painting, sculpture, to express itself vividly, and it has combined these elements with endless variation. Through continual change the theater has remained vital. The reader who wants to learn about theater development ought to consult Macgowan and Melnitz's handsomely illustrated *The Living Stage.*

One unchanging factor in the theater is the audience's desire to be entertained, though ideas as to what constitutes entertainment have varied greatly from age to age. Playwrights, with one eye on popular acclaim, have developed a sneaking fondness for the spectacular, the melodramatic, and the sentimental. In almost every age the plea of the minority—from Aristotle to Brooks Atkinson—has been for less show and more art.

Perhaps the best way to start reading plays is in a critical anthology such as Bentley's *The Play,* Brooks and Heilman's *Understanding Drama,* or Downer's *The Art of the Play*—all of which contain not only a variety of theater classics from the Greeks on, but also hints for developing a capacity to visualize imaginatively. Paperbound anthologies provide the most good plays for the least money. By browsing in them the reader can discover playwrights and periods of the drama that he wishes to explore further.

Earlier sections of this book contain material on the classic dramatic localities: Greece with its unsurpassed quartet of Aeschylus, Sophocles, Euripides, and Aristophanes; Tudor England with Marlowe, Shakespeare, Jonson; 17th-century France with Corneille, Molière, Racine; Restoration England with Congreve and Sheridan. All of these, and many others, helped build the solid foundations of modern drama.

Since the late 19th century the world has taken such a lively interest in drama that it has become a rival of the novel for popularity. Nine Nobel Prizes for literature have been awarded to playwrights. The familiarity of such names as Ibsen, Chekhov, Pirandello, O'Casey, Coward, Brecht, Lorca, Sartre, Eliot, Williams, Wilder, makes one realize how large the dramatist bulks in the total literary scene.

In 20th-century America the drama has flourished—quantitatively if not qualitatively—in the motion picture and in television as well as in the legitimate theater. Though realism has been the prevailing mode, experi-

mentation in other modes has fortunately never ceased.
In recent decades the theater has become at its best a
forum for provocative social thought: Shaw, O'Neill,
Anderson, Rice, Odets, Sherwood, Hellman, Miller, Inge,
Serling, have all written plays that are both eminently
theatrical and socially alert. To read representative contemporary American plays is to become aware of the
most challenging and disturbing developments in our
day.

A. Anthologies

BENTLEY, ERIC 1916– (ed.) *The Classic Theatre* (3 vols.) (1958–9).
Volume 1: six Italian plays by Machiavelli, Goldoni, etc.; Volume 2: five German plays by Goethe, Schiller, Kleist; Volume
3: Spanish plays by Cervantes, de Vega, Calderon. Other volumes in preparation. *Anch.*

——— *The Modern Theatre* (6 vols.) (1955–6–7). Contain 30
otherwise hard-to-find modern European and American plays,
including works by Anouilh, Brecht, Giraudoux, Gogol, Schnitzler. *Anch.*

——— *The Play: A Critical Anthology* (1951). One play each by
Sophocles, Molière, Ibsen, Strindberg, Rostand, Wilde, and
Miller, and two by Shakespeare, accompanied by illuminating
critical analyses. *Prentice-Hall $3.95.*

BENTLEY, GERALD E. 1901– (ed.) *The Development of English
Drama* (1950). 23 dramas from the miracle plays to Pinero.
Appleton-Century-Crofts $6.50.

CERF, BENNETT A. 1898– and VAN H. CARTMELL 1896– (eds.)
24 Favorite One-Act Plays (1958). An excellent collection of
short plays by all the leading modern masters of the form.
Doubleday $5.75.

CUBETA, PAUL M. (ed.) *Modern Drama for Analysis* (1955). Nine
modern plays (Ibsen to Williams) with critical analyses. *Holt
$3.60.*

DOWNER, ALAN S. 1912– (ed.) *The Art of the Play* (1955). A
basic guide to intelligent playreading; 9 great plays from the
Greeks to O'Neill. *Holt $4.75.*

Eight Famous Elizabethan Plays (1932, 1950). Representative of the
Golden Age of English drama. *ML, MLCE.*

Eight Great Comedies from Aristophanes to Shaw (1957). *NAL.*

Eight Great Tragedies from Aeschylus to O'Neill (1957). *NAL.*

Famous American Plays of the 20's (1959). *Dell.*

Four Great Comedies of the Restoration and 18th Century (1958).
The masterworks of Wycherley, Congreve, Goldsmith, and
Sheridan. *Ban.*

GASSNER, JOHN 1903– (ed.) *A Treasury of the Theater* (2 vols.) (1950–1). An imposing collection of 65 plays covering dramatic history from 5th-century B.C. Greece to 20th-century Europe and America—all with helpful introductions. *Holt-Dryden $12.50 for both vols.*

LIND, L. R. 1906– (ed.) *Ten Greek Plays in Contemporary Translations* (1958). The best inexpensive collection, with solid introductory material. *Houghton Mifflin $3, RivEd.*

Six Great Modern Plays (1959). Major "social" plays by Chekhov, Ibsen, Shaw, O'Casey, Williams, and Miller. *Dell.*

Six Restoration Plays (1959). With background essays by J. H. Wilson. *RivEd.*

TUCKER, S. M. 1876– and ALAN S. DOWNER 1912– (eds.) *25 Modern Plays* (1953). Representative European, English, American plays from Ibsen to the present. *Harper $6.*

WALLEY, HAROLD R. 1900– *The Book of the Play: An Introduction to Drama* (1950). 12 plays of all types and from many periods with first-rate introductions and extensive study aids. *Scribner $4.75.*

WATSON, E. BRADLEE 1879– and BENFIELD PRESSEY 1894– (eds.) *Contemporary Drama: 15 Plays* (1959). An excellent assembling of the best plays of modern masters; as up-to-date as Frings' *Look Homeward, Angel. Scribner $2.75.*

B. Classics of the Drama

For plays by, and studies about, the ancient Greek dramatists (AESCHYLUS, SOPHOCLES, EURIPIDES, ARISTOPHANES) see Chapter 1 on "Greece." For Roman drama see Chapter 2, "Rome." Elizabethan drama, including SHAKESPEARE, is treated in detail in the second part of Chapter 4, "The Renaissance." For 17th-century French drama (MOLIERE, CORNEILLE, RACINE) see Chapter 5. Representative plays from all the great dramatic periods are contained in many of the critical and standard anthologies cited above.

C. Modern Drama

Many plays by contemporary dramatists are inexpensively available in anthologies such as those listed above. Only collections of a single playwright's work, rather than single plays, are cited below. Since 1948 *Theatre Arts* magazine has published one new play in each monthly issue; a full listing can be consulted in any recent issue.

ANDERSON, MAXWELL 1888–1959 *Four Verse Plays* (1959). Contains the best plays—*Elizabeth the Queen, High Tor, Winterset, Mary of Scotland*—of a modern playwright who tried with varying success to wed poetry and social commentary. *Harv.*

ANOUILH, JEAN 1910– *Five Plays* (2 vols.) (1958, 1959). Ten plays of a contemporary French master of theatricalism. *Drama, Drama-h.*

BRECHT, BERTOLT 1898–1956 *Parables for the Theater* (1958). Contains *The Good Woman of Setzuan* and *The Caucasian Chalk Circle*—two of the best-known "epic theater" dramas by a leading Communist playwright. *Ever.*

CHEKHOV, ANTON 1860–1904 *Plays.* There are many inexpensive collections of this realist's subtle analyses of timeless human nature. *Ban, Evman, Evman-h, ML, MLP, Pen, UL, Vik, Vik-h.*

COWARD, NOEL 1899– *Plays* (1934–1957). Urbane drawing-room comedies. *British Book Centre 5 vols. $5.25 ea.*

ELIOT, T. S. 1888– *The Complete Poems and Plays* (1952). Contains three famous verse plays by the major poetic talent contributing to the modern theater. *Harcourt, Brace $4.50.*

GIRAUDOUX, JEAN 1882–1944 *Four Plays* (1958). Four theatricalist dramas, including *The Madwoman of Chaillot,* in Maurice Valency's translations and adaptations. *Drama.*

HELLMAN, LILLIAN 1905– *Four Plays* (1942). A moralist and realist analyzes contemporary society in skillfully wrought dramas; includes *The Children's House* and *The Little Foxes.* *ML.*

IBSEN, HENRIK 1828–1906 *Plays.* Naturalistic and symbolistic plays which have significantly influenced both form and content of modern drama. *Ban, Dell, Drama, Evman-h 4 vols., ML, MLCE, Nel, Pen, Rine, UL.*

INGE, WILLIAM 1913– *Four Plays* (1958). Sentimental realism; includes *Bus Stop* and *Picnic. Random House $5.*

IONESCO, EUGENE 1912– *Four Plays* (1958). Short antirealistic plays by a leading exponent of the experimental European theater. *Ever.*

LORCA, FEDERICO GARCIA 1898–1936 *Three Tragedies* (1955). Powerful poetic tragedies by the leading 20th-century Spanish writer. *New.*

MILLER, ARTHUR 1915– *Collected Plays* (1957). All the plays to date, mostly tragedies and all social parables, by the man whom many consider the greatest American theatrical talent since O'Neill. *Viking $4.95.*

O'CASEY, SEAN 1884– *Selected Plays of Sean O'Casey* (1955). Nine plays by the most important living Irish playwright. *George Braziller $5.* His best-known dramas, *Juno and the Paycock* and *The Plough and the Stars,* are available in *Three Plays* (SM).

ODETS, CLIFFORD 1906– *Six Plays* (1939). The early, most important plays of a once-powerful social critic. *ML.*

O'NEILL, EUGENE 1888–1953 *Nine Plays* (1941). Most of the plays—sometimes overlong but always deeply probing—that make O'Neill the major American playwright. *MLG.*

PIRANDELLO, LUIGI 1867–1936 *Naked Masks: Five Plays* (1958). Enigmatic but provocative dramatic inquiries into the nature

of reality by an Italian playwright of first importance. *Evman,
EvmanNA.*

SARTRE, JEAN-PAUL 1905– *No Exit and Three Other Plays*
(1955). Incisive dramatizations of French existentialist thought
by its leading spokesman. *Vin.*

SERLING, ROD 1924– *Patterns* (1957). Four long TV plays by a
brilliant new talent. *Simon & Schuster $3.95, Ban.*

SHAW, GEORGE BERNARD 1856–1950 *Plays.* Witty, talky dramas
dedicated to promoting rule of the goddess Reason among 20th-
century man. Individual plays in *Pen; collections: Dodd, Mead
$5, Dell, ML 2 vols., Rine.*

STRINDBERG, AUGUST 1849–1912 *Six Plays* (1955). New translations, by Elizabeth Sprigge, of a mordant Scandinavian dramatist. *Anch. Three Plays* available in *Pen.*

WILDE, OSCAR 1854–1900 *Plays.* Sophisticated comedies of manners by a master wit. *CoNc, ML, Nel, Pen, UL.*

WILDER, THORNTON 1897– *Three Plays* (1957). Experimental
but always lucid plays by a modern who retains his faith in
both man and God. *Harper $4.95, Ban.*

WILLIAMS, TENNESSEE 1914– *Plays.* Theatricalist tragedies of
warped, frustrated lives by the dramatic successor to Sherwood
Anderson. *The Glass Menagerie* in *6 Great Modern Plays, Dell;
The Rose Tattoo* and *A Streetcar Named Desire* in individual
volumes, *NAL.*

D. Histories and Guides

BENTLEY, ERIC 1916– *The Playwright As Thinker* (1955). An
analysis of the thought in drama of Cocteau, Ibsen, Pirandello,
Sartre, Shaw, Strindberg. Most useful after the reader knows
the plays discussed. *Mer.*

CHENEY, SHELDON 1886– *The Theatre: Three Thousand Years
of Drama, Acting, and Stagecraft* (rev. ed. 1952). A popular,
well-illustrated introductory history; particularly informative
on early periods. *Longmans, Green $6.35.*

DOLMAN, JOHN, JR. 1888–1952 *The Art of Play Production*
(1946). Analyses of interpretive and technical problems of play
production; a good guide for amateurs. *Harper $4.50.*

FERGUSSON, FRANCIS 1904– *The Idea of a Theatre* (1949). A
perceptive and often profound study of ten great plays from
Sophocles to Eliot with focus on the changing art of the drama.
Princeton Univ. $3.75, Anch.

GASSNER, JOHN 1903– *Masters of the Drama* (1954). A basic study
of the world's major playwrights. *Dover $5.95.*

MACGOWAN, KENNETH 1888– and WILLIAM MELNITZ *The
Living Stage: A History of the World Theater* (1955). A lively,
readable, handsomely illustrated history. *Prentice-Hall $7.25.*

NICOLL, ALLARDYCE 1894– *World Drama: From Aeschylus to
Anouilh* (1949). Readable scholarly history. *Harcourt, Brace $9.*

Oxford Companion to the Theatre (1951). Useful for quick reference. *Oxford Univ. $11.50.*

SAMACHSON, DOROTHY and JOSEPH *Let's Meet the Theatre* (1954). Compact introduction to all types of theater activity in America today. *Abelard-Schuman $4.*

SIMONSON, LEE 1888– *The Stage Is Set* (1932). Philosophical, beautifully illustrated study of the art of stage scenery from the Greeks to today by a leading designer of the 20th century. *Dover $4.50.*

WRIGHT, EDWARD A. *A Primer for Playgoers* (1958). A helpful guide to richer understanding and appreciation of stage, motion picture, and TV dramatic production. *Prentice-Hall $6.50.*

E. Drama on Records

Often more rewarding than reading plays, but usually less satisfying than seeing them, is listening to good dramatic readings on records. The following list of recorded plays, prepared by HARRY T. MOORE of Southern Illinois University, will provide many hours of good listening. Read the play first; then listen.

BECKETT, SAMUEL 1906– *Waiting for Godot.* A fine recording of a provocative and highly controversial symbolist drama (*Columbia, 2 LP*).

ELIOT, T. S. 1888– *Murder in the Cathedral:* Robert Donat and the "Old Vic" company (*Angel, 2 LP*). *The Cocktail Party:* Alec Guinness with the Broadway cast (*Decca, 2 LP*). Both offer expert performances of Eliot's two best-known verse plays.

EURIPIDES c. 484–408 B.C. *Medea.* Judith Anderson's sonorous Broadway performance of this tragedy of terror and passion is effectively recaptured (*Decca, LP*).

The First Stage: A Chronicle of the Development of English Drama from Its Beginnings to the 1580's (1960). 13 one-hour programs from the BBC's *Third Programme,* excellently tracing the development of English drama up to Shakespeare. Not all albums are yet (Jan. 1960) available. (*Spoken Word, 6 albums*).

MILLER, ARTHUR 1915– *Death of a Salesman.* Miller's most discussed drama is performed by the Broadway cast (*Decca, 2 LP*). Extra: *Arthur Miller Reads His Plays* presents an interesting medley (*Spoken Arts, LP*).

Monuments of Early English Drama. Some of the great pre-Shakespearean plays: Vol. 1—*Quem Quaeritis, The Deluge, Abraham and Isaac;* Vol. 2—*Second Shepherd's Play, Gammer Gurton's Needle,* and others; Vol. 3—*Everyman,* with Burgess Meredith; Vol. 4—Marlowe's *Dr. Faustus,* with Frank Silvera (*Caedmon, 4 LP*).

O'CASEY, SEAN 1880– *Juno and the Paycock* and *Pictures in the Hallway.* Fine dramatic performances, in brogue, of the works of the great Irishman, who also reads some excerpts from his own work on a Caedmon recording (*Angel, 2 LP; Riverside, 2 LP; Caedmon, LP*).

SARTRE, JEAN-PAUL 1905– *No Exit.* Betty Field stars in Sartre's tense short play about an existentialist afterlife (*Riverside, 2 LP*).

SHAKESPEARE, WILLIAM 1564–1616 Outstanding performances among the many Shakespearean recordings are those of the "Old Vic": John Gielgud in *Hamlet* (*Victor, 4 LP*) and Alec Guinness in *Macbeth* (*Victor, 2 LP*). Gielgud's *The Ages of Man* offers a variety of magnificently read scenes and passages (*Columbia, LP*); Helge Kökeritz's record of *Shakespeare's Pronunciation* is the most authoritative and exciting of its kind (*Columbia, LP*). Other excellent Shakespearean records now obtainable include:

> *Hamlet.* Laurence Olivier in excerpts (*Victor, LP*); Maurice Evans (*Columbia, 4 78 rpm*).
>
> *Merchant of Venice.* Michael Redgrave (*Caedmon, 2 LP*).
>
> *Othello.* Paul Robeson, José Ferrer (*Columbia, 3 LP*).
>
> *Richard III.* Laurence Olivier (*Victor, 3 LP; abr. Victor, LP*).
>
> *Romeo and Juliet.* John Gielgud and Pamela Brown (with *Hamlet* soliloquies) (*Decca, LP*); Claire Bloom with the "Old Vic" (*Victor, 3 LP; abr. Victor, LP*).
>
> The Cambridge University Marlowe Society has recorded *As You Like It, Coriolanus,* and *Troilus and Cressida,* the first on 3 disks, the latter two on 4 each (*London, LP*).

SHAW, GEORGE BERNARD 1856–1950 *Don Juan in Hell.* Charles Laughton, Charles Boyer, Agnes Moorhead, and Sir Cedric Hardwicke give a spirited reading of the third act of Shaw's *Man and Superman* (*Columbia, 2 LP*).

SHERIDAN, RICHARD BRINSLEY 1751–1816 *The School for Scandal.* A lively performance of this classic 18th-century comedy (*Angel, 3 LP*).

SOPHOCLES 496–406 B.C. *Oedipus Rex.* The soundtrack from the impressive film of this tragedy as performed by the Canadian Stratford Players (*Caedmon, 2 LP*).

SYNGE, JOHN MILLINGTON 1871–1909 *The Playboy of the Western World.* Cyril Cusack and Siobhan McKenna head a fine cast in an inspired reading of this roistering comedy (*Angel, 2 LP*).

THOMAS, DYLAN 1914–1953 *Under Milk Wood.* The author, one of the great reciters of our time, is the featured player in his lyrical Welsh comedy (*Caedmon, 2 LP*).

TWAIN, MARK 1835–1910 *Mark Twain Tonight.* Hal Holbrook's reading of his dramatizations from Twain's writings (*Columbia, LP*).

WILDE, OSCAR 1854–1900 *The Importance of Being Earnest.* An excellent cast supports John Gielgud and the incomparable Edith Evans (as a monstrous Lady Bracknell) in Wilde's dry, witty farce (*Angel, 2 LP*).

13. Biography

WAINO S. NYLAND, *University of Colorado*

The lives of famous men and women, or even of infamous
rascals, can make profitable as well as entertaining reading. If the purpose of creative composition is, as the
ancients said, to please and to instruct, then a good biography has everything: it entertains while it gives information. From the lives of others we learn to understand
ourselves and to respect the mysteries of relationship
between a self and the world.

Where shall you start reading in biography? One
method is to begin with something easy but substantial,
like Hamlin Garland's *A Son of the Middle Border*. The
next step would be to take on something a little more
remote and more stimulating, like *The Autobiography
of Benvenuto Cellini* or Maurois's *Byron*. Thus one
would be prepared to digest and enjoy the richness of
detail in such volumes as Sandburg's *Abraham Lincoln*.
Then even the masterpieces would be assimilable: such
works as Boswell's ample *Johnson* and the philosophic
Education of Henry Adams.

Another and less cautious plan is to begin with a few
of the greatest biographies and work out, or down, from
them. By this method, you might read Boswell first of all,
then Joseph Wood Krutch's modern interpretation of
Johnson. Similarly, the solid *Autobiography of John
Stuart Mill* might come before the saltier *Queen Victoria*
by Strachey.

A third system for biographical reading may be called
chronological. As Carlyle said, "History is the essence of
innumerable biographies." Certainly history reduced to
its elements is a combination of the lives of many folk.
To understand your own place in the present confusion,
it is helpful to look into the confused past. This is not
the first time that mankind has been at the crossroads of
fateful decisions. A mature reader may untangle some of

the apparent contradictions in the record of mankind by wisely adopting a chronological program of biographical reading.

The Bible is a good place to begin. The latter part of Genesis and all of Exodus constitute a life of Moses. Next should come several of Plutarch's parallel *Lives of Eminent Greeks and Romans,* with collateral reading of such modern interpretations as Evelyn Abbott's *Pericles.* The Four Gospels can be reread as parallel lives, with Renan's *Life of Jesus* included for comparison, or Sholem Asch's imaginative interpretations of Jesus, Paul, and Mary. Then, to see something of the two sides of Rome, the reader should proceed to the *Meditations* of the pagan emperor Marcus Aurelius and the *Confessions* of the Christian Saint Augustine. From the Middle Ages down to the development of atomic power and space missiles there has been such a profusion of life-writing, by and about both saints and sinners, that the systematic reader must select on some basis of specialized interest.

For every reader of biography there is a sharp and difficult question. Is it not self-evident that the first merit of a life should be its truth, its factual reliability? Yet, almost all biographies are tinted by the prejudices of their authors, and are more or less shaded to protect or condemn their subjects. Even Boswell, Strachey, Sandburg, and other noted biographers are necessarily limited by the bias of their social backgrounds. The reader naturally makes allowances for human fallibility.

Historical and other sections of GOOD READING include numerous additional biographies of artists, musicians, scientists, religious leaders, philosophers, and others.

ADAMS, HENRY 1838–1918 *The Education of Henry Adams* (1906). One man's earnest efforts to find a meaning for life. *Houghton Mifflin $5.50, ML.*

ALLEN, GAY WILSON 1903– *The Solitary Singer* (1955). The definitive biography of Walt Whitman: the scholarly evidence thoroughly sifted, the poems acutely criticized. *Macmillan $8, Ever.*

ARMITAGE, ANGUS 1902– *World of Copernicus* (1947). A life story of the great astronomer who overthrew the theory of the world as the center of the universe. *NAL.*

BARBELLION, W. N. P. (*pseud.*) 1889–1919 *The Journal of a Disappointed Man* (1919). The vivid diary of a man who, though stricken with progressive paralysis, maintained an undiminished interest in life. *Pen.*

BOSWELL, JAMES 1740–1795 *London Journal 1762–1763* (1950). Ed. by Frederick Pottle. The first, possibly the liveliest, of many projected volumes of Boswellian manuscripts recently uncovered. More frankly revealing than Pepys' *Diary. McGraw-Hill $6, NAL.*

————— *Samuel Johnson.* Perhaps the greatest of all biographies. See page 67.

BOWEN, CATHERINE DRINKER 1897– *John Adams and the American Revolution* (1950). Fascinating re-creation of a man and an era. *Little, Brown $7.50, UL.*

————— *Yankee from Olympus* (1944). Biographical record of a remarkable personality, Oliver Wendell Holmes, Justice of the Supreme Court. *Little, Brown $5, Ban (abr.).*

BROOKS, VAN WYCK 1886– *The Ordeal of Mark Twain* (1920). An important study of America's most famous humorist in the Gilded Age. *Mer.*

CELLINI *Autobiography.* Swashbuckler, braggart, artist. See page 48.

CHUTE *Geoffrey Chaucer of England.* See page 43.

————— *Shakespeare of London.* Factual, readable. See page 54.

CROCKETT, DAVID 1786–1836 *Autobiography.* Salty, vigorous story of a backwoods pioneer. *Scribner $3.75, NAL.*

CUNLIFFE, MARCUS *George Washington, Man and Monument* (1958). A successful effort to re-create Washington's life as it really was rather than as legend and myth have recorded it. *Little, Brown $4, NAL.*

CURIE *Madame Curie.* Portrait of a pure scientist. See page 243.

DANA, RICHARD HENRY 1815–1882 *Two Years Before the Mast* (1840). Young Harvard graduate's adventures and hardships aboard a windjammer a century ago. *Ban, Evman-h, Gtll, ML, Nel, Pen, Pyroy (abr.).*

DARWIN, CHARLES 1809–1882 *The Voyage of the Beagle* (1840). A trip around the world, both travel-adventure and significant scientific document. *Heritage $5, Ban, Evman-h.*

DE QUINCEY, THOMAS 1785–1859 *Confessions of an English Opium-Eater* (1822). Ever-popular story of a drug addiction told in brilliant and beautiful prose. *Evman-h, WoC.*

ELLMANN, RICHARD 1918– *James Joyce* (1959). The nearly definitive biography of the great novelist, meticulously researched and gracefully written. *Oxford $12.50.*

FISCHER *Gandhi.* The miracle of a great man's life. See page 27.

FRANK, ANNE 1929–1945 *Diary of a Young Girl* (1952). The unforgettable story of a Jewish girl who hid with her family in an Amsterdam attic before capture and death in a German concentration camp. *Doubleday $3.50, ML, PB.*

FRANKLIN *Autobiography*. America's first self-made man in letters, science, business, diplomacy, and philosophy. See page 68.

FREEMAN, DOUGLAS SOUTHALL 1886–1953 *Robert E. Lee*
(1934–1935). The American general enthusiastically delineated.
Scribner 4 vols. $7.25 ea.

GARLAND, HAMLIN 1860–1940 *A Son of the Middle Border*
(1917). Depicts the hardships endured by our pioneer fore-
fathers. *Macmillan $4.50.*

HART, MOSS 1904– *Act One* (1959). A gay, witty, frank story of
theatrical success by a leading playwright and director. *Random
House $5.*

HECHT, BEN 1894– *A Child of the Century* (1955). Tangy memoirs
of a bold, buoyant man with an insatiable zest for life. *Simon
& Schuster $5, NAL.*

JOHNSON, EDGAR 1901– *Charles Dickens* (2 vols.) (1952). A brilliantly realized picture of Dickens and his times plus discerning
analyses of his novels. *Simon & Schuster $10.*

JONES, ERNEST 1879–1958 *The Life and Work of Sigmund Freud*
(1953, 1955, 1958). Superb three-volume biography of one of the
shapers of the modern mind. Scholarly and readable. *Basic
Books vols. 1 & 2 $6.75 ea., vol. 3 $7.50.*

KENNEDY, JOHN F. 1917– *Profiles in Courage* (1956). Short readable studies of American statesmen who defied the majority and
endured calumny and vilification. *Harper $3.95, PB.*

LINDEMAN, EDUARD C. 1885–1953 (ed.) *Life Stories of Men Who
Shaped History; from Plutarch's Lives* (1950). The lives of six
famous Greeks and Romans are portrayed as they represented
the dictator, the lawgiver, the patriot, the traitor, the people's
advocate, the conqueror. *NAL.*

LOEWY, RAYMOND 1893– *Never Leave Well Enough Alone* (1951).
Spirited autobiography of a French-American who designed
fashions first, then industrial products in a dazzlingly successful
campaign against the inefficiency of ugliness. *Simon & Schuster
$5.*

LORANT, STEFAN 1901– *The Life of Abraham Lincoln* (1941).
A text-and-picture biography that presents Lincoln as a husband, father, student, and statesman. *NAL.*

LUDWIG, EMIL 1881–1948 *Cleopatra* (1937). The unquiet history
of Cleopatra as a lover, mother, warrior, and queen. *Ban.*

MATTHIESSEN, F. O. 1902–1950 *The James Family* (1947). A
century of American life reflected in the personalities, writings,
and relationships of four remarkable Americans. *Knopf $7.50.*

MAUGHAM, W. SOMERSET 1874– *The Summing Up* (1938). A
popular writer's disarmingly candid observations on himself as
a man and a writer, and on philosophical aspects of life.
Doubleday $3.95, NAL.

MENCKEN, HENRY L. 1880–1956 *Days of H. L. Mencken* (1940–
1943). Self-portrait by the great iconoclast of the 1920's, always
bold, sometimes devastating and bludgeoning. *Knopf 3 vols.
$4.50 ea., $12 set.*

MERTON, THOMAS 1915– *The Seven Storey Mountain* (1948). Account of an American poet who, converted to Roman Catholicism, entered a Trappist monastery in Kentucky. Direct, realistic, challenging. *Harcourt, Brace $3.95, NAL.*

MILL, JOHN STUART 1806–1873 *Autobiography* (1873). How an infant prodigy became one of the most important of modern economists. *Columbia Univ. $2.50, Lib, RivEd, WoC.*

MIZENER, ARTHUR 1907– *The Far Side of Paradise: A Biography of F. Scott Fitzgerald* (1951). Thorough, fascinating biography of one who epitomized the jazz age. *Houghton Mifflin $5, Vin.*

MONTAIGNE *Essays.* Unconventional, urbane autobiography. See page 49.

NEHRU *Toward Freedom.* The great leader of modern India recounts his struggle to achieve his ideals. See page 27.

NEWMAN, JOHN HENRY 1801–1890 *Apologia pro Vita Sua* (1864). Intimate account of the religious experience of one of the great minds of the 19th century. *Evman-h, Im, ML, RivEd.*

PARKMAN, FRANCIS 1823–1893 *The Oregon Trail* (1849). The classic, eyewitness story of the Westward trek. *Rinehart $3.75, ML, NAL.*

PASTERNAK, BORIS 1890– *Safe Conduct* (1949). The first work of the famous Russian author published in this country, containing an autobiography, selected letters, poems, and short stories. *New, NAL.*

PEARSON, HESKETH 1887– *Oscar Wilde* (1946). A discerning and compassionate biography that removes the atmosphere of sensationalism of previous accounts. *UL.*

PEPYS *Diary.* Delightfully revealing. See page 62.

PLUTARCH *Lives.* Great ancients vividly alive. See page 28.

POLO. MARCO *Travels.* First Western report on Orient. See page 42.

RENAN *The Life of Jesus.* Skeptical account. See page 37.

REYNOLDS, ERNEST E. 1894– *Nansen* (1932). The life story of the Norwegian who was Arctic explorer, humanitarian, and Nobel Peace Prize winner. *Pen.*

RIIS, JACOB A. 1849–1914 *The Making of an American* (1901). A classic in the literature of U. S. immigrants. Riis came from Denmark and became a successful journalist and an effective reformer. *Macmillan $4.50.*

ROOSEVELT, ELEANOR 1884– *This I Remember* (1949). Absorbing reading, chiefly for the intimate, candid glimpses of the democratic way of life at the White House. *Harper, o.p.*

ROUSSEAU *Confessions.* Revelations of a romantic. See page 69.

SANDBURG, CARL 1878– *Abraham Lincoln: The Prairie Years* (1926). Lincoln pictured against his natural background—the prairie. Rich in detail, poetic in phrasing. *Harcourt, Brace 2 vols. $18, 1 vol. ed. $5.95, Dell 3 vols.*

SCHWEITZER, ALBERT 1875– *Out of My Life and Thought* (1933). The life story of the remarkable teacher and theologian who became a doctor-missionary in Africa. *Holt $4, NAL.*

SELL, HENRY B. 1889– and VICTOR WEYBRIGHT 1903– *Buffalo Bill and the Wild West* (1955). Well illustrated life story of the man and the legend. *Doubleday $2.95, Oxford Univ. $6.95, NAL.*

SHERWOOD *Roosevelt and Hopkins.* See page 206.

SITWELL, DAME EDITH 1887– *Alexander Pope* (1930). A sympathetic biography of the famous 18th-century poet and satirist. *Pen.*

SOUTHEY, ROBERT 1774–1843 *Life of Nelson* (1813). This masterpiece among lives of heroes has been widely read for more than a century. *Evman-h.*

STEEGMULLER, FRANCIS 1906– *Flaubert and Madame Bovary* (1950). A brilliant account of how a classic novel came into being. *Farrar, Straus & Cudahy $4, Vin.*

STEFFENS, LINCOLN 1866–1936 *Autobiography* (1931). One of the most interesting reports about graft and corruption in American city politics a generation ago. *Grosset $2.95, Harcourt, Brace $7.50, HarB (abr.).*

STONE, IRVING 1903– *Lust for Life.* (1944). Romanticized biography of Vincent van Gogh. *ML, PB.*

STRACHEY, LYTTON 1880–1932 *Queen Victoria* (1921). The Queen-Empress in the enthusiasm of youth, the loneliness of middle age, and the eccentricities of age. *HarB.*

SUETONIUS *Lives of the Twelve Caesars.* Dictators both admirable and despicable. See page 35.

SYMONDS *Michelangelo.* Sculptor, painter, architect. See page 50.

THOMAS, BENJAMIN P. 1902– *Abraham Lincoln* (1952). The first modern one-volume biography to make extensive use of the new material from the papers of Robert Todd Lincoln. *Knopf $5.75.*

THOREAU *Walden.* Philosophy and nature study. See page 169.

TRUMAN, HARRY S. 1884– *Memoirs* (1955, 1956). Often fascinating memoirs of the recent President. *Doubleday 2 vols. $5 each.*

WEIZMANN, CHAIM 1874–1952 *Trial and Error* (1949). The first President of Israel modestly relates his life that began in a Russian ghetto, led to world fame as a chemist, and culminated in leadership of a new nation. *Harper $5.*

WRIGHT, RICHARD 1908– *Black Boy* (1945). Grim autobiography of a Southern Negro who yearned for the intellectual and physical freedoms forbidden where he was born. *Liv, NAL.*

WASHINGTON, BOOKER T. c.1859–1915 *Up From Slavery* (1901). How the Negro educator and scientist struggled to rise above his environment. *Doubleday $3, Houghton Mifflin $2.20, Ban.*

14. Essays, Letters and Criticism

CHARLES B. GOODRICH, *Indiana University*

It is unfortunate that the term *essay* may bring back to the present or former college student unpleasant memories of a book called *Freshman Essays* or the like which stifled in him any desire to read any more of them. It may be a shock for such a reader to learn that in his other reading he has encountered and enjoyed the essay unaware of the form. It is found, for example, on the editorial page and in the book and drama reviews of the daily newspaper. Much of our reading, whether Walter Lippmann, Norman Vincent Peale, advice to the lovelorn, the pages of *Time* or the *Nation*—almost all the nonfiction we read, in fact—is in essay form.

The essay, like most art forms, is difficult to define precisely; it is generally described as a short prose piece focusing on one subject and reflecting the personal thoughts and feelings of the writer. This vague definition suggests the wide range to be found: Bacon may pinpoint the nature of friendship, Lamb may joke about the origin of roast pig, Lippmann may discuss a meeting of foreign ministers, and T. S. Eliot may tell us that Shakespeare failed in writing *Hamlet*. Thus, there is no restriction on the subject matter or its treatment; the writer is free to choose his subject, whether trivial or earth shaking, and to treat it in any way he sees fit.

The important matter for the reader of an essay is the personality of the writer. We demand that he have something new, something interesting, to say on a subject. But, even more, we want him to attract us as a person, for we react to the essayist as to the people we meet daily: with some we come to an immediate understanding, others we have to know for some time before admitting them to our friendship, and still others we never want to meet again. Some of our feeling against the essay may be swept away when we realize that we must make the same effort to relate to the essayist as to a close friend. We have to explore with him those subjects which interest him and try to see in them what he sees. As in all good relationships, we will often find ourselves putting in a word or two of opposition. All in all, the appreciation of the essay is a personal matter, and we must approach it as such, choosing those writers we would like to know. Fortunately, the range is wide, and all of us can find many friends among the writers of essays from Montaigne to E. B. White.

The letter is the most personal of essays, since the writer reveals himself to his intimates. Often, through the letters of famous and not-so-famous people we come to know them and their times better than we might even through an autobiography. Those interested in history will find that the letters of those who lived in any era can bring back the times better than a history book; those who want to know more about a work of art will see in the artist's letters the agonizing steps which led to the finished work. One may follow the daily progress of *Madame Bovary* or see the changing ideas of D. H. Lawrence, and come away with greater appreciation of the man's work. Any confirmed reader of the "Letters to the Editor" section of his paper will recognize how the letter reveals the mind and soul of the writer; with the letters of great men the revelations are simply more rewarding.

Criticism is a specialized form of the essay, an interpretation of a work of art which aims at a better understanding of it. Like the essay, it is a late form, although one may be sure that as soon as the first cave artist drew his first bison on the wall, a friend soon came by to criticize the technique. In any case, when the Greeks developed drama and literature, Aristotle and Plato began to analyze the results; and the practice has continued.

As with the essay, criticism is found on many levels, from the hurried newspaper review of last night's opening play or TV show to the carefully formulated reflections of one who has spent a lifetime looking at plays, reading poetry or novels, viewing paintings, or listening to music. Again, the approach is personal, and the reader will finally choose those critics in whom he has most trust. It must be noted, however, that one can find in any fine critic new insights, even though one may not always agree with the critic's final conclusions; and one may learn much through being irritated. Since there are so many critical systems, almost as many as there are critics, the reader will have no difficulty in finding what he wants. One may enjoy the Romantic approach of Coleridge or Hazlitt, the psychological probing of F. L. Lucas, the close examination of the text by I. A. Richards, the theological views of T. S. Eliot, or any other of the multitudinous critical tactics. The acute reader will probably not accept completely any of the possible interpretations of a work, but he will find in each new insights which will send him back to the work itself and help him make up his own mind.

ESSAY ANTHOLOGIES. Good essay collections abound. The following paperbound anthologies represent the scope and variety of the essay and include examples from many essayists of diverse interests and techniques: *Great English and American Essays*, ed. by Douglass S. Mead, *Rine; Great Essays*, ed. by Houston Peterson, *PB; American Essays*, ed. by Charles B. Shaw, *NAL;* and *A Book of English Essays*, ed. by W. E. Williams, *Pen.*

ADDISON and STEELE *The Spectator.* Comments, both serious and satirical, on life in early 18th-century London. See page 66.

BACON *Essays.* Terse, shrewd, practical analysis of human conduct for an age when success was imperative. See page 53.

BATE, WALTER 1918– *Prefaces to Criticism* (1952). These introductions to the major critics, from Aristotle to T. S. Eliot, make a comprehensive history of literary criticism. *Anch.*

BENCHLEY, ROBERT C. 1889–1945 *Benchley Beside Himself* (1943). One of our great humorists reacts to the petty irritations of daily life. *Harper $3.*

BOTKIN, BENJAMIN ALBERT 1901– (ed.) *Treasury of American Folklore* (1944). Although not strictly essays, these tall tales, songs, and legends show the heroes and the bad men and make clear the vitality of our nation. *Crown $5.*

BOWRA, C. M. 1898– *The Creative Experiment* (1949). Lucid, sensitive interpretation of seven difficult modern poets, among them Lorca, Apollinaire, Pasternak, and Eliot. *Grove $3.50, Ever.*

BROOKS, VAN WYCK 1886– *The World of Washington Irving* (1944), *The Flowering of New England* (1936), *The Times of Melville and Whitman* (1947), *New England: Indian Summer* (1940), *The Confident Years* (1952). A comprehensive view of American literature and society by an astute but tolerant critic. *EvmanNA 5 vols.*

CAMUS, ALBERT 1913– *The Myth of Sisyphus and Other Essays* (1955). Searching personal essays on the absurdity of human life by a leading French Existentialist novelist. *Knopf $4, Vin.*

CERF, BENNETT 1898– (ed.) *An Encyclopedia of American Humor* (1954). Not an encyclopedia at all, but, better, a fine collection of American humor. *MLG.*

CHESTERFIELD, LORD 1694–1773 *Letters to His Son* (1774). Urbane 18th-century advice on manners and morals in an aristocratic world. *CoE, Evman-h.*

COLERIDGE, SAMUEL TAYLOR 1772–1834 *Coleridge's Writings on Shakespeare* (1959). Ed. by Terence Hawkes. Brilliant intuitive criticism by one of the greatest Romantics. *Cap.*

COWDEN, ROY W. (ed.) *The Writer and His Craft* (1956). Twenty contemporary writers and critics advise the hopeful writer. *AA.*

COWLEY, MALCOLM 1898– *Exile's Return* (1934, rev. ed. 1951). Recollections of the "lost generation" of writers by one who shared their lives and ideals. *Comp.*

————— *The Literary Situation* (1954). A writer and critic surveys books, authors' working conditions, and other literary matters. *Comp.*

CREVECOEUR, ST. JOHN DE 1731–1813 *Letters from an American Farmer* (1782). These letters to an imaginary friend in Europe reflect both an idealistic and a realistic view of life in the young America. *Evman, Evman-h.*

ELIOT, T. S. 1888– *Selected Essays* (1932). The poet and critic surveys literature and religion in one of the classics of modern criticism. *Harcourt, Brace $5.50.*

EMERSON, RALPH WALDO 1803–1882 *Essays: First and Second Series* (1841, 1844). Transcendental philosophy at work; Emerson's most influential book. *Crowell $5.50, Houghton Mifflin $4, Peter Pauper $4.50.*

————— *Selections. CoNC, Dell, Evman-h, ML, MLCE, NAL, Rine, RivEd, Vik.*

EMPSON, WILLIAM 1906– *Seven Types of Ambiguity* (1930, 1955). An analysis of poetry through the subtleties of language; not for the beginner. *Mer.*

FORSTER, E. M. 1879– *Aspects of the Novel* (1927). A conversational and penetrating treatment of the novel as a form by one of England's most civilized novelists and essayists. *Harcourt, Brace $2.75, Harv.*

FLAUBERT, GUSTAVE 1821–1880 *The Selected Letters of Gustave Flaubert* (1953). Ed. by Francis Steegmuller. Excellent selection, showing the life and work that went into the writing of *Madame Bovary*. *Vin.*

GIBBS, WOLCOTT 1902–1958 *More in Sorrow* (1958). Parodies, profiles, stories, and theater reviews by one of the most incisive and driest wits of our time. *Holt $4.*

GOLDEN, HARRY 1902– *Only in America* (1958). The warm, witty editor of *The Carolina Israelite* writes about New York's Lower East Side, segregation, and on America in general. *World $4, PB.*

HAZLITT, WILLIAM 1778–1830 *Table Talk* (1821). A most likable man writes of his personal reactions to people and the passing show. *Evman-h.*

———— *Hazlitt on Theater* (1895). Ed. by William Archer and Robert Lowe. One of the best of the Romantic critics writes on the theater and acting of his day and gives his views on Shakespeare and others. *Drama, Drama-h.*

HOWE, IRVING 1920– (ed.) *Modern Literary Criticism* (1959). A good introduction to modern British and American literary criticism: Richards, Woolf, Eliot, Yeats, and others. *Beacon $6.50.*

HYMAN, STANLEY EDGAR 1919– (ed.) *The Critical Performance* (1956). Seventeen British and American critics write on such diverse topics as *Oedipus Rex* and the detective story; a representative selection. *Vin.*

ISAACS, JACOB 1896– *The Background of Modern Poetry* (1952). A lucid and informative introduction to modern poetry addressed to the puzzled general reader. *Evman.*

JARRELL, RANDALL 1914– *Poetry and the Age* (1953). A poet writes about modern poetry and the conditions under which it is written. *Vin.*

KEATS, JOHN 1795–1821 *Letters 1814–1821* (1958). Ed. by Hyder Rollins. The definitive edition of Keats's letters, which read almost as well as his poetry. *Harvard Univ.* 2 vols. $20.

———— *Selected Letters.* Farrar, Straus & Cudahy $4.50, Anch, Nel, Pen, WoC.

KRUTCH, JOSEPH WOOD 1893– *The Measure of Man* (1954). Provocative thinking on freedom, human values, survival, and the modern temper. *UL.*

LAMB, CHARLES 1775–1834 *Essays of Elia* (1823). Sometimes gentle, sometimes incisive, these essays fit the definition of the form; the picture of a very likable man comes through. *Cambridge Univ. $1, Evman, Evman-h, Nel, SM, WoC.*

LAWRENCE, D. H. 1885–1930 *The Selected Letters of D. H. Lawrence* (1938). Ed. by Diana Trilling. The always natural, sometimes shocking, outpourings of one of England's most controversial writers. *Farrar, Straus & Cudahy $4.50.*

LINCOLN, ABRAHAM 1809–1865 *Speeches and Letters.* Lincoln's depth of character is easily seen in the dignity and directness of his personal communications. *Hendricks $2, Evman, Evman-h, Rine.*

LUCAS, F. L. 1894– *Literature and Psychology* (1957). An English critic shows the insight psychology can bring to great works of English and American literature. *AA*.

LYNN, KENNETH S. 1923– (ed.) *The Comic Tradition in America* (1958). An anthology which shows the wealth of American humor from Ben Franklin to Henry James. *Doubleday $5, Anch*.

MANN, THOMAS 1875–1955 *Essays* (1957). The noted novelist and critic discusses some of the great artists: Goethe, Tolstoy, Wagner, Freud, and Cervantes. *Vin*.

MAUGHAM, W. SOMERSET 1874– *Points of View* (1959). Essays, mostly on writers and writing, by one of our age's most urbane authors. *Doubleday $4.50*.

MENCKEN, H. L. 1880–1956 *Prejudices: A Selection* (1919–1927, 1948). Some of the best from the great shocker and debunker of the 20's. *Vin*.

———— *The Vintage Mencken. Vin*.

MONTAIGNE, MICHEL DE 1553–1592 *The Complete Works of Montaigne: Essays, Travel Journals, Letters* (1958). Trans. by Donald M. Frame. First complete edition in English of the writings of the man who first used the term "essay" and was the model for many who later used the form. *Stanford Univ. $12.50*. For other editions see page 49.

NEIDER, CHARLES 1915– (ed.) *Essays of the Masters* (1956). Stimulating collection of essays by novelists and poets: Balzac, Dostoevski, Goethe, Poe, Sartre, and many others. *Rinehart $2.25*.

ORWELL, GEORGE 1903–1950 *A Collection of Essays* (1954). The author of *1984* discusses books, humor, language, politics, and other important subjects. *Anch*.

———— *Homage to Catalonia* (1938). Reflections on the Spanish Civil War by one who saw what it would mean to the world. *Harcourt, Brace $3.50, Bea*.

RAHV, PHILIP 1908– *Image and Idea* (1957). The cofounder of the *Partisan Review* examines modern literature. *New*.

READ, HERBERT 1893– *The Tenth Muse* (1958). 40 essays on genius in the arts. *Horizon $4.50, Ever*.

RICHARDS, I. A. 1893– *Practical Criticism* (1929). A pioneer and a classic work in modern criticism, placing emphasis on close examination of the poem itself. *Harv*.

RUSKIN, JOHN 1819–1900 *Sesame and Lilies* (1865). His most popular work, which gives his views on the importance of education and the arts. *Evman-h, WoC*.

SARTRE, JEAN-PAUL 1905– *Literary Essays* (1957). French and American writers are considered from the Existentialist view by one of its most provocative philosophers. *WL*.

SEVIGNE, MARIE, MARQUISE DE 1626–1696 *Letters*. Charming, natural letters which give a fine picture of the times of Louis XIV. *Dutton 2 vols. $7.50*.

SEWALL, RICHARD B. 1908– *The Vision of Tragedy* (1959). Brilliant inquiry into the nature of tragedy through examination of eight works from Job to Faulkner. *Yale $4*.

STEVENSON, ROBERT LOUIS 1850–1894 *Virginibus Puerisque* (1881). Gracefully written penetrating essays in the Lamb tradition. *Evman, Evman-h, Nel, SM*.

THOREAU, HENRY DAVID 1817–1862 *Walden; or Life in the Woods* (1854). A great individualist records his experience in living alone with nature; direct and powerful, an antidote against "togetherness." *Hendricks $2.50, Peter Pauper $4.50, Evman-h, GtIl, Harp, MLCE, NAL, Rine, RivEd, Vik, Vik-h*.

THURBER, JAMES 1894– *The Owl in the Attic* (1931). One of our greatest humorists discusses the English language and other difficulties of modern life. *UL*.

———— *Thurber Country* (1953). Very informal essays and sketches in the best Thurber tradition. *Simon & Schuster $3.75*.

TOLSTOY, COUNT LEO 1828–1910 *Recollections and Essays.* A more intimate view of the great Russian novelist. *WoC*.

Treasury of the World's Great Letters (1940). Ed. by M. L. Schuster. The most interesting letters from ancient times to the present. *Simon & Schuster $5*.

TRILLING, LIONEL 1905– *The Liberal Imagination* (1950). A liberal examination of literature and society, from Wordsworth to the Kinsey report. *Anch*.

WALPOLE, HORACE 1717–1797 *Selected Letters.* The civilized 18th century comes to life in these letters about his friends and their activities. *Evman-h*.

WELLEK, RENE 1903– and AUSTIN WARREN 1899– *Theory of Literature* (1956). An excellent introduction to the "New Criticism" (concentration on the structure and detail of a work rather than on its historical and social background). *Harv*.

WHITE, E. B. 1899– *One Man's Meat* (1942). Random, personal thoughts about such things as hay fever and coon hunting, from one of the *New Yorker's* finest minds. *Harp*.

———— and K. S. WHITE (eds.) *Subtreasury of American Humor* (1941). The classic collection of American humor. *MLG, PB*.

WILLIAMS, WILLIAM CARLOS 1883– *In the American Grain* (1925). An important American poet discusses the makers of American history. *New*.

WILSON, EDMUND 1895– *A Piece of My Mind* (1956). The critic, at 60, brings his vast reading and observation to bear on such topics as religion, science, and sex. *Farrar, Straus & Cudahy $3.75, Anch*.

———— (ed.) *The Shock of Recognition* (1943, 1955). A collection of literary documents from Lowell to Sherwood Anderson, critics writing mostly about their contemporaries. *UL 2 vols*.

WOOLF, VIRGINIA 1882–1941 *The Common Reader* (1932). Comments on literary themes and people by one of England's most perceptive novelists and critics. *Harv 2 vols*.

Magazines

The little magazines of the 20's—*Dial, Broom, transition, Hound and Horn*—invigorated the creative impulse of their times, nourishing Eliot, Pound, and Cummings among the poets, Stein, Hemingway, and Faulkner among the prose writers. Today's quarterly magazines of literature—larger, more sedate, longer lived—abet the critical rather than the creative. In the vanguard of the "schools" are critics like Edmund Wilson and Malcolm Cowley, poet-critics like John Ciardi and John Crowe Ransom, novelist-critics like Robert Penn Warren. All contribute regularly to the modern quarterlies. Although poems, short stories, and even segments of novels in progress do appear, the chief function of these magazines is to illuminate—to explicate—the work of art (or some integral part of it). Despite an occasional descent to pedantry or a flight into the bizarre, the quarterly magazines provide their readers with insights into modern literature unavailable in either newspaper book reviews or in popular literary journals.

But literature does not hold the field alone. Nonliterary quarterlies offer informed and provocative discussions in many other areas. These journals range widely and probe deeply into politics and contemporary affairs (regional and global), economics, history, philosophy, religion, art, and psychology. In most of these magazines the writing is lucid, the arguments cogent, and the tone intellectual—though rarely academic or pompous.

Good reading abounds in weekly and monthly magazines too. Factual and interpretive surveys of current events are presented in *Time, Newsweek, The Reporter,* and *U.S. News and World Report.* Each month *Harper's* and *Atlantic Monthly* appraise social and political developments and trends with high seriousness and acute perceptivity that have characterized these magazines for a century. *Commentary,* though only a quarter century old, has won respect for its outstanding essays on social and cultural problems. *Saturday Review* provides valuable weekly reports on new books, plays, films, and records both classical and popular, plus stimulating, challenging articles and editorials. Finally, no lover of good reading should neglect *The New Yorker*. Weekly, it relies on brilliant, urbane wit to point its gently satiric thrusts at the doings and inhabitants of an absorbing but mad world.

Accent: A Quarterly of New Literature (Univ. of Illinois). Publishes fiction, poetry, literary criticism, new translations by unknown as well as by established authors. ($1.50 per year)

Atlantic Monthly (Boston, Mass.). Fiction, poetry, and informal essays on a consistently high level for the general reader. ($7.50 per year)

Beloit Poetry Journal (Beloit, Wisconsin). A quarterly devoted exclusively to presenting poetry by new and established poets. ($1.50 per year)

Botteghe Oscure: An International Review of New Literature (Rome, Italy). A semiannual of book size, it prints the most important writing of the *avant garde* of all nationalities. ($4.50 per year)

Chicago Review (Chicago). Prints fiction, poetry, and criticism by new writers quarterly. ($1.75 per year)

Criticism (Wayne State Univ., Detroit). A quarterly review of serious essays on the arts designed for the advanced reader. ($6 per year)

Etc.: A Review of General Semantics (Chicago, Ill.). Edited by the distinguished semanticist, S. I. Hayakawa, its articles consider the impact of language on human behavior and aim toward promoting more effective communication. ($4 per year)

Foreign Affairs: An American Quarterly Review (Council on Foreign Relations, New York). Contains authoritative articles on world affairs contributed by outstanding statesmen. ($6 per year)

Harper's Magazine (New York). One of the oldest publications in the country, it publishes monthly fiction and essays for the general reader. ($6 per year)

Hudson Review (New York). One of the most important literary quarterlies, publishing fiction, poetry, drama, and criticism by some of the most sensitive and astute writers of our day. ($4 per year)

Kenyon Review (Kenyon College, Ohio). Like the *Hudson,* an influential quarterly, but especially partial to the "New Criticism." ($4 per year)

Modern Fiction Studies (Purdue Univ.). Committed to criticism of American, English, and European fiction since 1880, it devotes two issues a year to a single author. ($2 per year)

The New Yorker (New York). Urbane, witty fiction, criticism, and biography, plus cartoons, pointing up the madness of our modern world. Weekly. ($7 per year)

Partisan Review (New York). Living up to its name, this magazine publishes monthly not only creative and critical material, but also essays on politics, sociology, and philosophy which are often irritating but always interesting. ($4 per year)

Psychoanalysis: Journal of Psychoanalytic Psychology (New York). Essays illustrating the theory and practice of psychoanalysis, and its relationship to society. ($4 per year)

Sewanee Review (Univ. of the South, Tennessee). The oldest literary quarterly in the United States (1892) and the most important critical publication in the South, its point of view is in no way limited by regional interests. ($4 per year)

Virginia Quarterly Review: A National Journal of Literature and Discussion (Univ. of Virginia). Perceptive, well-written essays on national and international affairs as well as on the specific problems of the South. ($4 per year)

Yale Review: A National Quarterly (Yale Univ.). A major periodical whose articles range from philosophy to international politics, from poetry to economics. ($3.50 per year)

HUMANITIES AND
SCIENCES

---

15. Fine Arts

ATWOOD H. TOWNSEND, *New York University*

Art begins in primitive, practical handicraft; it climaxes as ultimate, exalted expression of truth and beauty.

The first sub-men who shaped sticks, stones, shells, and bones into useful implements contrived—generation after generation—to make their hammers, scrapers, stabbers, ever better and neater, more efficient and more shapely. Thus, countless millennia ago, they illustrated one basic principle of artistic design: the interrelation of form and function, or, if you will, of beauty and truth. This principle seems to be valid generally both in the plant and animal worlds, and in man-made artifacts: that whatever is proper, true, and good for its function is also beautiful and pleasing in its form.

Our paleolithic progenitors not only designed hand tools, clay pots, and clothing, but also built huts and daubed them with colored mud, or carved patterns on their timbers (Architecture). Very early they began to make pictures of animals, people, things—scratched on bone or wood or shell, hewed from logs or shaped from clay, drawn in color on cliffs and cavern walls (Painting and Sculpture). On joyous occasions and at solemn rituals they jigged and chanted, clapped hands and banged on hollow logs (Music and Dance). Out of such primitive folkways evolved those sophisticated refinements of artistic creation which we call ballet, symphony, opera—just as the supreme glory of the Parthenon is an idealized refinement of cabins made of logs set on their butts, the crude structures in which the early Greeks sheltered themselves and their gods.

A false notion is widespread that Art is fancy, special, remote from the facts of life. People who call themselves "practical" sometimes sneer at Art as trivial and trifling, mere foolish ornament, silly extravagance beneath the dignity of solid citizens. In truth, any genuine, vital Art is the essence of Life itself in finest, truest expression. Art is not rare, remote, precious, restricted to old pictures in museums or symphonies in concert halls. Art is intimately, essentially interwoven with every thread of daily life—in the neckties, scarves, clothes we wear; in the design of our chairs, rugs, and kitchens; in the style of the homes we build and the autos we buy; in the shows we enjoy on stage, screen, and TV; in the melodies we whistle or sing or dance to. A life deprived of the treasures and pleasures that Art affords us would be no life at all—at least not on the human level. Man *is* man, significantly more than a dumb beast, because man as man has always been a creative artist, and still is. Man's creativity is what makes progress possible, and what makes the human adventure continuously exciting.

From another point of view, Art can be defined as lying between the Ignorance of fumbling beasts, morons, or savages who know not what to do, and the Science which (insofar as it comes close to perfect knowledge) permits exact mastery over materials and forces toward predetermined ends. Art is wiser than Ignorance, but never as precise as Science. Art is always more free, more casual, and more personal, in a certain sense even more experimental than Science itself. Two scientists performing the same experiment will normally arrive at exactly the same result. Two artists painting the same scene must, if they are genuinely creative, produce pictures characteristically individual. That is one reason why Art is so much fun: it is ever-changing, various as the waves of the sea, never to be fixed, standardized, or routinized (even though certain cults or styles have prevailed for centuries); always zestfully seeking the unknown and the untried.

It is conventional to restrict the label "Fine Arts" to a few traditionally honored fields of artistic endeavor, and to call other arts "crafts" and their practitioners "artisans."

In the broad sense, however, silversmiths, gardeners, industrial designers, modistes, hairdressers, rug weavers can be and often are as truly artists in their respective lines as sculptors, composers, or choreographers.

As a rule, before you can care for a person deeply, you have to get to know him pretty well. Similarly, before you can really grasp what it is you like in various forms of Art, you will have to take time to acquire a certain amount of informed understanding so as to appreciate fully. You can take delight in Beethoven and Tschaikovsky, or Renoir and Matisse, without knowing a thing about the men or their works; but if you do know something about the personalities involved and their backgrounds, something about Classicism and Romanticism in music, about Impressionism and Modernism in painting, then you are prepared to hear in the symphonies or to see in the pictures significances and subtleties which the uninformed never know are there. By cultivating sympathetic understanding of what artists are striving toward, you develop your capacity to live more fully, to probe more deeply, to enjoy more keenly and richly.

The books listed below are means whereby your eyes and ears can be opened wider, and your intelligence keyed up, so that you may be among those equipped to relish fully the finest achievements of the greatest creative artists of all times. With the help of such books you can qualify yourself for a full, rich, truly civilized life. By cultivating the raw material of your native intellect, and by preparing it to react sympathetically to the most admirable products of the mind of man, you will ripen yourself to appreciate the sometimes sharp, sometimes exquisite delights of "the adventure of a soul among masterpieces."

A. Basic Principles

EDMAN, IRWIN 1896–1954 *Arts and the Man* (1939). A primer of esthetics attempting to explain why objects have beauty. *Norton $2.50.*

FRY, ROGER E. 1866–1934 *Transformations* (1926). The esthetics of changing art styles. *Anch.*

_____ *Vision and Design* (1920). A famous art critic and former curator of the Metropolitan Museum explains the relation between perception and esthetic form. *Peter Smith $6, Mer.*

GHISELIN, BREWSTER 1903– (ed.) *The Creative Process: A Symposium* (1952). Anthology by artists, musicians, writers about the processes of creation. *Univ. of California $5, NAL.*

GOMBRICH, E. H. 1909– *The Story of Art* (6th rev. ed. 1954). The artistic aims of architecture, painting, sculpture, in their historical development. *Phaidon $7.50.*

JOHNSON, MARTIN C. 1896– *Art and Scientific Thought* (1949). Attempts to show that art and science are not basically antagonistic. *Dov.*

MUNRO, THOMAS 1897– *The Arts and Their Interrelations* (1949). Films, animated cartoons, etc., against their cultural and historical backgrounds. *Liberal Arts $7.50.*

PANOFSKY *Meaning in the Visual Arts.* Relation of art to life in the Middle Ages and the Renaissance. See page 50.

B. Painting, Sculpture, Photography

NOTE: To enjoy fully great works of art, reading about them is much less valuable than looking at them, studying them, getting to know them—as originals in museums, as prints on your own walls, as reproductions in one or another of the rich variety of excellent art books now available. Three series are outstanding:

Library of Great Painters. Portfolio Edition series of beautifully illustrated books on individual artists, including Cézanne, El Greco, Renoir, Toulouse-Lautrec, Van Gogh. *Abrams $12.50– $17.50 ea.*

Phaidon Press Books. A series of excellent volumes of reproductions (only partly in color), from Etruscan sculpture to Cézanne. Each includes informative discussions of painters, places, and periods. *Doubleday $2.95 up.*

Skira Art Books. Scores of magnificent volumes with illuminating text and accurate, full-color reproductions of painting by particular artists (e.g., Botticelli, Rembrandt, Goya, Renoir, Degas, Modigliani), of significant countries or periods or places (Venice, Paris, Holland), etc. *Skira $3.50 up.*

Also useful are these smaller, less expensive series:

Aldine Library of Artists. Pocket series, including brief introductory essays and color reproductions of works of individual artists. *Tudor $1 ea.*

Hyperion Press Art Books. Small paperbound, illustrated books on individual artists. *Macmillan $1.95 up.*

Pocket Library of Great Art. Illustrated series of 24 volumes, each with brief essay about the artist and text for each picture. Artists from Michelangelo to the present are presented. *PB.*

ADAM, LEONHARD 1891– *Primitive Art* (3rd ed. 1954). Social meaning of art and anthropology from prehistory to today. *Pen.*

BARR, ALFRED H., JR. 1902– (ed.) *Masters of Modern Art* (1958). 350 fine reproductions, some in color, of chief treasures of the Museum of Modern Art in New York, summarizing major trends of modern experimentation. *Doubleday (Museum of Modern Art) $16.50.*

_____ *What Is Modern Painting?* (1946). A clear introductory explanation. *Doubleday (Museum of Modern Art) $1.25.*

BERENSON, BERNARD 1865–1959 *Aesthetics and History in the Visual Arts* (1948). A master critic analyzes the reasons for changing styles in art. *Anch.*

BETHERS, RAY 1902– *Composition in Pictures* (2nd ed. 1956). Graphic description of pictorial composition. *Pitman $5.95.*

BOAS *Primitive Art.* A classic study. See page 238.

BOWIE, HENRY *On the Laws of Japanese Painting* (1952). Clear, fascinating explanation. *Dov.*

CELLINI *Autobiography.* Portrait of the Renaissance. See page 48.

CHENEY, SHELDON 1886– *Primer of Modern Art* (rev. ed. 1958). Readable explanation of modern techniques. *Liveright $5.*

CLARK, SIR KENNETH 1903– *The Nude: A Study in Ideal Form* (1956, 1959). A witty, learned analysis of the nude as a complete expression of imaginative experience—both sensual and divine. *Pantheon $7.50, Anch.*

COVARRUBIAS *Indian Art of Mexico and Central America.* See page 84.

CRAVEN, THOMAS 1889– *Famous Artists and Their Models* (1949). *PB.*

_____ *Pocket Book of Greek Art* (1950). Useful introduction. *PB.*

_____ *The Story of Painting* (1943). From cave pictures to contemporary art. *Simon & Schuster $5.*

_____ (ed.) *Treasury of Art Masterpieces* (rev. ed. 1958). Full color reproductions from the Renaissance to the present. *Simon & Schuster $7.95.*

DAVIDSON, MORRIS 1898– *Painting for Pleasure* (1938). Sound instruction and persuasion to do-it-yourself. *Branford $3.95.*

DA VINCI *Notebooks.* An intimate record of genius. See page 48.

Family of Man (1955). Reproducing the famous photographic exhibition—503 pictures from 68 countries—created by Edward Steichen for the Museum of Modern Art. *Simon & Schuster $2.95, PB.*

FLANAGAN, GEORGE A. *How to Understand Modern Art* (rev. ed. 1955). Readable explanation of the backgrounds, meaning, motivations of modern art. *Crowell $6.50.*

FLEXNER, JAMES THOMAS 1908– *Pocket History of American Painting* (1950). Useful, compact introduction. *PB.*

GARDNER, HELEN d. 1946 *Art Through the Ages* (4th. ed. 1959).
A standard one-volume history, profusely illustrated; somewhat
dated but still useful. *Harcourt, Brace $8.95.*

GOYA, FRANCISCO DE 1746–1828 *The Disasters of War* (1956).
85 etchings plus an essay on his life and work by Xavier de
Salas. *Anch.*

GROSSER, MAURICE R. 1903– *The Painter's Eye* (1951). How to
look at paintings. *Rinehart $3, NAL.*

HAUSER, ARNOLD 1892– *The Social History of Art* (1951). A
thousand pages with scores of illustrations summarizing the interrelation of social forces and the graphic arts. *Vin 4 vols.*

LARKIN, OLIVER W. 1896– *Art and Life in America* (1949). A
Pulitzer Prize-winning study of the relationship of the visual-
plastic arts to the development of American civilization. *Rinehart $7.50.*

MYERS, BERNARD S. 1908– *Fifty Famous Artists* (1953). *Ban.*

_____ *Modern Art in the Making* (1950). Unexcelled guide for
professional and layman. *McGraw-Hill $7.50.*

NEWTON, ERIC 1893– *European Painting and Sculpture* (1949).
Excellent introduction and summary. *Pen.*

OZENFANT, AMEDEE 1886– *The Foundations of Modern Art*
(new Am. ed. 1952). A scholarly investigation of backgrounds.
Dov.

POLLACK, PETER *The Picture History of Photography* (1958).
From earliest experiments to the latest triumphs of the greatest
photographers. *Abrams $17.50.*

PRAZ *The Flaming Heart.* 17th-century baroque art. See page 63.

READ, HERBERT 1893– *Art Now* (rev. ed. 1948). Good introduction to the theory of modern painting and sculpture. *Pitman
$7.50.*

_____ *The Philosophy of Modern Art* (1955). *Mer.*

RICE, D. TALBOT 1903– *Byzantine Art* (rev. ed. 1954). *Pen.*

ROBB, DAVID M. 1903– *The Harper History of Painting* (1951).
A first-rate survey of Western painting since the Old Stone Age,
with over 500 illustrations. *Harper $7.50.*

STONE *Lust for Life.* Colorful life of Van Gogh. See page 162.

STRUPPECK, JULES 1915– *The Creation of Sculpture* (1952).
Analysis of the nature and techniques of sculpture for those
who wish to appreciate or to produce it. *Holt $8.*

SYPHER *Four Stages of Renaissance Style.* See page 50.

TAYLOR, FRANCIS HENRY 1903– *Fifty Centuries of Art* (1954).
A thorough survey of art history from Egyptian to modern
times. *Harper $6.*

VAN LOON *R.V.R.: The Life of Rembrandt.* See page 63.

VASARI *Lives of the Painters.* Italian masters. See page 49.

WILLETTS *Chinese Art.* See page 80.

C. Architecture and Design

FAULKNER, RAY N. 1906– et al. *Art Today* (3rd ed. 1956). Traces the influence of form, color, and design in our daily lives. *Holt $6.95.*

GIEDION, SIGFRIED 1888– *Space, Time, and Architecture* (3rd ed. 1954). A fundamental text illuminating our times and the interrelation of materials, techniques, and human needs in terms of architectural design and city planning. Fascinatingly illustrated. *Harvard Univ. $12.50.*

———— *Walter Gropius* (1954). The essential facts about a creative genius of modern architecture. *Reinhold $5.*

GLOAG, JOHN 1896 *Guide to Western Architecture* (1958). Comprehensive and illuminating. *Macmillan $12.50, Ever.*

GREENOUGH, HORATIO 1805–1852 *Form and Function* (1957). Selected writings by a prophet of modern architecture. *Calif*

HAMLIN, TALBOT FAULKNER 1889–1956 *Architecture Through the Ages* (rev. ed. 1953). Excellent illustrated survey. *Putnam $8.*

HITCHCOCK *Latin American Architecture Since 1945.* See page 84.

HORNUNG, CLARENCE PEARSON 1899– *Handbook of Designs and Devices* (2nd ed. 1946). *Dov.*

KAUFMANN, EDGAR, JR. 1910– *What Is Modern Interior Design?* (1953). Principles of design in home furnishings. *Doubleday (Museum of Modern Art) $1.25.*

LAVEDAN, PIERRE 1885– *French Architecture* (1956). Readable introduction. *Pen.*

LAWRENCE, ARNOLD WALTER 1900– *Greek Architecture* (1957). A monumental study. *Penguin $12.50.*

LOEWY *Never Leave Well Enough Alone.* Industrial design. See page 60.

MUMFORD, LEWIS 1895– *The Culture of Cities* (1938). The past, present, and hoped-for future of the city—and of civilization. *Harcourt, Brace $5.*

———— *From the Ground Up* (1956). *Harv.*

———— *Sticks and Stones* (2nd ed. 1955). *Dov.*

PEVSNER, NIKOLAUS 1902– *An Outline of European Architecture* (1953). A first-rate introduction and survey. *Pen.*

RICHARDS, JAMES M. 1907– *Introduction to Modern Architecture* (1956). New ways of building to fit today's needs. *Pen.*

SCOTT *The Architecture of Humanism.* See page 50.

SCOTT, ROBERT GILLAM 1907– *Design Fundamentals* (1951). Analysis of problems of visual relationships illustrated through step-by-step designing of this book. *McGraw-Hill $8.*

TUNNARD, CHRISTOPHER 1910– *The City of Man* (1953). Stimulating and richly illustrated commentary on the development of American city design out of ancient models and pioneer experiments. *Scribner $6.25.*

———— and HENRY HOPE REED *American Skyline* (1955). Traces the growth and form of American cities. *Houghton Mifflin $5, NAL.*

VITRUVIUS *On Architecture.* Standards of 27 B.C. See page 35.

WRIGHT, FRANK LLOYD 1869–1959 *When Democracy Builds* (1945). Famous architect's ideal city for a new world. *Univ. of Chicago o.p.*

D. Music

ABRAHAM, GERALD 1904– *This Modern Music* (1952). An ideal short guide for those who find modern music puzzling. *Norton $2.50.*

AUDEN, W. H. 1907– et al. (eds.) *An Elizabethan Songbook* (1955). Lute songs, madrigals, and rounds. *Doubleday $5, Anch.*

BACHARACH, A. L. 1891– (ed.) *British Music of Our Time* (1954). Essays on contemporary composers. *Pen.*

BARZUN, JACQUES 1907– *Berlioz and His Century* (1956). Splendid evocation of a man and his time. *Mer.*

BAUER, MARION 1889–1955 and ETHEL PEYSER 1887– *Music Through the Ages* (rev. ed. 1951). Useful basic text summarizing chief composers and main trends. *Putnam $4.50.*

BERNSTEIN, MARTIN 1904– *An Introduction to Music* (2nd ed. 1951). Good guide to intelligent listening. *Prentice-Hall $6.25.*

BLOM, ERIC 1888–1959 (ed.) *Mozart's Letters* (1956). The intimate record of genius. *Pen.*

BROCKWAY, WALLACE 1905– and HERBERT WEINSTOCK 1905– *Men of Music* (rev. ed. 1950). Critical biographies. *Simon & Schuster $1.95.*

BURK, JOHN N. 1891– *The Life and Works of Beethoven* (1946). Comprehensive biography and analysis. *ML.*

COPLAND, AARON 1900– *Our New Music* (1941). Illustrated talks on European and American composers. *McGraw-Hill $4.50.*

CROSS, MILTON 1897– *Stories of the Great Operas* (1955). *Perm.*

DARRELL, R. D. 1903– *Good Listening* (1953). A guide to the best on records. *NAL.*

DENT, EDWARD J. 1876–1957 *Opera* (1940). Readable basic introduction. *Pen.*

EINSTEIN, ALFRED 1880–1952 *A Short History of Music* (1936). *Knopf $5, Vin.*

FEATHER, LEONARD 1914– *The Encyclopedia of Jazz* (1955). Contains a brief history of jazz; thumbnail biographies of instrumentalists, vocalists, composers; glossary of terms; bibliography; and a selected list of jazz records. *Horizon $10.*

GROUT, DONALD JAY *Short History of Opera* (1947). The best introduction. *Columbia Univ. $6.*

HILL, RALPH 1900–1950 (ed.) *The Concerto* (1952). Excellent guide to the understanding of musical structure. *Pen.*

⸻ *The Symphony* (1949). Basic guide to an understanding of symphonic masterpieces. *Pen.*

HODEIR, ANDRE 1921– *Jazz: Its Evolution and Essence* (1956). Traces the evolution of jazz. *Grove $3.50, Ever.*

HOWARD, JOHN TASKER 1890– and JAMES LYONS *Modern Music* (rev. 1957). A popular guide explains the experiments of modern composers (Debussy, Stravinsky, Gershwin, Bartók, etc.) with dissonance, impressionism, atonality, polytonality, jazz rhythms, etc. *Crowell $3.95, NAL.*

⸻ *Our American Music* (3rd ed. 1955). Historical survey to the present. *Crowell $8.50.*

LANG, PAUL HENRY 1901– *Music in Western Civilization* (1941). The definitive one-volume history—sound, detailed, readable. *Norton $7.50.*

LEONARD, RICHARD ANTHONY *The Stream of Music* (1943). Illustrated history of 300 years of music. *Doubleday $5.*

MACHLIS, JOSEPH *The Enjoyment of Music* (Shorter ed. 1957). Persuasive instruction in music appreciation for the average listener. *Norton $4.50.*

MCKINNEY, HOWARD D. 1889– and W. R. ANDERSON 1891– *Music in History* (1940). Relationship of music to other fine arts, including film and ballet. *American Book $6.50.*

NEWMAN, WILLIAM S. 1912– *Understanding Music* (1953). Basic approaches to melody, rhythm, texture, form in a survey of music in Western civilization. *Harper $4.*

SACHS, CURT 1881–1959 *The History of Musical Instruments* (1940). The definitive text. *Norton $7.95.*

SALAZAR, ADOLFO 1890– *Music in Our Time* (1946). Analysis of the main currents in music of the last century as an expression of the life and aims of the age. *Norton $5.95.*

SANDBURG, CARL 1878– *The American Songbag* (1927). Unexcelled for background of 280 songs, ballads, ditties with music. *Harcourt, Brace $5.75.*

SHAPIRO, NAT and NAT HENTOFF (eds.) *The Jazz Makers* (1957). Colorful factual sketches by various jazz critics on 21 key figures, such as Morton, Beiderbecke, Waller, Goodman, Ellington, Gillespie. *Rinehart $4.95, Ever.*

SULLIVAN, J. W. N. 1886–1937 *Beethoven: His Spiritual Development* (1927). Masterly interpretation of perhaps the greatest composer of them all. *Knopf $3.50, NAL.*

TURNER, W. J. 1889–1946 *Mozart* (1938). Highly readable biography and well-balanced interpretation. *Anch.*

E. The Dance

AMBERG, GEORGE 1901– *Ballet in America* (1949). Excellent introduction to ballet, and survey of its growth in the U.S.A. *NAL.*

BOWERS, FAUBION 1917– *Theatre in the East* (1956). Panorama of dance and drama in Asia. *Nelson $7.50.*

CONYN, CORNELIUS *Three Centuries of Ballet* (1953). Survey of dance as an art since 1600, giving insight into the evolution of the ballet. *Elsevier Press o.p.*

DE MILLE, AGNES 1908– *Dance to the Piper* (1952). Entertaining autobiography of a significant contributor to the development of ballet today. *Grosset $1.98, Ban.*

HASKELL, ARNOLD 1903– *Ballet* (1938). Illustrated guide to an appreciation of ballet as an art form. *Pen.*

KROKOVER, ROSALYN *The New Borzoi Book of Ballets* (1956). Explains what modern dance is and discusses those who have contributed to it creatively. *Knopf $6.75.*

MARTIN, JOHN 1893– *World Book of Modern Ballet* (1952). A leading critic discusses informatively, entertainingly, companies, dancers, composers, designers, choreographers. *World o.p.*

MAYO, MARGOT *The American Square Dance.* A complete guide to do-it-yourself. *Sent.*

16. Philosophy

LOYD D. EASTON, *Ohio Wesleyan University*

Like mountain climbing, philosophy undertakes hazardous but challenging tasks—exhilarating because of their difficulties and rewarding because of the significant vistas they yield. To scan the very horizons of human experience through the lens of sustained reflection can yield a panoramic view of man and his place in the universe. Philosophy is often chastised for its high abstractions and its detachment from everyday life, but these are, in part, the price of its final satisfactions. The perspectives of philosophy require objectivity and distance to correct the distortions of familiar but fragmentary views of life.

Through many ages philosophical thinking has had essentially one basic goal—a reflective view of experience in all its ramifications and relationships. The philosopher is primarily preoccupied with over-all connections, not, as the scientist, with the details of a limited area. Thus, in all its varieties philosophy has maintained a unity of aim, no matter how much men have argued over specific answers.

To the general reader, a philosophy is best understood as a personally synthesized view of life or as a rationale for the way of life of a culture or an historical period. To the scholar, however, the history of philosophy is a succession of possible answers to particular technical problems involving theories of mind, knowledge, morality, or existence—and perhaps also general theories concerning the nature of beauty, society, or man's historical destiny.

To read philosophers in historical sequence provides a panorama of the development of man's basic values and ideas. As one surveys the ever-changing cultural setting, he sees the continuing function of philosophy as a guide through the problems of life and as a record of the paths

of solution men's minds have followed. The great thinkers loom as signposts, junction points, on the highways
of man's intellectual journeyings. Sometimes pleasant
and smooth, at other points rugged and steep, the road
of great thinkers beckons the amateur as well as the
professional philosopher. Often, too, great thinkers have
the gift of a pleasing, vivid style—for example, Plato,
Voltaire, William James. But those who write more
difficult prose—Aristotle, Kant, or Dewey—cannot be by-
passed on the highroads of philosophy.

The beginning reader can well start on the paths laid
out by the great Greeks—Plato, Aristotle, Epictetus—and
by Romans such as Lucretius and Marcus Aurelius.
Then, with classical humanism behind him, he can follow the harder foothill pathways of Plotinus and of early
Christian thought to reach St. Augustine's confessional
Platonism. Next, even if he sidesteps the technicalities
of Anselm and Abelard, he must survey the world view
of St. Thomas Aquinas—the great medieval synthesis of
Aristotelian and Christian thought which even today is
fundamental for Roman Catholicism. And so on—
through the Renaissance humanism of Bruno and Bacon;
the 17th-century geometrical reasoning of Descartes,
Spinoza, and Leibniz; the emphasis on physics and scientific method in Hobbes and Locke; the 18th-century
rationalism, culminating in Voltaire and Kant; 19th-
century philosophies of history and evolution by Hegel,
Marx, and Spencer; down to the 20th-century emphasis
on practice, process, and logical analysis in Dewey,
Whitehead, and Russell.

You need not, however, retrace twenty-five centuries to
understand the present. You can quite as well begin with
the problems of contemporary thought and trace them
back to their roots in the past. But if you seek philosophic
insight, you cannot rest content with the flat-projection
map of historical lines and connections. Some integrating
and organizing focus is needed to place before the mind's
eye a living landscape, a viable understanding of the
actualities of your lives. Such understanding, as rewarding
as it is rare, comes only from that unusually persistent
questioning and reflection which philosophy demands of
its devotees.

A. General Anthologies and Histories

ANDERSON, PAUL R. 1907– and MAX FISCH 1900– (eds.) *Philosophy in America from the Puritans to James* (1939). Substantial selections from major writings in their historical setting. *Appleton-Century-Crofts $4.50.*

COMMINS, SAXE 1892?–1958 and ROBERT N. LINSCOTT 1886– (eds.) *The World's Great Thinkers.* Generous selections from all the major speculative, social, political, and scientific philosophers. *Random House 4 vols. $14.95.*

DURANT, WILL 1885– *The Story of Philosophy* (1926). A deservedly popular, selective account of Western thought from Socrates to Dewey. *Simon & Schuster (rev. ed. 1933) $5, PB.*

EDMAN, IRWIN 1896–1954 and HERBERT W. SCHNEIDER 1892– (eds.) *Landmarks for Beginners in Philosophy* (1941). Selections and whole writings ranging from Plato to Bergson, with brief introductions. *Holt $7.50.*

HOFFDING, HARALD 1843–1931 *A History of Modern Philosophy* (1955). Detailed but readable account of men and movements from the Renaissance to late 19th century. *Dov 2 vols.*

LAMPRECHT, STERLING P. 1890– *Our Philosophical Traditions* (1955). Chronological presentation of the major thought of Western civilization arranged to highlight influential traditions. *Appleton-Century-Crofts $5.50.*

LIN YUTANG *The Wisdom of China and India.* Major writings from Hindu, Buddhist, Confucian, and Taoist traditions. See page 77.

WINDELBAND, WILHELM 1848–1915 *A History of Philosophy* (1958). A thorough account of major movements, widely regarded as a classic. *Torch 2 vols.*

B. Ancient and Medieval Thought

The Age of Belief: The Medieval Philosophers (1954). Ed. by Anne Fremantle. Selections from Augustine to Ockham with connecting commentaries and interpretations. *Houghton Mifflin $3, NAL.*

ARISTOTLE *Works.* The most encyclopedic Greek thinker. See page 27.

AUGUSTINE, SAINT *Confessions.* The odyssey of a powerful mind to Christian belief. See page 33.

KIRK, G. S. and J. E. RAVEN *The Presocratic Philosophers* (1957). Scholarly collection, clearly interpreted, of the writing of early cosmologists from Thales to Democritus. *Cambridge Univ. $9.50.*

LUCRETIUS *On the Nature of Things.* A philosophic poem following Epicurus on pleasure and atoms. See page 34.

MARCUS AURELIUS *Meditations.* The Stoic creed of self-possession and brotherhood in a rationally determined world. See page 34.

PLATO *Dialogues.* Perennially provocative conversations revealing Socrates's logical irony and Plato's theory of Ideas. See page 28.

PLOTINUS A.D. 205?–270 *The Enneads.* Plato lives again in this philosophical search for the ineffable One. *Oxford Univ. $3.*

Stoic and Epicurean Philosophers (1940). Ed. by Whitney J. Oates. Complete extant writings, in standard translations, of Epicurus, Lucretius, Epictetus, Marcus Aurelius. *MLG.*

THOMAS AQUINAS, SAINT *Writings.* Synthesis of Aristotelian and Christian thought. See page 43.

C. Modern Thought

The Age of Ideology: Nineteenth Century Philosophers (1956). Ed. by Henry Aiken. Selections, with connecting interpretations, from Kant, Spencer, and others, including Marx's influential "Theses on Feuerbach" (1845). *Houghton Mifflin $3, NAL.*

BERKELEY, GEORGE 1685–1753 *Three Dialogues Between Hylas and Philonous* (1713). Provocative conversations on whether things are really different from ideas. *Lib.*

DESCARTES *Discourse on Method.* How doubt can lead to indubitable truths. See page 60.

English Philosophers from Bacon to Mill. Ed. by E. A. Burtt. Generous selections plus several whole writings. *MLG.*

HEGEL, GEORG 1770–1831 *The Philosophy of History* (1837). Sees the panorama of civilizations as the struggle toward rational freedom or wholeness, a view attacked by Kierkegaard, revised by Marx. *Dov, Lib.*

HOBBES, THOMAS 1588–1679 *The Leviathan* (1651). Defense of state power to end, by compact, the "war of all against all." *Oxford Univ. $2, EvmanNA, Gate, Lib.*

HUME, DAVID 1711–1776 *Enquiry Concerning Human Understanding* (1748). Knowledge of self and causality as based on experience rather than on logical necessity. The view that "awakened" Kant. *Open Court $1.25, Oxford Univ. $2.40, Gate, Lib.*

KANT, IMMANUEL 1724–1804 *Prolegomena to Any Future Metaphysic* (1783). How knowledge is tied to perception, though God, freedom, and immortality may be rationally established through ethics. *Barnes & Noble $2.20, Open Court $1.10, Lib.*

KIERKEGAARD, SOREN 1813–1855 *Fear and Trembling* (1843) and *The Sickness Unto Death* (1849). A father of existentialism vividly examines faith and despair and attacks Hegel's system. *Princeton Univ. 2 vols. $3 ea., Anch.*

LOCKE, JOHN 1632–1704 *Essay Concerning Human Understanding* (1690). A classic of empiricism. Seminal attack on innate ideas, appealing to experience for knowledge of nature. *Oxford Univ. $1.70, Evman-h, Gate.*

MILL, JOHN STUART 1806–1873 *Utilitarianism* (1863) and *On Liberty* (1859). Vivid defenses of the greatest happiness principle as the basis of justice and individual freedom. Both in *EvmanNA;* former in *Lib;* latter in *Macmillan $2.50, Gate, Lib, WoC.*

NIETZSCHE, FRIEDRICH 1844–1900 *Philosophy.* Protagonist of power philosophy and defender of noble individuality against mediocrity. Collection of his writings in *The Portable Nietzsche* (1954), *Vik, Vik-h; Thus Spake Zarathustra* (1883 ff.) alone in *Evman-h, ML.*

PASCAL, BLAISE 1623–1662 *Pensées (Thoughts)* (1670). Reflections of a sensitive mathematician on nature, man, and God. *World $1.75, Evman, Evman-h, ML, SM.*

SCHOPENHAUER, ARTHUR 1788–1860 *Philosophy.* Pessimistic view of the world as ever-struggling Will crystallized in ideas. *Lib, ML, Scrib.*

SPINOZA, BARUCH 1632–1677 *Philosophy.* Mysticism and mathematics blend to view mind and matter as demonstrable attributes of God (Nature). *Dov 2 vols., ModSL, Scrib.*

VOLTAIRE The great 18th-century rationalist. See page 70.

D. Contemporary Thought

The Age of Analysis: Twentieth Century Philosophers (1955). Ed. by Morton White. Selections, with connecting interpretations, from Moore, Croce, Wittgenstein, and others. *Houghton Mifflin $3, NAL.*

AYER, ALFRED J. 1910– *Language, Truth and Logic* (1951). Lucid exposition of logical empiricism, viewing metaphysics as meaningless, ethics as emotive, philosophy as analysis. *Dov.*

BERGSON, HENRI 1859–1941 *Introduction to Metaphysics* (1912). Best preface to Bergson's other writings, memorably explaining how reality can be reached through intuition rather than by the intellect. *Lib.*

CASSIRER, ERNST 1874–1945 *An Essay on Man* (1944). The particular human significance of symbolic forms in religion, art, history, and science. *Anch.*

COHEN, MORRIS R. 1880–1947 *Reason and Nature* (1931, rev. ed. 1953). Readable account of how science and philosophy reveal the rational structure of existence. *Free Press $6.*

Contemporary Philosophy (1954). Ed. by Sterling McMurrin and James Jarrett. Essays and chapters from influential thinkers. *Holt $6.50.*

DEWEY, JOHN 1859–1952 *Art as Experience* (1934). A renowned, influential explanation of how both fine and useful arts are "integral experiences." *Putnam $4.50, Cap.*

————— *Reconstruction in Philosophy* (1920). Trenchant first presentation of the experimental philosophy as a coherent whole. *Bea.*

Existentialism from Dostoevsky to Sartre (1956). Ed. by Walter Kaufmann. Selections and whole writings, several newly translated, from Jaspers, Heidegger, and others who view truth as "subjectivity." *Peter Smith $3.50, Mer.*

JAMES, WILLIAM 1842–1910 *Pragmatism* (1907). Highly influential and delightful interpretation of truth in terms of practical consequences. *Longmans, Green $3.25, Mer.*

LOVEJOY, ARTHUR O. 1873– *The Great Chain of Being* (1948). The William James Lectures, vividly tracing the unit-idea of Being through Western thought. *Harvard Univ. $6.*

PEIRCE, CHARLES S. 1839–1914 *Philosophical Writings* (1955). Ed. by Justus Buchler. Key ideas on logic, evolution, and the cosmos which unlocked new doors in American thought. *Dov.*

RUSSELL, BERTRAND 1872– *Mysticism and Logic* (1917). Sharp, witty, popular essays by a distinguished living philosopher. Contains "A Free Man's Worship" and close analyses of knowledge and causality. *Barnes & Noble $2.75, Anch.*

SANTAYANA, GEORGE 1863–1952 *Writings.* Various books trace the adventures of Mind in a world of Matter. *AA, Anch 2 vols., ML, Torch 2 vols.*

TILLICH, PAUL 1886– *The Courage to Be* (1952). A philosopher-theologian relates courage to historic philosophies, existentialism, despair, and "the God above God." *Yale Univ. $2.80.*

UNAMUNO, MIGUEL DE 1864–1936 *The Tragic Sense of Life in Men and Peoples* (1912). Masterpiece of a Spanish thinker in quest of the saving incertitude to alleviate life's despair. *Peter Smith $3.75, Dow.*

WHITEHEAD, ALFRED NORTH 1861–1947 *Science and the Modern World* (1925). Sweeping, path-breaking, but difficult interpretation of the universe in terms of events or organisms-in-process. *Macmillan $5, NAL.*

Additional Recommended Paperbounds

BERLIN, ISAIAH (ed.) *The Age of Enlightenment: the 18th Century Philosophers. NAL.*

BROAD, C. D. *Five Types of Ethical Theory. Lita.*

DEWEY, JOHN *Experience and Nature. Dov.*

————— *Philosophy of Education. Lita.*

HEINEMANN, F. H. *Existentialism and the Modern Predicament. Torch.*

HUME, DAVID *Dialogues Concerning Natural Religion. Haf.*

_____ *Moral and Political Philosophy. Haf.*

JAMES, WILLIAM *Essays in Pragmatism. Haf.*

_____ *The Will to Believe. Dov.*

KANT, IMMANUEL *Foundations of the Metaphysics of Morals* and *What Is Enlightenment? Lib.*

_____ *Perpetual Peace. Lib.*

LANGER, SUSANNE K. *Philosophy in a New Key. NAL.*

LEWIS, C. I. *Mind and the World Order. Dov.*

MEYERHOFF, HANS (ed.) *Philosophy of History in Our Time. Anch.*

MILL, J. S. *Nature and Utility of Religion. Lib.*

MILLER, PERRY (ed.) *American Thought. Rine.*

MOORE, G. E. *Philosophical Studies. Lita.*

PETERSON, HOUSTON (ed.) *Essays in Philosophy. PB.*

ROYCE, JOSIAH *Religious Aspect of Philosophy. Torch.*

RUSSELL, BERTRAND *Analysis of Matter. Dov.*

_____ *Problems of Philosophy. GB.*

SANTAYANA, GEORGE *Scepticism and Animal Faith. Dov.*

SUZUKI, D. T. *Zen Buddhism. Anch.*

WHITEHEAD, A. N. *The Concept of Nature. AA.*

_____ *Modes of Thought. Cap.*

17. Religion

C. HUGH HOLMAN, University of North Carolina

In one sense all learning is a record of man's quest for meaning. Religion is the specific form of learning that states the question in spiritual terms: "What is man's spirit? His individual worth? His goal? Unto what far reaches does his imagination carry him? How can he express the perceptive flashes by which in certain moments the universe around him seems ordered?" Religion emphasizes individual and personal values, the nonphysical and immeasurable qualities of man, life, and God.

Nearly every religion exists in three forms: its basic scriptures, wherein are expressed, often in poetic or narrative forms, the fundamental perceptions on which it rests; its theology, the conceptualized statements of its beliefs and dogma; and its church, the formal institution which has been created by this belief.

The sacred scriptures, like all great literature, defy effective paraphrase. Fortunately the major documents of the world's religions are available to us in good or even excellent English translations, and reading them is not only an intellectual experience, but also an experience that quickens the spirit and the imagination. For most of us the greatest of these documents is the King James Version of the Holy Bible, one of the literary masterworks of our language; other versions may be more clear or more accurate, but they lack the poetry of the King James Version. The low-priced Mentor Religious Classics series has first-rate translations of some of the leading Oriental scriptures—Buddha, *Bhagavad-Gita,* Lao-tzu, the Koran. Frazer's *The Golden Bough* is a valuable guide to primitive religions.

Theology is a highly specialized study, but a meaningful view of the major formulations of the Christian faith can be gained from two compilations of theological writings in the Modern Library Giant series, *The Wisdom of Catholicism* and *Great Voices of the Reformation*.

Almost all organized churches publish denominational handbooks. It is well for us to have the acquaintance with the dogma and structure of our particular church which can be gained from such books. Leo Rosten's *A Guide to the Religions of America* gives a general picture of the variety of religious organization and life in the United States.

A. The Basic Scriptures

The Holy Bible (800 B.C.–A.D. 300). The Sacred Scriptures of Israel and Christendom. *The Apocrypha* contains religious writings similar to the books of the Old and New Testaments but not universally accepted as authentic. The most famous of the English translations is the King James Version (1611), rich in literary and religious associations for English-speaking people and a monument of the English language (available in numerous editions from many publishers). The recent American Revised Standard Version (1946–52) is careful, scholarly, clear, but lacks the literary excellence of the King James Version (*Nelson*). The Ronald Knox translation is the scholarly and readable version favored today by most Roman Catholics (*Sheed & Ward*).
The Bible Designed to Be Read as Living Literature (1926), edited by Ernest Sutherland Bates, is a handsomely printed modern arrangement of the King James text, with some omissions. *Simon & Schuster $7.50.*
The Modern Reader's Bible (1907), edited by Richard G. Moulton. Although old, this volume, because of the wealth of its notes and comments, remains the most useful single book for the examination of the Bible as literature. *Macmillan $7.50.*

Bhagavad-Gita. The epic of the Hindu faith. See page 26.

BUDDHA 563–483 B.C. *The Teachings of the Compassionate Buddha.* An anthology of material from the basic texts of Buddhism, with introduction and notes by E. A. Burtt. *NAL.*

BULFINCH *Mythology*. A convenient handbook. See page 28.

CONFUCIUS *Analects*. Pivotal Chinese document. See page 78.

FRAZER *The Golden Bough*. Primitive religions. See page 29.

GRAVES *The Greek Myths*. Greek gods and heroes assembled. See page 29.

HAMILTON *Mythology*. Classic myths in brief. See page 29.

LAO-TZU *Way of Life*. Basic document of Taoism. See page 79.

LIN YUTANG *The Wisdom of China and India*. See page 77.

MOHAMMED *Koran*. The sacred book of Islam. See page 76.

B. Writings of the Great Theologians

AUGUSTINE, SAINT *The City of God.* Christian study of history. See page 33.

_____ *Confessions.* Conversion of the greatest Church Father. See page 33.

FOSDICK, HARRY EMERSON 1878– (ed.) *Great Voices of the Reformation.* The major documents in the Protestant Reformation. *MLG.*

FRANCIS OF ASSISI, SAINT *The Little Flowers.* See page 41.

PEGIS, ANTON C. 1905– (ed.) *The Wisdom of Catholicism* (1949). The best writings of the Church Fathers and of others in the Catholic Church. *MLG.*

Sayings of the Fathers (rev. ed. 1945). Ed. by J. H. Hertz. A manual for students of the Jewish Law (Torah), drawn from the Talmud and Midrash. *Behrman $1.50.*

THOMAS A KEMPIS *The Imitation of Christ.* The greatest of Christian inspirational books. See page 42.

THOMAS AQUINAS, SAINT *Writings.* The major works of the greatest medieval theologian. See page 43.

C. Books on Religion and the Churches

BAINTON, ROLAND H. 1894– *The Church of Our Fathers* (1941). An elementary and exceedingly readable general history of the Christian Church. *Scribner $3.95.*

_____ *Here I Stand* (1950). A biography of Martin Luther, perhaps the greatest figure of the Protestant Reformation. *NAL.*

BRUNINI, JOHN GILLAND 1899– *Whereon to Stand* (1946). Objective, informative handbook for non-Catholics about the Roman Catholic Church and its doctrines. *Harper o.p.*

BURROWS, MILLAR 1889– *The Dead Sea Scrolls* (1955). The most detailed and scholarly account of the discovery and contents of the Dead Sea Scrolls, recently found manuscripts which are profoundly affecting Biblical studies. *Viking $6.50.* See page 76 for Edmund Wilson's book on the same subject.

CHASE, MARY ELLEN 1887– *The Bible and the Common Reader* (1944). An elementary, inspiring introduction to the Bible as literature, with emphasis on the Old Testament. *Macmillan $4.95.*

FOSDICK, HARRY EMERSON 1878– *The Man from Nazareth* (1949). A careful and fascinating study of the known facts about Jesus in the light of contemporary scholarship. *Harper $3.*

GUILLAUME *Islam.* Mohammedanism explained. See page 76.

HARRISON *Prolegomena to the Study of Greek Religion.* Ancient Greek religions. See page 29.

HILL, CAROLINE MILES 1866– (ed.) *The World's Great Religious Poetry* (1938). An extensive anthology of the poetic expression of man's religious thought, feeling, and experience. *Macmillan $4.95.*

HUMPHREYS *Buddhism.* Summary of its various teachings. See page 77.

JAMES, WILLIAM 1842–1910 *Varieties of Religious Experience* (1902). An historically great and still impressive psychological and pragmatic inquiry into the nature of the religious experience. *ML, NAL.*

JURJI, E. J. 1907– (ed.) *The Great Religions of the Modern World* (1946). Ten authorities explain simply and objectively the ten great living religions. *Princeton Univ. $4.50.*

LATOURETTE, KENNETH S. 1884– *A History of Christianity* (1953). A solid account of the birth of Christianity and of its influence on Western civilization. *Harper $9.50.*

LIU, WU-CHI 1907– *A Short History of Confucian Philosophy* (1955). A record, for the general reader, of the philosophy that has shaped Chinese religion and life for 25 centuries. *Pen.*

MARTINDALE, CYRIL C. 1879– *The Faith of the Roman Church* (1951). A lucid statement of Catholic beliefs. *Sheed & Ward $2.50.*

NICHOLS, JAMES HASTINGS 1915– *Primer for Protestants* (1949). Clear exposition of the basic beliefs of Protestants. *Association Press $1.50, Refl (abr.).*

NOSS, JOHN B. *Man's Religions* (rev. ed. 1956). The best text on the world's religions and their development. *Macmillan $5.90.*

ROSTEN, LEO C. 1908– (ed.) *Religions of America* (1955). A collection of accurate factual statements about the major religious organizations of America. *Simon & Schuster $3.50 (cloth) and $1 (paper).*

SPERRY, WILLARD L. 1882– *Religion in America* (1946). A graceful, comprehensive, stimulating account. *Cambridge Univ. $3.50.*

STEINBERG, MILTON 1903– *Basic Judaism* (1947). A nontechnical presentation of the beliefs, ideals, and practices of Jews. *HarB.*

SWEET, WILLIAM WARREN 1881– *The Story of Religion in America* (1939). The religious sects in our national life in relation to social, economic, and political trends. *Harper $3.75.*

UNDERHILL, EVELYN 1875–1941 *Mysticism* (1911). The classic study of the history and manifestation of mysticism, with material drawn from St. Teresa of Avila, Meister Eckhart, St. John of the Cross, and William Blake. *Mer.*

WATTS, HAROLD H. 1906– *The Modern Reader's Guide to the Bible* (rev. ed. 1958). The best introduction to the Bible as literature—richly detailed and lucid. *Harper $4.50.*

18. History

DANIEL H. THOMAS, *University of Rhode Island*

"Not to know what happened before one was born is always to be a child." So wrote Cicero, who believed that history was the "teacher of life" and the "torch of truth." Lord Chesterfield disagreed, charging that "history is only a confused heap of facts." Anatole France said that when history contains no lies, "it is always tedious"; and Napoleon remarked cynically, "We learn from history only that men do not learn from history." Even professional historians have two definitions, some defining history as "that which has happened," and others as "an account of that which has happened."

Nevertheless, a well-written story about the past is a drama to be enjoyed. It has quantities of conflict and suspense, of heroes and villains, of disasters and triumphs. Many a piece of historical writing reads as excitingly as any novel, is usually a more penetrating interpretation of life, and has the virtue of being factually true. The cultural values in the reading of history are obvious, for it surveys the natural sciences, the social sciences, and the humanities—in fact, everything which we think has happened. All can agree with Judge Arthur T. Vanderbilt that it "gives a third dimension to subjects which would otherwise be flat"—particularly to economics, politics, geography, anthropology, and sociology.

At one time, mathematics and logic were considered the subjects most useful in developing mental discipline; now it is realized that many subjects can serve that purpose. For instance, historians are continuously seeking the "why," the logical method of presenting a complicated narrative, the significant results, and any analogies that may be found.

Furthermore, sound history is a foe of careless decisions and of snap judgments, for all careful historians insist on collecting sufficient evidence before reaching conclusions. History makes plain that members of a special race or votaries of a particular religion have never had a monopoly on civilization; neither has any nation, or social class, or other limited group. Hence a knowledge of history is an antidote for sectionalism, narrow nationalism, and racism, leading one instead to realize the eternal interdependence of all peoples.

History's ability to create a "better-informed citizenry" is sometimes exaggerated; yet what are historical records if not the laboratory data of past experiences? The price of actual experience may be high, but the same wisdom may be secured relatively painlessly if one will only turn to the record of the past. Such knowledge can give the intelligent reader a balance, a more considered judgment, even a happier existence, because it can make him feel more at home in his own times.

Some prefer to read history backward, beginning with our own country in our own time; they may wish to start with such books as Truman's *Memoirs* or Eisenhower's *Crusade in Europe*. As Montaigne has said, most travelers see in a foreign country only what they take with them from their own; the same may be true about the time-traveling involved in reading history. Any of the lively one-volume surveys of the American saga could follow— perhaps Adams's *Epic of America*. No one should overlook *The Chronicles of America* volumes, which are convenient in size, found in most libraries, and offer in about 200 pages each readable, even entertaining, accounts of each stage of our past.

Others may prefer a geographical approach, perhaps beginning by crossing the border via Strode's *Timeless Mexico* or the earlier and very colorful *Conquest of Mexico* by Prescott.

For the major countries of Europe, distinguished national histories include Green's *Short History of the English People* and Trevelyan's more modern *History of England;* Romier's *History of France;* and Henderson's *Short History of Germany*. For China, books by Latourette and the Lattimores give the rich record of Oriental history.

Still another approach is by historical periods, starting perhaps with Wells's *Outline of History*. Coon's *Story of Man* describes the Old and New Stone Ages, while Breasted's *Conquest of Civilization* presents a superior introduction to Egyptian and other early cultures. George B. Adams has written brilliantly in *Civilization During the Middle Ages* and Ferdinand Schevill concisely in *History of Europe from the Reformation to the Present Day*.

After you have read substantial portions of the history of the ancients, the moderns, and those between, and have come to feel the need for a synthesis, then you are ready to examine the works of the historian-philosophers. Gibbon's *Decline and Fall of the Roman Empire* is a work of majestic sweep, written in a style full of conscious artifice and almost Roman rhetoric, but fascinating for the feel it gives of the long panorama of history between the downfall of Rome and the collapse a thousand years later of the Eastern Roman Empire. Scholars are much less in accord about the merits of two other interpretative sweeps. Spengler's gloomy *Decline of the West* is stimulating reading, but his theory of the cyclic rise and fall of civilizations is questionable. Toynbee's *Study of History* compares various civilizations and their leaders and concludes that our own appears to be best; therefore he is generally recognized as a more comfortable guide than Spengler.

Today, when almost every daily headline records new history, it is particularly important that the educated minority which must lead our nation be not ignorant of the wisdom of the past.

Many important historical books, too numerous for cross reference here, are listed in other chapters of this book. See especially HISTORICAL AND REGIONAL CULTURES (GREECE through LATIN AMERICA). For more recent history, see POLITICS, ECONOMICS, GEOGRAPHY AND TRAVEL, ANTHROPOLOGY AND SOCIOLOGY, and PHYSICAL SCIENCES. For dates and other reference data, extremely useful volumes include *An Encyclopedia of World History*, edited by W. L. Langer; *Dictionary of American History*, edited by J. T. Adams; and *Encyclopedia of American History*, edited by R. B. Morris.

A. General

Special histories listed in other sectons of GOOD READING include:
CRAVEN *The Story of Painting*, DAMPIER *A Shorter History of Science*, GARDNER *Art Through the Ages*, MACAULAY *History of England*, MOULTON *Autobiography of Science*.

The Berkshire Studies in European History. A series of popularizations by distinguished historians. Extremely helpful for those who wish to supplement brief surveys and texts by reading 100–150 page monographs such as those by RICHARD A. NEWHALL *The Crusades*, WALLACE K. FERGUSON *The Renaissance*, or GEORGE L. MOSSE *The Reformation*. Twenty volumes now in print. *Holt $1.40 each (paper).*

BRINTON, CLARENCE CRANE 1898– *Ideas and Men: The Story of Western Thought* (1950). A stimulating and lucid review of many questions concerning ethics, religion, politics, and science, with some of the ideas men have supplied as answers. *Prentice-Hall $6.50.*

———— *et al. A History of Civilization* (1955–6). A general text on Western civilization which is superior in style and content. *Prentice-Hall 2 vols. $7.25 & $7.50.*

CLOUGH, SHEPARD B. 1901– and CHARLES W. COLE 1906– *Economic History of Europe* (3rd ed. 1952). A survey clarifying some rather complicated aspects of history since the 7th century. *Heath $7.25.*

CREASY, EDWARD S. 1812–1878 *Fifteen Decisive Battles of the World* (1851). Popular treatment of battles from Marathon to Waterloo. *Evman-h.*

CURTIS, EDMUND 1881–1943 *A History of Ireland* (6th rev. ed. 1950). A balanced survey from the earliest times to the establishment of the Irish Free State in 1922. *Barnes & Noble $4.50.*

GOODSELL, WILLYSTINE 1870– *A History of Marriage and the Family* (1934). Revised edition of one of the best historical studies of the family. *Macmillan o.p.*

GRAS, NORMAN S. B. 1884– *A History of Agriculture in Europe and America* (1925). Important developments in rural life and their relationship to national economy. *Appleton-Century-Crofts o.p.*

GREEN, JOHN R. 1837–1883 *A Short History of the English People* (1874). The political and social advance of the people, rather than of kings or conquests. *Evman-h 2 vols.*

GUNTHER, JOHN 1901– *Inside Africa* (1955). Reviews the past, emphasizes the present, and considers the potentialities of various areas and states. *Harper $6.50.*

HENDERSON, ERNEST F. 1861–1928 *A Short History of Germany* (1916). Still the standard history of moderate length about Germany to World War I. *Macmillan o.p.*

HITTI, PHILIP KHURI 1886– *The Arabs: A Short History* (1949). Compact history of the Arabic-speaking peoples from earliest times to the Ottoman conquest. *Gate.*

JARVIS, HENRY WOOD *Pharaoh to Farouk* (1955). A successful attempt to review 5,000 years of Egypt's history in 300 pages. *Macmillan $4.50.*

KIRK *A Short History of the Middle East from the Rise of Islam to Modern Times.* See page 75.

LATOURETTE, KENNETH S. 1884– *The Chinese: Their History and Culture.* See page 193.

_____ *A History of Christianity.* A definitive survey. See page 193.

_____ *History of Japan* (rev. ed. 1947). A condensed but dependable review by an American Orientalist. *Macmillan $5.*

LATTIMORE, OWEN 1900– and ELEANOR LATTIMORE 1895– *China: A Short History* (rev. 1947). Compact and readable account, from preliterary times to the present. *Norton o.p.*

MAHAN, ALFRED T. 1840–1914 *The Influence of Sea Power upon History, 1660–1783* (1890). An American admiral sustains his thesis that sea power has frequently been the decisive factor in international relations. *Little, Brown $7.50.*

MOTLEY *The Rise of the Dutch Republic.* A brilliant history of The Netherlands, 1555–1584. See page 50.

MULLER, HERBERT J. 1905– *The Uses of the Past; Profiles of Former Societies* (1952). Although a professor of English, the author interprets history much more like the great majority of historians than do Spengler and Toynbee—and much more briefly. *GB, NAL.*

NAMIER, LEWIS B. 1888– *Avenues of History* (1952). Essays and reviews by a leading English historian; the first one, "History," has been called the best essay on the nature and use of that subject. *Macmillan $3.*

ROBB *The Harper History of Painting.* Western painting since the Old Stone Age. See page 178.

ROBINSON, JAMES HARVEY 1863–1936 *The Mind in the Making: The Relation of Intelligence to Social Reform* (1921). "Study of how man has come to be as he is and to believe as he does." *Harp.*

ROMIER, LUCIEN 1885–1944 *History of France* (Tr. and completed for the period after 1789 by A. L. Rowse 1903–) (1953). Particularly good in reflecting the role of individuals. *St. Martins $6.50.*

SANSOM, GEORGE B. 1883– *Japan: A Short Cultural History* (rev. 1943). Brilliantly written history of Japan from prehistoric times to 1868, by a former British envoy. *Appleton-Century-Crofts $5.*

SPENGLER, OSWALD 1880–1936 *Decline of the West* (1918–22). Detailed attempt to demonstrate that cultures follow a cycle of growth and decline and that Western culture has passed its peak. Most historians are skeptical of his mystical conclusions. *Knopf 2 vols. $16.50.*

SULLIVAN, J. W. N. 1886–1937 *The Limitations of Science* (1933). An exceptionally clear interpretation of developments in science through the ages, written for the layman. *NAL.*

TOYNBEE, ARNOLD J. 1889– *A Study of History* (1934–54). An inquiry into the causes of the rise and decline of civilizations. Unconventional and philosophical in approach and treatment. *Oxford Univ. 10 vols. $75.* A 2-volume abridgment edited by D. C. SOMERVELL, *A Study of History* (1947, 1957), preserves the method, atmosphere, and texture of the original. *Oxford Univ. $6 & $5.*

TREVELYAN, GEORGE M. 1876– *History of England* (3rd ed. 1945). Admired for excellent scholarship and style. *Longmans, Green $5.*

VALENTIN, VEIT 1885–1947 *The German People: Their History and Civilization from the Holy Roman Empire to the Third Reich* (1946). Comprehensive account, especially good on the 19th century. *Knopf o.p.*

WELLS, H. G. 1866–1946 *The Outline of History* (rev. ed. 1956). Heroic, successful work; a brief "plain history of life and mankind." *Gar.*

The World of History (1954). Ed. by C. C. Brinton *et al.* An approach to history that complements the ways suggested in the introductory essay—by sampling thirty historians at their best on topics ranging from the ancient Egyptians to the better comprehension of the Soviet rulers. *NAL.*

B. Ancient and Medieval

Among the books on ancient history recommended in earlier sections are: *The Bible,* BURY *History of Greece,* CAESAR *Commentaries,* DURANT *Caesar and Christ, Life of Greece, Age of Faith,* GIBBON *Decline and Fall of the Roman Empire,* HERODOTUS *History,* PLUTARCH *Lives,* THUCYDIDES *Peloponnesian Wars.*
  Medieval and early Renaissance titles listed elsewhere include: ADAMS *Mont-Saint-Michel and Chartres,* BURCKHARDT *Civilization of the Renaissance in Italy,* DAVIS *Life on a Medieval Barony,* FROISSART *Chronicles,* LAMB *The Crusades* and *Genghis Khan,* MEREJKOWSKI *Romance of Leonardo da Vinci,* POLO *Travels,* YOUNG *The Medici.*

BREASTED, JAMES H. 1865–1935 *The Conquest of Civilization* (rev. ed. 1938). Ancient history lucidly summarized in a single volume by an eminent Egyptologist. *Harper $6.*

CHIERA, EDWARD 1885–1933 and GEORGE G. CAMERON 1905– *They Wrote on Clay* (1938). Describes life in ancient Babylonia and draws some astonishing parallels with modern times. *Univ. of Chicago $4.50, Phoen.*

CHILDE, V. GORDON 1892–1957 *Man Makes Himself* (1936). Probably the best treatment of the stages of primitive man as he settled into communities. *NAL.*

_____ *What Happened in History* (1942). Supplements the above work; traces man's development in crafts, economics, religion, art, and science from paleolithic times to the Roman Empire. *Pen.*

COON, CARLETON S. 1904- *Story of Man: From the First Human to Primitive Culture and Beyond* (1954). A stimulating description by an anthropologist of early man and his society and one of the best reviews of the old and the new stone ages. *Knopf $7.50.*

HAMILTON *The Greek Way.* Authors and their influence. See page 29.

_____ *The Roman Way.* Richly informative. See page 36.

KITTO *The Greeks.* Social analysis. See page 29.

PAINTER, SIDNEY 1902- *A History of the Middle Ages, 284–1500* (1953). Witty and authoritative, with an emphasis on political history of northwestern Europe. *Knopf $6.*

PIRENNE *Economic and Social History of Medieval Europe.* Sound in scholarship, brilliant in style, realistic in presentation. See page 44.

POWER *Medieval People.* Typical people go about their day's work. See page 44.

SCHEVILL, FERDINAND 1868–1954 *The Medici* (1949). The political and cultural story of the Medici's control of Florence, the greatest Renaissance city at its height. *Harcourt, Brace o.p.*

URE, PERCY N. 1879–1950 *Justinian and His Age* (1951). Life and times of the Byzantine ruler (527–565) as recorded by his contemporaries. *Pen.*

C. Modern, 1500-1900, Other Than American

See also these volumes described in other sections: CARLYLE *The French Revolution,* CORVO *History of the Borgias,* PRESCOTT *Conquest of Mexico* and *Conquest of Peru,* PEPYS *Diary.*

ALBRECHT-CARRIE, RENE 1904- *A Diplomatic History of Europe Since the Congress of Vienna* (1958). A superior account of the international relations of European states from 1814 to 1956. *Harper $7.50.*

ALLEN, HARRY C. *Great Britain and the United States: A History of Anglo-American Relations, 1783–1952* (1955). An Oxford University professor reviews our relations with the British. *St Martin's $10.*

BRUUN, GEOFFREY 1898- *Europe and the French Imperium, 1799–1814* (1938). The rule of Napoleon Bonaparte. Part of *The Rise of Modern Europe* series. *Harper $4.50.*

BRYANT, ARTHUR 1899- *Age of Elegance: England 1812–1822* (1951). Life in England during and immediately following the French Revolution and the Napoleonic era. *Harper $5.*

CHAPMAN *Colonial Hispanic America* and *Republican Hispanic America.* See page 84.

CREIGHTON, DONALD G. 1902– *Dominion of the North: A History of Canada* (1958). Considered superior to all other short histories of Canada. *Houghton Mifflin $7.50.*

FLORINSKY, MICHAEL T. 1894– *Russia: A History and an Interpretation* (1953). A well-balanced history. *Macmillan* 2 vols. *$15.*

GILMORE, MYRON P. 1910– *The World of Humanism, 1453–1517* (1952). The second volume in *The Rise of Modern Europe* series, analyzing the prominent factors of the era. *Harper $4.50.*

GRIMM, HAROLD J. 1901– *The Reformation Era, 1500–1650* (1954). A balanced account of the Protestant Reformation and the Catholic Counter Reformation. *Macmillan $6.50.*

HECHT, J. JEAN 1915– *The Domestic Servant Class in Eighteenth Century England* (1956). It has usually been the ones who were served who have occupied the center of the stage of history, but in this volume it is those who served. *Humanities Press $5.*

IRVINE, WILLIAM 1906– *Apes, Angels and Victorians: The Story of Darwin, Huxley and Evolution* (1955). Summarizes the controversy over the theory of evolution. *McGraw-Hill $5.*

LUCAS *The Renaissance and the Reformation.* See page 49.

MATHIEZ, ALBERT 1874–1932 *After Robespierre, The Thermidorean Reaction* (1931). An example of a superior French historian's treatment of the French Revolution in 1794–95. *Knopf o.p.*

MATTINGLY *The Armada.* Brilliantly delineated story of the Spanish invasion of English waters. See page 50.

PALMER, ROBERT R. 1909– *Twelve Who Ruled: The Committee of Public Safety during the Terror* (1941). A volume which captures much of the atmosphere of the most radical period of the French Revolution. *Princeton Univ. o.p.*

PENROSE, BOIES 1902– *Travel and Discovery in the Renaissance, 1420–1620* (1952). A lucid account of explorations from the time of Prince Henry the Navigator to the first settlements on our shores. Good reading for "armchair navigators." *Harvard Univ. $5.50.*

POSTGATE, RAYMOND 1896– *Story of a Year: 1848* (1956). The memorable year of revolutions shown by vignettes of plotters and barricades, officials and council chambers, Chartists and petitions—and also maids and butlers at play. *Oxford Univ. $4.50.*

RANKE, LEOPOLD VON 1795–1886 *Memoirs of the House of Brandenburg* and *History of Prussia during the Seventeenth and Eighteenth Centuries* (1849). Two of the 54 volumes by the eminent German historian who did the most to set the pattern for training professional historians to write the past "as it actually was." *O.p.*

The Rise of Modern Europe. A series of 13 reliable interpretations by specialists in various eras; two volumes cover the 1250–1517 period, nine carry the story from 1610 to 1832, and two from 1852 to 1900. Another example (see BRUUN and GILMORE above) is FREDERICK L. NUSSBAUM, *The Triumph of Science and Reason, 1660–1685* (1953). *Harper $4.50 ea.*

STRODE, HUDSON 1893– *Timeless Mexico* (1944). An absorbing history of Mexico since the conquest by Cortez. *Harcourt, Brace $4.75.*

TAWNEY *Religion and the Rise of Capitalism.* See page 63.

TARLE, EVGENII V. 1874– *Napoleon's Invasion of Russia, 1812* (1942). Makes use of numerous eyewitness accounts and is particularly clear in its explanation of the psychological attitude of the Russian defenders. *Oxford Univ. o.p.*

THOMPSON, JAMES M. 1878–1956 *The French Revolution* (5th ed. 1955). An English scholar's brilliant account of the Revolution from 1789 to 1794. *Oxford Univ. $6.*

WILSON, EDMUND 1895– *To the Finland Station* (1940). The development of European radicalism from the French Revolution through the life and work of Karl Marx to the outbreak of the Russian Revolution. *Anch.*

D. Contemporary (Since 1900), Other Than American

BELOV, FEDOR *The History of a Soviet Collective Farm* (1955). A reliable account of the way a kolkhoz operates and its relation to the officials, by a former chairman of a collective farm. *Praeger $5.50.*

BRENNER *The Wind That Swept Mexico.* Compact history of the Mexican revolution. See page 84.

BRINTON, CLARENCE CRANE 1898– *The Temper of Western Europe* (1953). Are Europeans decadent? Is Europe in decline? This observer does not think so, as he analyzes the history of Europe since World War II. *Harvard Univ. $2.50.*

CHURCHILL, SIR WINSTON S. 1874– *The Gathering Storm* (1948), *Their Finest Hour* (1949), *The Grand Alliance* (1950), *The Hinge of Fate* (1950), *Closing the Ring* (1951), *Triumph and Tragedy* (1953). The very wording of the titles is an indication of the forceful style which Sir Winston uses in *The Second World War,* his personal narrative of the dramatic years of the recent war. *Houghton Mifflin $6.50 ea; $32.50 set.*

EISENHOWER, DWIGHT D. 1890– *Crusade in Europe* (1948). The commander's report to the public on his assignment; clear, concise, judicious, and interesting. *Doubleday $3.95. Gar.*

FAY, SIDNEY B. 1876– *Origins of the World War* (2nd ed. rev. 1948). The causes of World War I traced from 1871 to 1914. *Macmillan $7.*

HISTORY 203

FEIS, HERBERT 1893– *Road to Pearl Harbor: The Coming of the War between the United States and Japan* (1950). A documented review of the diplomatic events from 1937 to the outbreak of hostilities. *Princeton Univ. $5.*

FLORINSKY, MICHAEL T. 1894– *Toward an Understanding of the U.S.S.R.: A Study in Government, Politics and Economic Planning* (rev. ed. 1951). A liberal scholar's account of the last two decades of the Russian Empire and of the Soviet era to 1950. *Macmillan $3.50.*

HERSEY, JOHN 1914– *Hiroshima* (1946). What happened when the first atomic bomb fell on a city. A stark but subdued report of interviews with six survivors. *Knopf $3, Ban.*

HOFER, WALTHER 1920– *War Premeditated–1939* (1955). Immediate background of World War II told logically and briefly. *Longmans-Toronto $3.25.*

KOGON, EUGEN 1903– *Theory and Practice of Hell: The German Concentration Camps and the System Behind Them* (1950). A calm, objective description of the Nazi practices and a Christian's six years in Buchenwald. *Farrar, Straus and Cudahy o.p.*

KOHN, HANS 1891– *The Twentieth Century: A Mid-Way Account of the Western World* (rev. ed. 1957). A brief interpretation of the trends, issues, and ideologies, by one whose liberal attachments show. *Macmillan $3.40.*

LIE, TRYGVE H. 1896– *In the Cause of Peace* (1954). The United Nations' first Secretary-General gives an account of the first seven years of that organization. *Macmillan $6.*

SETON-WATSON, HUGH 1916– *From Lenin to Malenkov: The History of World Communism* (1953). A survey and analysis of the successes and failures of the Communist movement in various states. *Praeger $6.*

SHIRER, WILLIAM L. 1904– *Berlin Diary: The Journal of a Foreign Correspondent, 1934–41* (1941). A graphic account of Germany from the year after Hitler came into power until the Nazi war machine had overrun much of northern and western Europe. *Knopf o.p.*

———— *The Challenge of Scandinavia: Norway, Sweden, Denmark and Finland in Our Time* (1955). A recent history (primarily since the start of World War II) and description of conditions in these countries which have such a high level of social and economic well-being. *Little, Brown $5.*

SNYDER, LOUIS L. 1907– (ed.) *Fifty Major Documents of the Twentieth Century* (1955). Includes the Austro-Hungarian ultimatum to Serbia in 1914, the Munich agreement of 1939, the enfranchisement of women in Britain and the United States in 1918–19, the Nuremberg Laws on race, Churchill's "Blood, Toil, Tears and Sweat" address, the secret Yalta agreement, and the Truman Doctrine. *Van Nostrand $1.25 (paper).*

WOLFE, BERTRAM D. 1896– *Three Who Made a Revolution* (1948). A biographical history of the men and the forces that brought on the Russian Revolution, focused on Lenin, Trotsky, and Stalin. *Peter Smith $4, Bea.*

E. United States

ADAMS, JAMES T. 1878–1949 *The Epic of America* (rev. ed. 1933). Stirring pageant of our national spirit and character, stressing "the American dream" of a better life for the common man. *Little, Brown $6.50, Gar.*

ALLEN, FREDERICK L. 1890–1954 *Only Yesterday* (1931). The years following World War I, treating the Teapot Dome scandals and the "flaming youth" period with equal charm and deftness. *Harper $4, Ban.*

BAILEY, THOMAS A. 1902– *A Diplomatic History of the American People* (6th ed. 1958). A popular, authoritative survey. *Appleton-Century-Crofts $7.*

BEARD, CHARLES A. 1874–1948 and MARY BEARD 1876–1958 *Rise of American Civilization* (rev. ed. 1949). An outstanding historical analysis of the factors behind the emergence of modern America. *Macmillan $6.75.*

BISHOP, JAMES A. 1907– *The Day Lincoln Was Shot* (1955). A tense account of the actions of Lincoln's family and of Federal officials on that Friday in 1865. *Harper $3.95, Ban.*

BOWERS, CLAUDE G. 1879–1958 *The Tragic Era* (1929). Dramatic, vigorous account of the decade following the Civil War, sternly critical of those who made the era more tragic than necessary. *Houghton Mifflin $6.*

BURLINGAME, ROGER 1889– *March of the Iron Men* (1938), *Engines of Democracy* (1940) and *Backgrounds of Power* (1949). A social history of the U.S.A., told in terms of the chief inventions and technological developments which have helped shape our destiny. Learned and stimulating. *Scribner $6 ea.*

CARSON, GERALD 1899– *Old Country Store* (1954). An informal, humorous, accurate story of the village general store from the late 1700's to the 1920's. *Oxford Univ. $5.75.*

CATTON, BRUCE 1899– *A Stillness at Appomattox* (1953). A Pulitzer Prize winner's account of the Northern Army of the Potomac's final victories told so that the reader feels he is a participant. *Doubleday $5.* Preceding volumes are *Mr. Lincoln's Army* (1951) and *Glory Road* (1952). *Doubleday $4 & $4.50.*

Chronicles of America (1918–51). Small volumes written by distinguished scholars. Extraordinarily readable, accurate accounts of all phases of our history. *Yale Univ. 56 vols. about $3 ea.*

COMMAGER, HENRY STEELE 1902– (ed.) *America in Perspective: The United States Through Foreign Eyes* (1947). To see ourselves as others have seen us when traveling through our country. *NAL (abr.).*

———— and ALLAN NEVINS 1890– (eds.) *The Heritage of America* (rev. ed. 1949). A source book of firsthand narratives illuminating American history from Leif Ericsson to the A-bomb. *Little, Brown $8.*

CRAVEN, AVERY O. 1886– *The Growth of Southern Nationalism, 1848–1861* (1953). How sectionalism developed in the South, resulting in the Civil War. *Louisiana State Univ. $6.50.*

CURTI, MERLE E. 1897– *The Growth of American Thought* (2nd ed. 1951). A Pulitzer Prize-winning history of American social, intellectual, and scientific thought. *Harper $6.*

DANIELS, JONATHAN 1902– *A Southerner Discovers the South* (1938). An able Southern journalist describes his section's social and economic conditions with rare insight and urbane pen. *Macmillan o.p.*

DE VOTO, BERNARD A. 1897–1955 *The Course of Empire* (1952), *The Year of Decision, 1846* (1943), and *Across the Wide Missouri* (1947). These volumes on the American West have been called the best since Parkman. *Houghton Mifflin $6.50, $6, $10.*

EATON, CLEMENT 1898– *A History of the Southern Confederacy* (1954). An account of how the Southern civilian, soldier, and official felt and acted during the Civil War. *Macmillan $5.75.*

FREEMAN, DOUGLAS S. 1886–1953 *Lee's Lieutenants* (3 vols., 1942–4). The campaigns of the Confederate Army of Northern Virginia; usually compared with Catton's superb treatment of the Union Army of the Potomac. *Scribner $8.25 ea.*

GRANT, ULYSSES S. 1822–1885 *Personal Memoirs of U. S. Grant* (1885–6). A straightforward account of his recollections. *World o.p.*

HACKER, LOUIS M. 1899– *The Triumph of American Capitalism* (1947). American history to 1900, in terms of economic and political forces that have molded our culture. *Columbia Univ. $4.50.*

HEFFNER, RICHARD D. (ed.) *A Documentary History of the United States* (1952). Twenty-five basic American "documents," each with an introduction and some interpretation. Includes not only such standard selections as Washington's Farewell Address and F. D. Roosevelt's Four Freedoms, but also Turner's explanation of the influence of the frontier, Hoover's views on rugged individualism, and the Marshall Plan. *Indiana Univ. $3, NAL.*

History of American Life Series (1927–48). Economic, social, and cultural life in the United States. Examples are GREEN *Revolutionary Generation, 1763–1790;* COLE *Irrepressible Conflict, 1850–1865;* NEVINS *Emergence of Modern America, 1865–1878;* and WECTER *Age of the Great Depression, 1929–1941. Macmillan 13 vols. $6.75 ea.*

HOFSTADTER, RICHARD 1916– *The American Political Tradition and the Men Who Made It* (1948). A dozen biographical essays interpret and review the American political tradition from the Founding Fathers through F.D.R. *Knopf $5, Vik.*

HOOVER, HERBERT C. 1874– *Memoirs* (1951–52). One of the most controversial figures in American history recounts his terms as cabinet member and President. *Macmillan 3 vols. $5 ea.*

JOHNSON, GERALD W. 1890– *Incredible Tale: The Odyssey of the Average American in the Last Half-Century* (1950). An informal and witty history about the people and the events which have influenced John Q. Public, about his own influence, and even about his probable future. *Harper o.p.*

MUMFORD, LEWIS 1895– *The Brown Decades: A Study of the Arts in America, 1865–1895* (1931). A study and criticism of three decades of American art—primarily architecture, city planning, landscaping, and painting. *Dov.*

NIEBUHR, REINHOLD 1892– *The Irony of American History* (1952). Survey of American history from the point of view of Christian ethics. *Scribner $3.50.*

PERKINS, DEXTER 1889– *History of the Monroe Doctrine* (rev. ed. 1955). The definitive account of this famous policy. *Little, Brown $5.*

PYLE, ERNIE 1900–1945 *Brave Men* (1944). The very "human" war correspondent (beloved by G.I.'s and readers alike) describes what he saw and heard from the landing in Sicily to the liberation of Paris in World War II. *Grosset $1.98.*

The Rivers of America. Each volume of this popular series gives the history and folklore of the area through which a river flows, and the collection now consists of 46 rivers—from the Allegheny to the Yazoo. Forty-three authors have contributed. *Rinehart $3.50–$5 ea.*

SCHLESINGER, ARTHUR M. 1888– *Paths to the Present* (1949). Entertaining and enlightening essays on 13 characteristics of Americans—why we are "joiners," the role of food in American life, our spirit in wartime, cycles of liberalism and conservatism, etc. *Macmillan $5.25.*

SCHLESINGER, ARTHUR M., JR. 1917– *The Age of Jackson* (1945). Provocative restudy of the era of Jacksonian democracy by one of our ablest historians. *Little, Brown $6.50, NAL (abr.).*

SHERWOOD, ROBERT E. 1896–1955 *Roosevelt and Hopkins: An Intimate History* (rev. ed. 1950). Superlative portrayal of crucial years by an intimate friend of both men. *Harper $8.50, Ban 2 vols.*

TURNER, FREDERICK J. 1861–1932 *The Frontier in American History* (1920). An historically important essay analyzing the characteristics of the shifting frontier and developing the theory that the frontier gave Americans certain distinctive national traits. *Holt $4.75.*

VAN DOREN, CARL 1885–1950 *Secret History of the American Revolution* (1941). A book club selection and a best seller; much attention is given to conspiracies, particularly that of Benedict Arnold. *Viking $6.*

WILEY, BELL I. 1906– *The Life of Billy Yank* (1952). The common soldier of the Union armies. His counterpart in the Confederate service is found in *The Life of Johnny Reb* (1943). *Bobbs-Merrill $6 ea.*

———— *The Road to Appomattox* (1956). A superior analysis of why the South was defeated. *Bobbs-Merrill $6.*

Additional Recommended Paperbounds

ALBRIGHT, W. F. *The Archaeology of Palestine. Pen.*

ANGLE, PAUL (ed.) *The Lincoln Reader. PB.*

ARON, RAYMOND *The Century of Total War. Bea.*

ASHLEY, MAURICE *England in the 17th Century. Pen.*

ATIYAH, EDWARD *The Arabs. Pen.*

BAINTON, ROLAND H. *The Reformation of the Sixteenth Century. Bea.*

BARROW, R. H. *The Romans. Pen.*

BINDOFF, S. T. *Tudor England. Pen.*

BREBNER, JOHN B. *The Explorers of North America, 1492–1806. Anch.*

BURCKHARDT, JAKOB *The Age of Constantine the Great. Anch.*

BURKE, EDMUND *Reflections on the Revolution in France. LLA-Lib.*

COLE, SONIA *The Prehistory of East Africa. Pen.*

COOPER, JAMES FENIMORE *The American Democrat. Vin.*

COULTON, G. G. *Medieval Panorama. Mer.*

COWELL, F. R. *Cicero and the Roman Republic. Pen.*

DAWSON, CHRISTOPHER *The Making of Europe. Mer.*

DE BURGH, W. G. *The Legacy of the Ancient World. Pen 2 vols.*

FISCHER, LOUIS *Gandhi: His Life and Message for the World. NAL.*

GASTER, THEODOR (trans.) *The Dead Sea Scriptures. Anch.*

GEORGE, M. DOROTHY *England in Transition. Pen.*

GHIRSHMAN, R. *Iran. Pen.*

GIBBON, EDWARD *Portable Gibbon* (ed. D. A. Saunders). *Vik.*

GOLDMAN, ERIC F. *Rendezvous with Destiny. Vin.*

GUILLAUME, ALFRED *Islam. Pen.*

HADAS, MOSES (ed.) *A History of Rome, from Its Origins to 529 A.D., as Told by the Roman Historians. Anch.*

HEGEL, G. W. F. *Philosophy of History. Dov.*

HOOK, SIDNEY *The Hero in History. Bea.*

JAMESON, FRANKLIN *The American Revolution Considered as a Social Movement. Bea.*

KENNAN, GEORGE *American Diplomacy 1900–1950. NAL.*

LATOURETTE, K. S. *A History of Modern China. Pen.*

MORPURGO, J. E. and R. B. NYE *A History of the United States. Pen 2 vols.*

MYERS, A. R. *England in the Late Middle Ages.* Pen.

ORWELL, GEORGE *Homage to Catalonia.* Bea.

PADOVER, SAUL K. *The Living U. S. Constitution.* NAL.

PARES, BERNARD *Russia.* NAL.

PARKMAN, FRANCIS *The Oregon Trail.* NAL.

———— *The Discovery of the Great West: La Salle.* Rine.

PATMAN, WRIGHT *Our American Government.* Ban.

PIGGOTT, STUART *Prehistoric India.* Pen.

PLUMB, J. H. *England in the 18th Century.* Pen.

RICHMOND, IAN *Roman Britain.* Pen.

ROBINSON, C. E. *Hellas: A Short History of Ancient Greece.* Bea.

ROSTOW, W. W. *et al. The Dynamics of Soviet Society.* NAL.

STENTON, DORIS M. *English Society in the Early Middle Ages.* Pen.

THOMSON, DAVID *England in the 19th Century.* Pen.

THUCYDIDES *Complete Writings.* MLCE.

———— *The Peloponnesian War.* Pen.

TOCQUEVILLE, ALEXIS DE *The Old Régime and the French Revolution.* Anch.

VAILLANT, GEORGE C. *The Aztecs of Mexico.* Pen.

VAN LOON, H. W. *The Story of America.* Dell, Prem.

———— *The Story of Mankind.* PB.

WHEELER, SIR MORTIMER *Rome Beyond the Imperial Frontiers.* Pen.

WHITELOCK, DOROTHY *The Beginnings of English Society.* Pen.

WILSON, JOHN DOVER *Life in Shakespeare's England.* Pen.

WILSON, WOODROW *Congressional Government: A Study in American Politics.* Mer.

WINT, GUY *Spotlight on Asia.* Pen.

WOODWARD, C. VANN *Reunion and Reaction.* Anch.

WULF, MAURICE *Philosophy and Civilization in the Middle Ages.* Dov.

XENOPHON *The Persian Expedition.* Pen.

YOUNG, G. M. *Victorian England: Portrait of an Age.* Anch.

19. Politics

JAMES TRACY CROWN, *New York University*

Politics may be simply defined as the study of the theory and practice of government. Political scientists—as opposed to those of us who just "talk politics"—attempt to systematize and refine political observations and perceptions.

But contributions to the study of politics are made by many writers other than scholars. Politics provided the stuff of tragedy and comedy for Sophocles and Aristophanes as well as for Shakespeare and Shaw because it displays both man's highest aspirations and his deepest depravity, presents a being who seems at times not distantly related to the angels and at times nearly kin to the devil. For George Orwell in *1984,* Aldous Huxley in *Brave New World Revisited,* and C. Wright Mills in *The Causes of World War III,* new developments in politics have inspired thrillers whose final chapters are yet to be written—presumably by readers, who must determine whether in the world of tomorrow mankind can survive, or will even want to. Very many thoughtful people read these books, though they seem absurd exaggerations. Why? Why do people gather together in more and more homes, cafés, libraries, and classrooms, not to plot the overthrow of governments, but to discover more about them? The reason is that in this supposed age of complacency more and more people are seriously questioning most of the age-old basic assumptions about government.

Many American citizens today seek new answers to old questions which once intrigued only philosophers, such as Plato, Aristotle, Machiavelli, Marx, and John Stuart Mill. They want to probe the strategic political problems: Why do we have states? Who should rule, and to what ends? How can power be obtained and maintained? What is the proper line separating state control and in-

dividual freedom? How far should the state carry out
the wishes of its people? The study of political theory
and constitutions ponders these questions, among others.

How government really works and how we can get it
to work the way we want it to—this is the important
province of "practical politics." Yet even at its most
practical, politics cannot wholly divorce itself from
philosophy—cannot evade the question put to Alice by
Humpty Dumpty (though in a different context): "Which
is to be master?" Is it to be the philosopher-king of
Plato? The proletariat of Marx? The "elites" of Mosca
or Ortega? "The people"? Or, in terms of the next American election, the Democrats or Republicans? The endeavor to answer the last question can reduce political
writing to the level of the racing form, but it can also
serve as an introduction to sound political research—as
in Samuel Lubell's valuable *The Future of American
Politics*.

International affairs examines the relations of sover-
eign nations with one another, considers the ways in
which they can live together. We can understand international affairs only after we know something about comparative government, the area of politics that attempts to
explain why various societies have evolved different kinds
of governments, and with what consequences.

For the purpose of organizing good reading in politics,
then, books have been divided into categories of Theory,
Constitutions, Practical Politics and Government in General, and International Affairs and Comparative Government. In this highly selective list the discriminating
reader can find, in readable prose, most of the possible
answers to the basic questions in politics.

A. Theory

ACTON, LORD 1834–1902 *Essays on Freedom and Power* (1955).
Perceptive, learned, and readable essays on political fundamentals. *Mer.*

ARISTOTLE *Ethics* and *Politics.* Classic treatment of individual
and political morals. See page 27.

CASSIRER, ERNST 1874–1945 *The Myth of the State* (1946). Essays
on the various symbols of government, their uses and effects.
Anch.

CROSSMAN, RICHARD H. S. 1907– (ed.) *The God That Failed* (1949). Essays by famous ex-Communists or fellow travelers on why they sympathized with and then left communism. *Ban.*

EBENSTEIN, WILLIAM 1910– (ed.) *Great Political Thinkers: Plato to the Present* (2nd ed. 1956). Selected readings from famous theorists with an excellent commentary. *Rinehart $7.50.*

GABRIEL, RALPH H. 1890– *The Course of American Democratic Thought* (1940). Lucidly traces democratic thought in this country from 1815 to the present. *Ronald $6.*

HOBBES, THOMAS 1588–1679 *Leviathan* (1651). A frank justification of autocratic rule. *Macmillan $2.85, Oxford Univ. $2, EvmanNA.*

LENIN, NIKOLAI 1870–1924 *Imperialism* and *The State and Revolution* (1917). Basic statements of Russian Communist theory by the U.S.S.R.'s first dictator. The second volume is particularly important. *International 60¢ & 50¢ (paper).*

LINDSAY, A. D. 1879–1952 *The Modern Democratic State* (1947). The first volume of an uncompleted study; nevertheless a very fine analysis of Western thought. *Oxford Univ. $3.*

LOCKE, JOHN 1632–1704 *Two Treatises of Civil Government* (1689). The source of much of the early political theory of America, especially that of Jefferson. *Hafner $1.25, Evman-h; Second Treatise* only: *Macmillan $2.50, LLA-Lib.*

MACHIAVELLI *The Prince.* Realistic handbook written for the guidance of an autocratic Renaissance ruler. See page 48.

MARX, KARL 1818–1883 *Capital* (1867). The bible of modern communism and socialism. *Evman-h 2 vols., ML (abr.), MLG.*

———— and FRIEDRICH ENGELS 1820–1895 *The Communist Manifesto* (1847). A statement of the ends and purposes of early communism. *Gate.* Also in Ebenstein, above.

MOSCA, GAETANO 1858–1941 *The Ruling Class* (1939). An explanation of ruling groups in terms of invariable "laws" of human relationship. *McGraw-Hill $10.*

ORTEGA Y GASSET, JOSE 1883–1955 *The Revolt of the Masses* (1932). A frank plea for the assumption of rule by an intellectual aristocracy and for the suppression of "mass-man." *Norton $3.50.*

ORWELL *1984.* A frightening description of future totalitarianism. See page 115.

PLATO *The Republic, The Statesman,* and *The Laws.* Plato's chief political writings. See page 28.

ROUSSEAU *The Social Contract.* The theory of majority rule based on free association was influential upon early American radicals. See page 69.

SABINE, GEORGE H. 1880– *A History of Political Theory* (rev. ed. 1950). An excellent summary of political thought from the Greeks to the present. *Holt $7.25.*

WILSON *To the Finland Station.* How Marxism evolved. See page 202.

B. Constitutions

BARNES, WILLIAM R. 1866–1945 (ed.) *Constitution of the United States* (1956). A surprisingly fascinating starting point for reading about American government. *B&N.*

CORWIN, EDWARD S. 1878– *The Constitution and What It Means Today* (12th ed. 1958). A phrase-by-phrase exposition of fundamental American law. *Princeton Univ. $6.*

HAMILTON *et al. The Federalist Papers.* The best, clearest political analysis yet produced by Americans. See page 67.

MARKE, JULIUS 1913– (ed.) *Holmes Reader* (1955). The core thought of a foremost American jurist. *Oceana $3.50, Oce.*

NEWMAN, EDWIN S. 1922– (ed.) *The Freedom Reader* (1955). Essays on the theory and practice of individual liberties. *Oceana $3.50, Oce.*

ZURCHER, ARNOLD J. 1902– (ed.) *Constitutions and Constitutional Trends Since World War II* (rev. ed. 1955). The best analysis. *New York Univ. $5.*

C. Practical Politics and Government in General

BARTH, ALAN 1906– *The Loyalty of Free Men* (1951). A critical look at our loyalty program and our hunt for "security." *Viking $3.*

BEARD, CHARLES A. 1874–1948 *An Economic Interpretation of the Constitution of the United States* (1913). An early attempt to give a realistic explanation of the forces which led to the Constitution. *Macmillan $4.75.*

BRYCE, JAMES 1838–1922 *The American Commonwealth* (1888). A brilliant analysis by an Englishman of the American people and their government. *Macmillan $6.50 (abr.), Cap 2 vols., Saga (abr.).*

CORWIN, EDWARD S. 1878– *The President: Office and Powers* (4th ed. 1957). A standard examination of an amazingly flexible American institution. *New York Univ. $6.50.*

DIMOCK, MARSHALL E. 1903– *A Philosophy of Administration* (1958). Emphasizes the creative and cooperative nature of successful administration; challenges some traditional power concepts. *Harper $3.50.*

GOLDMAN, ERIC F. 1915– *Rendezvous with Destiny* (1956). Perceptive description of modern American reform movements, both for beginners and advanced readers. *Knopf $5.75, Vin.*

GROSS, BERTRAM 1912– *The Legislative Struggle* (1953). Highly intellectual and realistic approach to the legislative process. *McGraw-Hill $6.50.*

HOFSTADTER *The American Political Tradition.* Good reading for the beginner or specialist in politics. See page 205.

Hoover Commission Report (1949). A condensation of the most searching appraisal ever made of the American executive branch. *McGraw-Hill o.p.*

HUXLEY, ALDOUS 1894– *Brave New World Revisited* (1958). Envisions future trends in society and government. *Harper $3, Harp.*

KEY, V. O. 1908– *Politics, Parties, and Pressure Groups* (4th ed. 1958). A clear, scholarly exposition of how politics works. *Crowell $6.50.*

KOHN, HANS 1891– *Nationalism, Its Meaning and History* (1955). An authoritative examination of the strongest emotional force in modern politics. *Anv.*

LASSWELL, HAROLD 1902– *Politics: Who Gets What, When, How?* (1958). A good introduction to how practical politics works. *Mer.*

LIPPMANN, WALTER 1889– *The Public Philosophy* (1955). A rather suspicious look at the basic workings of American democratic government. *Little, Brown $3.75, NAL.*

LUBELL, SAMUEL 1911– *The Future of American Politics* (1956). A readable and provocative attempt to explain the present-day American party system and its paradoxes; analyzes recent changes in the American electorate. *Harper $2.75, Anch.*

PARKINSON, C. NORTHCOTE 1909– *Parkinson's Law and Other Studies in Administration* (1957). How all forms of social organization tend to strangle themselves by organizational hypertrophy. *Houghton Mifflin $3.*

PARTEN, MILDRED B. 1902– *Surveys, Polls and Samples* (1950). Comprehensive examination of the methods and proper uses of opinion-measuring devices. *Harper $6.*

PELTASON, JACK W. 1923– and JAMES M. BURNS 1918– *Functions and Policies of American Government* (1958). A sound yet imaginative introduction to the subject. *Prentice-Hall $4.95.*

TOCQUEVILLE, ALEXIS DE 1805–1859 *Democracy in America* (1835, 1840). The views of an observant Frenchman on American government in the Age of Jackson. *NAL (abr.), Vin 2 vols., WoC.*

D. International Affairs and Comparative Government

ADAM, THOMAS R. 1900– *Government and Politics in Africa, South of the Sahara* (1959). An up-to-date treatment. *Ran.*

CHILDS, J. RIVES 1893– *American Foreign Service* (1948). Describes lucidly and in detail how American diplomacy works. *Holt o.p.*

DEAN, VERA M. 1903– *The Nature of the Non-Western World* (1957). A thoughtful general introduction to how most people live. *NAL.*

214 GOOD READING

DULLES, JOHN FOSTER 1888–1959 *War or Peace* (1950). Some intelligent views on the international situation by the late Secretary of State. *Macmillan $4.75.*

Everyman's United Nations (1953). A handy brief reference book on the organization and work of the U.N. *Columbia Univ. $1.50.*

KENNAN, GEORGE F. 1904– *Realities of American Foreign Policy* (1954). A series of lectures by one of our experts on Russia. *Princeton Univ. $2.75.*

LOWER, ARTHUR 1889– *Canadians in the Making* (1958). A pleasant way to end ignorance about our great neighbor. *Longmans, Green $7.50.*

MACDONALD, AUSTIN F. 1898– *Latin American Politics and Government* (2nd ed. 1954). A short but comprehensive text on the governments of Central and South America. *Crowell $6.*

MILLIS, WALTER 1899– (ed.) *Foreign Policy and the Free Society* (1958). A thoughtful prescription for achieving desirable qualities leading toward a free society. *Oceana $2.75, Oce.*

MILLS, C. WRIGHT 1916– *The Causes of World War III* (1958). Deliberately provocative arguments about political responsibility at the top level. *Simon & Schuster $3.50, S&S.*

MORGENTHAU, HANS J. 1904– *Politics Among Nations* (1954). The classic modern defense of the power-centered view of international relations. *Knopf $6.*

NEUMANN, ROBERT 1916– *European and Comparative Government* (2nd ed. 1955). Clear explanation of several governmental systems with some thoughtful comparisons of their relative values. *McGraw-Hill $6.75.*

NUSSBAUM, ARTHUR 1877– *A Concise History of the Law of Nations* (rev. ed. 1954). A fine review of what international law is and of how it got that way. *Macmillan $5.*

RIENOW, ROBERT 1907– *Introduction to Government* (2nd ed. 1956). Simplified but nevertheless sound presentation of comparative political systems. *Knopf $5.75.*

ROBERTS, HENRY L. 1916– *Russia and America: Dangers and Prospects* (1956). Illuminating examination of the historic patterns of the two countries' relations. *NAL.*

SCHUMAN, FREDERICK 1904– *International Politics* (6th ed. 1958). A provocative presentation of the case for international organization and law. *McGraw-Hill $7.50.*

STOUT, HIRAM 1905– *British Government* (1953). Clear, sound general introduction. *Oxford Univ. $5.50.*

20. Economics

RICHARD A. LESTER, *Princeton University*

Economists analyze the processes by which man makes his
living and the problems encountered in operating an industrial economy. It is enlightening to learn how production and employment are guided and what affects the
wealth and material strength of nations. And one need
not accept the Marxian theory of economic determination to recognize that the economy of a country directly
influences not only the inhabitants' living standards but
also individual freedom, the distribution of political
power, and the country's culture.

The ramifications of economic inquiry are wide indeed, ranging from modern technology to human motives, from the individual's wage to the clash between
capitalism and communism.

Within its broad scope, economics provides intellectual
stimulus and interesting reading for persons with widely
different tastes and talents. Some look upon economics as
a science which is primarily theoretical and deals with
uniformities and causal relationships. To others it is
essentially an art which combines practical experience
with policy recommendations for both industry and government. Almost every economist is, of course, a mixture
of the pure and applied, part theoretician and part in-
stitutionalist.

For the general reader, the historical approach to
economics provides a good introduction and orientation,
combining theory and practice in a meaningful manner.
One can begin with an engaging popular account of the
ideas and lives of the great economists, such as Robert
Heilbroner's *The Worldly Philosophers* or George
Soule's *Ideas of the Great Economists*. Then he can move
in two directions: read about the development of national economies in economic histories like those of
Huberman and Ware, and get to know some of the

classics in economics by men such as Adam Smith, Alfred Marshall, and John Maynard Keynes, perhaps along with their biographies.

Another approach would be to select a lively, provocative textbook like Samuelson's *Economics: An Introductory Analysis* as a jumping-off point. If Samuelson seems a bit difficult as a starter, simpler works like Soule's and Crane's might be sampled first. Thereafter, one could examine in more detail the operations and the economic institutions of American capitalism in books by Berle and Means, Galbraith, and Ross. Reading about the Russian economy in Schwartz would provide a good contrast.

Whether one starts with the historical or the modern approach, he will wish to read some recent works on the defense and reform of our economic system, since the struggle between capitalism and communism is the overriding issue of our time.

BERLE, ADOLPH A. 1895– and GARDINER C. MEANS 1896– *The Modern Corporation and Private Property* (1932). A thorough study of the ownership and control of huge corporations; almost a classic. *Macmillan $6.50.*

BEVERIDGE, WILLIAM H. 1879– *Full Employment in a Free Society* (1945). The foundations for a full-employment economy presented in simple language by a world-renowned political economist. *Norton $3.75.*

BURNS, ARTHUR F. 1904– (ed.) *Wesley Clair Mitchell: The Economic Scientist* (1952). Essays on the life and contributions of a great American student of business cycles who applied quantitative methods to social science. *Princeton Univ. $4.*

CLARK, JOHN MAURICE 1884– *An Alternative to Serfdom* (1948). Explorations into some of the broad economic issues of our time. *Knopf o.p.*

———— *Economic Institutions and Human Welfare* (1957). A vigorous analysis of the relation of economic thought to the broad issues of modern life. *Knopf $4.*

CRANE, BURTON *Getting and Spending: An Informal Guide to National Economics* (1956). A thoroughly understandable and wise, though sometimes oversimplified, analysis of economic problems. *Harcourt, Brace $4.95.*

ELLIS, HOWARD S. 1898– (ed.) *A Survey of Contemporary Economics* Vol. 1 (1948) and BERNARD F. HALEY 1898– (ed.) Vol. 2 (1952). A careful survey and appraisal of recent scholarly achievement in various branches of economics. *Irwin $4.75 & $5.50.*

GALBRAITH, JOHN KENNETH 1908– *American Capitalism* (1956). A challenging critique of current economic thought and an analysis of the economy based on the thesis that power begets countervailing offsets. *Houghton Mifflin $3.50.*

————— *The Affluent Society* (1958). A stimulating antidote to conventional thinking about the operation and goals of our economy. *Houghton Mifflin $5.*

HANSEN, ALVIN H. 1887– *The American Economy* (1957). Explains the transformation to a mixed economy and the applications of advances in economic analysis to present-day problems. *McGraw-Hill $5.*

————— *A Guide to Keynes* (1953). A clear, helpful guide to Keynes's *General Theory. McGraw-Hill $4.90, McGH.*

HAYEK, FRIEDRICH AUGUST VON 1899– *The Road to Serfdom* (1944). Tract opposing government controls and intervention, and favoring free markets. *Univ. of Chicago $5, Phoen.*

HAZLITT, HENRY 1894– *The Failure of the "New Economics": An Analysis of the Keynesian Fallacies* (1959). A systematic, vigorous, sometimes convincing attack on Keynes's *General Theory. Van Nostrand $7.50.*

HEILBRONER, ROBERT L. *The Worldly Philosophers* (1953). Lively, exciting accounts of the great economic thinkers and their doctrines. *Simon & Schuster $5, S&S.*

HOOVER, CALVIN B. 1897– *The Economy, Liberty and the State* (1959). General analysis of the transformation of American capitalism and of the development of the Soviet economy and of the mixed economies of Western Europe by an expert on economic systems. *Twentieth Century Fund $5.*

HUBERMAN, LEO 1903– *Man's Worldly Goods* (1936). Skillful exposition of the development of economic institutions and doctrines by a socialist writer. *Harper $3.*

KEYNES, JOHN MAYNARD 1883–1946 *Essays and Sketches in Biography* (1933). Engaging biographical studies of the Cambridge economists—Malthus, Marshall, and Edgeworth—as well as of political figures in the 1920's. *Mer.*

————— *The General Theory of Employment, Interest and Money* (1936). The most influential economic tract published in this century. Although sparkling in spots, it is written primarily for economists, and the general reader may prefer to approach its logic through popular interpretations such as those by Beveridge or Hansen, above. *Harcourt, Brace $5.*

MALTHUS *Essay on the Principles of Population.* See page 69.

MARSHALL, ALFRED 1842–1924 *Principles of Economics* (1890). A restatement of the whole structure of economic thought in the grand tradition and with a view toward economic progress. *Macmillan $6.90.*

MARX *Capital.* A ponderous critique of mid-19th-century capitalism; the fundamental text of modern socialism. See page 211.

Rockefeller Brothers Fund *The Challenge to America: Its Economic and Social Aspects* (1958). An assessment of the challenges confronting America during the next decade by a panel of 17 experts. *Doubleday 75¢.*

ROSS, ARTHUR M. 1916– *Trade Union Wage Policy* (1956). A realistic analysis of American unionism in political as well as economic terms. *Univ. of California $3.*

SAMUELSON, PAUL A. 1915– *Economics: An Introductory Analysis* (4th ed. 1958). The leading elementary text since first publication in 1948, skillfully written by an outstanding American economist. *McGraw-Hill $6.75.*

SCHUMPETER, JOSEPH A. 1883–1950 *Capitalism, Socialism, and Democracy* (3rd ed. 1950). An economist–philosopher examines two competing economies, forecasting the supplanting of capitalism by socialism though favoring the former. *Harper $4.50.*

SCHWARTZ, HARRY 1919– *Russia's Soviet Economy* (2nd ed. 1954). Comprehensive picture of the operation of the Soviet economy, based on discriminating use of factual material. *Prentice-Hall $7.50.*

SMITH *The Wealth of Nations.* The classic case for a free economy. See page 69.

SOULE, GEORGE 1887– *Ideas of the Great Economists* (1952). Concise, deft treatment of the panorama of economic thought from the Greeks to Keynes. *Viking $3.50, NAL.*

———— *Introduction to Economic Science* (1951). A first reader written clearly and interestingly. *Viking $2.50, NAL.*

TAWNEY *Religion and the Rise of Capitalism.* A brilliant development of the thesis that Protestantism made possible the triumph of capitalism in Western Europe. See page 63.

TAYLOR, OVERTON H. 1897– *Economics and Liberalism* (1955). Philosophical, thought-provoking essays on the foundations and limitations of classical liberalism. *Harvard Univ. $5.*

VEBLEN, THORSTEIN 1857–1929 *The Theory of the Leisure Class* (1899). Barbed, pungent study of the "conspicuous consumption" of the rich and near-rich. *Viking $3.75, ML, NAL.*

———— *The Portable Veblen* (1948). Contains the first half of *Theory* and selections from other works, including essays on economists. *Vik, Vik-h.*

WARE, NORMAN JOSEPH 1886– *Wealth and Welfare* (1949). Popular history detailing the background of American economic structures and issues. *Holt-Dryden $1.90.*

WILSON *To the Finland Station.* See page 202.

21. Geography

TRUMAN M. TALLEY, New American Library

The science of geography arises from man's exploration of our planet. The desire for conquest, the search for trade routes, scientific curiosity, missionary efforts, or simply the love of travel and adventure—all have played their part in discovering the world we live in.

This process of discovery—still very much with us today —had its origins in prehistoric times. There is evidence, for example, that—about 5000 B.C.—trade routes had already been established to bring obsidian blades from Lake Van in Turkey and shells from the Red Sea to the tiny communities on the foothills around the Tigris and Euphrates Valley. Coastal and river transport was well developed by 3000 B.C. By 1400 B.C. the Phoenicians had opened trading stations throughout the Mediterranean; a thousand years later their maritime network included the west coast of Africa, the Atlantic coast of Europe, and even the Azores.

The maritime trade of the Greek city states, the conquests of Alexander, and the rise of the Roman Empire each gave impetus to new explorations extending as far eastward as China. Then, for almost twelve hundred years after the collapse of the Roman Empire, the curtain came down, and in Christian Europe "the conception of the globe degenerated to that of a flat disc with Jerusalem at the center."

Only in northern Europe and the Moslem world was the spark of exploration kept alive. In the middle of the 9th century the Vikings discovered the North Cape, and about a century later Leif Ericson sailed to America. In the Middle East, Arabic geographers continued to develop the science of cartography. The geographic renaissance in Europe began in the 13th century with the Asian travels of Carpini and Marco Polo. Two hundred years later the magnetic compass and the astrolabe led to exploration of the oceans and exploitation of the New World.

As the unknown became more and more known, geography began to take on a new dimension: systematic comparison of geographic regions. Many different kinds of geographies evolved—economic, political, social, biological, botanical, and physical. Recently the minds of men have turned to the ocean depths and outer space as new areas for exploration. Concepts of geography have been modified and extended—forerunners of a new comprehension of our planet, still unknown.

ANDERSON, CMMDR. WILLIAM R. 1921– *Nautilus 90 North* (1959). Full account of the first voyage under the top of the world. *World $3.95, NAL.*

ARCINIEGAS, GERMAN 1900– *Amerigo and the New World* (1955). A brilliant, scholarly reappraisal of the first explorer to proclaim that a new world had been found. *Knopf $5.75.*

AYRES, EUGENE 1891– and CHARLES A. SCARLOTT *Energy Sources: The Wealth of the World* (1952). Where sources of energy are found today, and where they may come from in the future. *McGraw-Hill $5.*

BATES, MARSTON 1906– *Where Winter Never Comes* (1952). The tropics interpreted in a "new and truer light." *Scribner $3.50.*

BROWN, LLOYD A. 1907– *The Story of Maps* (1949). An account of mapping and map makers throughout history. *Little, Brown $10.*

CALDER, RITCHIE 1906– *After the Seventh Day* (1960). Fascinating new history of human geography. *Simon & Schuster.*

CARMER, CARL 1893– *The Hudson* (1939). Delightful collection of facts and legends. One of the *Rivers of America* series, 45 titles of great regional interest. *Rinehart $4.50.*

CARSON *The Sea Around Us.* An absorbing account of the mystery and meaning of the sea, its relationship to man and the earth. See page 251.

COOK, JAMES 1728–1779 *Captain Cook's Voyages of Discovery* (1954). Ed. by John Barrow. The three voyages of one of the world's greatest navigators. Cook sailed around the South Pole and for the first time scientifically charted the islands of the Pacific. *Evman-h.*

COUSTEAU, JACQUES-YVES 1910– and FREDERIC DUMAS *The Silent World* (1953). Pioneers of "skin diving" report their first undersea explorations. *Harper $5, PB.*

CRESSEY, G. B. 1896– *Asia's Lands and Peoples* (2nd ed. 1951). A geography of one third of the earth and two thirds of its people. *McGraw-Hill $8.95.*

DARWIN *The Voyage of the Beagle.* See page 159.

DE TERRA, HELMUT 1900– *Humboldt: The Life and Times of Alexander von Humboldt, 1769–1859* (1955). A biography of the founder of scientific geography, who was also explorer, naturalist, and humanist. *Knopf $5.75.*

DE VOTO *The Course of Empire.* Discovery and exploration of North America. See page 205.

DOUGHTY *Travels in Arabia Deserta.* See page 75.

FISHER, WILLIAM B. 1916– *The Middle East: A Physical, Social and Regional Geography* (2nd ed. 1952). Peoples, human society, and historical geography of a complex region. *Dutton $6.50.*

FREEMAN, O. W. 1889– (ed.) *Geography of the Pacific* (1951). The Pacific Ocean, its climates, currents, and features; the Pacific islands; the peoples, resources, and industries. *Wiley $8.50.*

FREUCHEN, PETER 1886–1957 *Peter Freuchen's Book of the Seven Seas* (1957). A gifted storyteller communicates his great feeling for the seas. *Messner $8.95.*

FUCHS, SIR VIVIAN 1908– and SIR EDMUND HILLARY 1919– *The Crossing of Antarctica: The Commonwealth Trans-Antarctic Expedition 1955–8* (1958). Fascinating account of first voyage across the bottom of the world. *Little, Brown $7.50.*

GHEERBRANT, ALAIN 1921 *Journey to the Far Amazon: An Expedition into Unknown Territory* (1954). A dramatic account of the Orinoco–Amazon expedition by four young men who covered thousands of miles in Indian canoes through hazardous territory among primitive peoples. *Simon & Schuster $5.*

GOTTMAN, JEAN 1915– *A Geography of Europe* (rev. ed. 1954). A leading presentation of newer ideas on human geography. *Holt $8.25.*

GOUROU, PIERRE 1900– *The Tropical World* (1953). A geographic analysis of a large, little-understood area. *Longmans, Green $4.*

GREENHOOD, DAVID 1895– *Down to Earth: Mapping for Everybody* (rev. ed. 1951). An introduction to maps and mapping for the general reader. *Holiday House $6.*

HAKLUYT *Voyages.* See page 53.

HARE, FREDERICK K. 1919– *The Restless Atmosphere* (1953). An authoritative study of climatology designed for the general reader; principles of atmospheric circulation and also the climates of major regions. *Rinehart $1.50.*

HERRMANN, PAUL 1905– *Conquest by Man* (1954). How man, from the Stone Age to historical times, driven by curiosity, greed, accident, and ingenuity, discovered the lands and seas around him. *Harper $6.*

HUNTINGTON, ELLSWORTH 1876–1945 *Mainsprings of Civilization* (1945). Explains how human vitality was affected by climate, geography, migration and the concept of kiths. *NAL.*

HURST, HAROLD E. 1880– *The Nile* (1952). A general account of the river and the utilization of its waters, essential to the understanding of a huge section of Africa. *Macmillan $6.*

JAMES, PRESTON E. 1899– *Latin America* (rev. ed. 1950). Covers South America, Mexico, Central America, and the islands of the Caribbean. *Odyssey $7.50.*

JONES, CLARENCE F. 1893– and GORDON G. DARKENWALD 1906– *Economic Geography* (rev. ed. 1954). A clear discussion of the distribution of economic resources. *Macmillan $6.75.*

KIMBLE, G. H. T. 1908– and DOROTHY GOOD 1906– (eds.) *Geography of the Northlands* (1955). Systematic and regional geography includes physiography, weather, climate, marine life, and peoples. *Wiley $10.50.*

LEBON, JOHN H. G. *An Introduction to Human Geography* (1952). Clear, readable survey of man's relationship to his environment. *Rinehart $6.50.*

LEITHAUSER, JOACHIM G. 1910– *Worlds Beyond the Horizon* (1955). Engrossing narrative of exploration and discovery, from ancient times to the space age, that emphasizes exploits in the Western Hemisphere. *Knopf $6.75.*

MOORE, W. G. 1907– *Dictionary of Geography* (1953). An exploration of terms basic to the understanding of geography. *Pen.*

MORISON *Christopher Columbus, Mariner.* The story of the great seafarer told by America's foremost naval historian. See page 50.

Oxford Economic Atlas of the World (1954). Basic information about world economics. *Oxford Univ. $6.75.*

POLO, MARCO *Travels.* Medieval Asia. See page 42.

PRESCOTT *Conquest of Mexico* and *Conquest of Peru.* See page 50.

RUSSELL, RICHARD J. 1895– and FRED B. KNIFFEN 1900– *Culture Worlds* (1951). Regional human geography integrated with that of physical resources. *Macmillan $6.50.*

SHOR *After You, Marco Polo.* Fine reporting by a young American couple attempting to follow in Marco Polo's steps. See page 79.

SPATE, OSKAR H. K. *India and Pakistan: A General and Regional Geography* (1954). A comprehensive study by one of the greatest living authorities on the Indian subcontinent: geography, people, and economy. *Dutton $11.75.*

———— and W. GORDON EAST 1902– (eds.) *The Changing Map of Asia* (2nd ed. 1953). A good political geography. *Dutton $4.95.*

STAMP, LAURENCE DUDLEY 1898– *Africa: A Study in Tropical Development* (1953). A survey of the geography of Africa, including historical summaries of the African peoples, European exploration, and colonization. *Wiley $9.25.*

STEFANSSON, VILHJALMUR 1879– (ed.) *Great Adventures and Explorations* (rev. ed. 1952). Outstanding narratives in the history of exploration. *Tudor $2.98.*

TREWARTHA, GLENN THOMAS 1896– *An Introduction to Climate* (3rd ed. 1954). The best presentation of climatic factors. One of the *Geography* series. *McGraw-Hill $7.75.*

_____ and VERNOR C. FINCH 1883– *Elements of Geography, Physical and Cultural* (3rd ed. 1949). Valuable introductory text. *McGraw-Hill $7.50.*

VAN VALKENBURG, SAMUEL 1891– and CARL L. STOTZ 1908– *Elements of Political Geography* (1954). Geographical factors having to do with national power. *Prentice-Hall $8.65.*

WHITE, C. L. 1897– and E. J. FOSCUE 1899– *Regional Geography of Anglo-America* (2nd ed. 1954). A geography of the United States, Canada, and Alaska. *Prentice-Hall $10.60.*

WOOLDRIDGE, S. W. 1900– and W. GORDON EAST 1902– *The Spirit and Purpose of Geography* (1951). Two distinguished geographers trace the evolution of the science and suggest lines of future development. *Rinehart $1.50.*

22. Language

DONALD A. SEARS, *Upsala College*

Language—the peculiarly human vehicle of communication distinguishing us from the animals—has always fascinated man. But the past two hundred years have been especially fruitful in developing systematic approaches to language study.

The first scholarly technique was that of dictionary making. Early dictionaries were glossaries of hard words; no attempt was made to list anything like the complete vocabulary of a language. But the rational spirit of the 18th century was soon brought to bear on language. Attempts were made to reduce modern languages to orderly rules such as had been worked out for Greek and Latin. Rather complete dictionaries and grammars resulted. In England the monument of these efforts is Dr. Samuel Johnson's *Dictionary of the English Language* of 1755. In America this was followed in 1828 by Noah Webster's *American Dictionary of the English Language*.

The motive behind these dictionaries was an urge to determine the "correct" words and their "correct" spelling and usage. Thus the 19th century became an age of spellers and grammars. Along with these came studies into the history of language. Great scholars like Grimm in Germany linked English to the Germanic branch of the Indo-European language family. Their work developed into the branch of learning known as philology. In this tradition is Baugh's *A History of the English Language*.

By the beginning of the 20th century, a new approach to language was being made by the new science of anthropology. Franz Boas studied the American Indian languages and discovered communication systems other than that of Indo-European. He was followed by Edward

Sapir, whose *Language* (1921) is still a classic statement of the relationship of language to culture, and by Benjamin L. Whorf.

Almost concurrently Leonard Bloomfield pioneered in the field of linguistics and semantics. This latter, the science of meanings, was broadened by the work of Korzybski and popularized by Stuart Chase's *The Tyranny of Words* (1938).

All approaches to the study of language have been valuable. From the Tower of Babel to the latest mathematical formula or psychological theory of perception man still seeks to learn more about his most human activity—language behavior.

AYER *Language, Truth and Logic.* Words in philosophic thinking, that of neo-positivism. See page 187.

BAUGH, ALBERT C. 1891– *A History of the English Language* (rev. ed. 1957). A classic history of the development of our native tongue. *Appleton-Century-Crofts $5.50.*

BROWN, ROGER W. 1925– *Words and Things* (1958). A psycholinguist looks at language. *Free Press $6.75.*

CAREY, GORDON V. 1886– *Mind the Stop* (rev. ed. 1958). Brief, clear guide to punctuation. *Cambridge Univ. 95¢.*

CARROLL, JOHN B. 1916– *The Study of Language* (1953). "A survey of linguistics and related disciplines in America" written for the general reader. *Harvard Univ. $4.75.*

CHASE, STUART 1888– *The Tyranny of Words* (1938). Popular application of semantics to general communications. *Harv.*

COON, HORACE C. 1897– *Speak Better—Write Better—English* (1954). Informative, readable self-help to reading, writing, and speaking. *NAL.*

DEAN, LEONARD F. 1909– and KENNETH G. WILSON 1923– (eds.) *Essays on Language and Usage* (1959). Excellent collection of readable authoritative essays. *Ox.*

ESTRICH, ROBERT M. 1906– and HANS SPERBER 1885– *Three Keys to Language* (1952). Relationship of language to cultural and political history, religion, sociology, and psychology. *Rinehart $5.*

FOWLER, H. W. 1858–1933 *Dictionary of Modern English Usage* (1926). Classic and witty desk guide to good usage. *Oxford Univ. $3.75.*

FRIES, CHARLES C. 1887– *American English Grammar* (1940). Pioneer study of present-day English by a distinguished linguist. Establishes class dialects. *Appleton-Century-Crofts $3.25.*

GOAD, HAROLD 1878–1956 *Language in History* (1958). Stimulating development of the thesis that language and culture are so linked that their survival or decline depends on the loyalty of the speech community to a common purpose. *Pen.*

HALL, ROBERT A. 1911– *Leave Your Language Alone!* (1950). Spirited discussion of the problem of usage. A popular presentation which does not sacrifice scholarship. *Linguistica $3.*

HAYAKAWA, S. I. 1906– *Language in Thought and Action* (rev. ed. 1949). Fascinating semantic study of human interaction through communication, stressing the need for cooperation. *Harcourt, Brace $3.*

HOCKETT, CHARLES 1916– *A Course in Modern Linguistics* (1958). Broad survey of descriptive linguistics. Technical terms and concepts are explained en route. *Macmillan $7.50.*

HOOK, JULIUS N. 1913– and ERNST GARLAND MATHEWS 1903– *Modern American Grammar and Usage* (1956). Based on the language used by writers today, offers guidance on current language structure. *Ronald $5.*

HUPPE, BERNARD F. 1912– and JACK KAMINSKY 1922– *Logic and Language* (1956). Brief and illuminating discussion of language as it relates to logical thinking. *Knopf $1.75.*

JESPERSEN, OTTO 1860–1943 *Growth and Structure of the English Language* (1905, 1955). Brilliant description of the growth of English, particularly as a literary medium. *Macmillan $2.25 (9th ed.), Anch.*

JOHNSON, ALEXANDER BRYAN 1786–1867 *A Treatise on Language* (1836). 1959 edition edited by David Rynin. A pioneer study of the crucial issues in semantics. Still vital and readable. *Calif.*

LAIRD, CHARLTON G. 1901– *The Miracle of Language* (1953). A readable survey of language and English grammar for the general reader. *World $4, Prem.*

LEE, DONALD W. 1910– *Harbrace Vocabulary Guide* (1956). A systematic guide to vocabulary building through practice with prefixes, roots, and suffixes. *Harcourt, Brace $1.50.*

McKNIGHT, GEORGE H. 1871– *Modern English in the Making* (1928). Traces development of English and attitudes toward it from the time of Chaucer to the present. *Appleton-Century-Crofts $4.25.*

MARCKWARDT, ALBERT 1903– *American English* (1958). Brief history of the development of our language in the United States. "Reads like a novel," reports one young reader. *Oxford Univ. $4.50, Ox.*

MATHEWS, MITFORD M. 1891– *Words: How to Know Them* (1956). A vocabulary builder that offers basic information on our language, plus a history of dictionaries. *Holt $1.25.*

MENCKEN, HENRY L. 1880–1956 *The American Language* (4th ed. 1936). A treasure house of information written with verve and punch. Later expanded by two more heavy tomes, *Supple-*

ments I and *II* (1945, 1948), following the pattern of the original. *Knopf $8.75 ea., $23 set.*

The Merriam-Webster Pocket Dictionary (1951, 1958). Based on Webster's New International Dictionary, 2nd ed. Authoritative, accurate, inexpensive. *PB.*

OGDEN, C. K. 1889– and I. A. RICHARDS 1893– *The Meaning of Meaning* (1923, 1959). Famous study of the influence of language and symbols on thought and action. For the intellectually tough. *Harv.*

PARTRIDGE *Shakespeare's Bawdy.* The lusty language of the Elizabethans. See page 55.

PERRIN, PORTER G. 1896– *Writer's Guide and Index to English* (rev. ed. 1950). An unusually complete and workable reference handbook to good usage. A "must" for every desk. *Scott, Foresman $3.75.*

POTTER, SIMEON 1898– *Our Language* (1950). Delightful history of the adaptiveness of English. *Pen.*

RANDOLPH, VANCE 1892– *Down in the Holler* (1953). Language of the Ozarks described by a writer who has spent most of his life there. Fascinating, and in spots hilarious. *Univ. of Oklahoma $5.*

RAPOPORT, ANATOL 1911– *Science and the Goals of Man* (1950). A scientist reviews the relations between words and objective reality. Cogent and illuminating. *Harper o.p.*

ROBERTS, PAUL 1917– *Patterns of English* (1956). Although arranged as a high school text, a short, readable introduction to the new structural grammar which seems to be replacing the traditional Latinized English grammar of our schools. *Harcourt, Brace $2.88.*

ROGET, PETER M. 1779–1869 *Thesaurus.* The classic word finder. *Grosset $2.39, Longmans, Green $3.95, PB.*

SAPIR, EDWARD 1884–1939 *Language* (1921). A classic analysis of speech, the variability of language in time and place, and its relationship to culture. *Harv.*

SHEFTER, HARRY *Short Cuts to Effective English* (1955). Self-help, presented without technical jargon. *PB.*

SLOANE, EUGENE H. 1902– *Words and Their Ways: A Primer of Philology and Philosophy* (1955). Good introduction to the power and limitations of words. *Owl.*

SMITH, LOGAN PEARSALL 1865–1946 *The English Language* (rev. ed. 1952). Eminently readable and concise history of English. *Ox.*

VALLINS, G. H. 1897–1956 *The Pattern of English* (1956). Lucid account of the changes in structure of the English sentence. *Oxford Univ. $3.50, Pen.*

WALDHORN, ARTHUR 1918– and ARTHUR ZEIGER 1916– *English Made Simple* (1954). A useful book for learning correct English. *Made.*

WHATMOUGH, JOSHUA 1897– *Language: A Modern Synthesis* (1956). Thought-provoking study relating language to communication theory, statistics, symbolic logic, acoustics, and neurology. *NAL, SM.*

WHITEHALL, HAROLD 1905– *Structural Essentials of English* (1956). Clear and important presentation of the structure of English, adapted from the findings of linguistic science. *Harcourt, Brace $3.*

23. Psychology

DOUGLAS H. FRYER, *Richardson, Bellows, Henry & Co., Inc.*

People seek to enter the world of knowledge through many doors. They may enter the doorway of psychology through the reading of literature, history, and philosophy in which human behavior is described in detail. Magazines and the daily newspapers constantly remind them of men's various characteristics. Through such reading they develop their own practical psychology—their basis for understanding the happenings in the world.

Others enter the doorway of psychology through the study and writings of psychologists. Frequently they begin with a college text in general psychology and then broaden their knowledge through the reading of books according to their interest in such specialized areas as educational, social, industrial, clinical, abnormal, personnel, military, and physiological psychology. Good books in all of these areas are available in inexpensive paperbound editions. Indeed, for about $30 the modern reader can collect a first-class basic psychology library.

The psychologist is interested in all human activities. He deals with everything that man senses, all his patterns of thought, why he thinks as others do, how he learns to speak and write, how he develops his values and makes judgments, what motivates him and causes his tensions, how social groups are formed and what causes antisocial behavior, how man's behavior differs from that of his fellows and from that of other animals.

Psychologists try to deal with these subjects precisely, unemotionally, scientifically. In more informal and personal treatment these matters are at the basis of all fiction and biography. The reading of books on specialized subjects in psychology opens the door wide to a scientific evaluation of human behavior however and wherever portrayed.

The goal of a scientist is to contribute to human knowledge. The goal of the applied scientist is to put his knowledge to work for human welfare. Psychologists are employed in schools, industrial companies, department stores, mental hygiene clinics, advertising firms, guidance bureaus, consulting firms, and many units of government and military services. Psychologists deal with such problems as personnel selection, mental therapy, employee training, management development, propaganda, morale, reading efficiency, crime detection, public opinion, performance evaluation, motivation research, and the engineering of machines for human operation. The books that follow illustrate what is being done in the ever-expanding professional work of psychologists.

A. General Psychology

CROW, LESTER D. 1897– and ALICE CROW 1894– (eds.) *Readings in General Psychology* (1955). 195 short selections by specialists on various areas of psychological investigation provide an easy orientation to the science. *B&N.*

DREVER, JAMES 1873–1950 *A Dictionary of Psychology* (1952). Contains 4,500 generally excellent definitions. Weak on explaining terms used by contemporary American psychologists. *Pen.*

EYSENCK, H. J. 1916– *Uses and Abuses of Psychology* (1953). Controversial in its evaluations but freighted with useful information on the use of tests, psychotherapy, the roots of prejudice, national character, etc. *Pen.*

FIELD, JOANNA 1900– *A Life of One's Own* (1952). Fascinating exploration of what constitutes normal thought, behavior, and imagination growing out of the author's own psychoanalysis. *Pen.*

FRYER, DOUGLAS H. 1891– *et al. General Psychology* (1954). Digest of the principles and facts of the science. *B&N.*

KNIGHT, MARGARET 1903– (ed.) *William James* (1950). Excellent selections from the writings of a pioneer American psychologist. *Pen.*

SARGENT, S. STANSFELD 1906– *Basic Teachings of the Great Psychologists* (1944). Informative, interesting summary. *B&N.*

SMITH, GEORGE MILTON 1902– *A Simplified Guide to Statistics for Psychology and Education* (rev. ed. 1946). Fairly inclusive about useful techniques. *Rinehart $1.50.*

B. Comparative Psychology (Animal)

BERRILL, N. J. 1903– *Sex and the Nature of Things* (1953). A zoologist reviews in depth the facts about sex. *PB*.

KATZ, DAVID 1884–1953 *Animals and Men* (1937). A basic book for the reader interested in comparative psychology. *Pen*.

C. Child Psychology

BOWLBY, JOHN *Child Care and the Growth of Love* (1953). A readable and sound introduction for parents. *Pen*.

CROW (see same two authors above) *Child Psychology* (1953). Explains lucidly the basic facts about growth and tells the story of development of communications, creative activity, mechanical and social skills, and their integration in the child. *B&N*.

FLESCH, RUDOLF 1911– *Why Johnny Can't Read* (1955). Though some of his diagnoses and prescriptions are controversial, Flesch's exposé of the disease of illiteracy produced by "progressive" education is provocative. *Harper $3.50, Pop*.

GESELL, ARNOLD 1880– and FRANCES ILG 1902– *Infant and Child in the Culture of Today* (1943). Current theory of child care, with emphasis on patterns of development and growth. *Harper $4.95*. Equally recommended, and equally useful, are *The Child from Five to Ten* (1946), *Harper $4.95*, and *Youth: The Years from Ten to Sixteen* (1956), *Harper $4.50*.

PIAGET, JEAN 1896– *Language and Thought of the Child* (1955). Another basic account for parents who want to know. *Humanities Press $4.50, Mer*.

VALENTINE, C. W. 1879– *The Normal Child and His Abnormalities* (1956). An excellent introduction to child psychology. *Pen*.

D. Educational Psychology

COLE, LUELLA W. 1893– *Psychology of Adolescence* (5th ed. 1958). Comprehensive survey of the critical years of mental, emotional, and physical development. *Rinehart $7*.

LEWIS, NORMAN 1912– *How to Read Better and Faster* (3rd ed. 1957). Simple rules for increasing speed and comprehension, complete with exercises and achievement tests. *Crowell $2.50*.

PINTNER, RUDOLPH 1884–1942 *et al. Educational Psychology* (1951). Sections describing the natural equipment for growth, the learning process, measurement of achievement, mental hygiene, and the psychology of teaching. *B&N*.

E. Industrial and Military Psychology

BORING, EDWIN G. 1886– *et al. Psychology for the Fighting Man* (1944). Discusses the proper use of the senses in war, aptitudes for different military jobs, control of emotions, development of leadership, and the problems of maintaining morale. *Pen.*

BROWN, J. A. C. 1911– *The Social Psychology of Industry* (1954). A lively account of challenging issues paramount in industrial relations. *Pen.*

CHILD, IRVIN L. 1915– and MARJORIE VAN DE WATER 1900– (eds.) *Psychology for the Returning Serviceman* (1945). Sane information on adjustment to home and job and on helping the injured. *Pen.*

MILLS, C. WRIGHT 1916– *White Collar: American Middle Classes* (1951). Tart, provocative writing about those who wear ties and receive salaries. *Oxford Univ. $6, GB.*

F. Social Psychology and Psychic Research

ALLPORT, GORDON W. 1897– and LEO J. POSTMAN *The Psychology of Rumor* (1947). How rumors start, grow, and arouse hatred toward special groups. *Holt o.p.*

BRITT, STEUART H. 1907– (ed.) *Selected Readings in Social Psychology* (1950). Fifty readings introducing various aspects of the field. *Rinehart $3.50.*

RHINE, JOSEPH B. 1895– *The Reach of the Mind* (1954). Interesting accounts of experiments by the originator of parapsychology, the study of extrasensory perception. *Pen.*

RIESMAN *The Lonely Crowd*. The individual in the crowd. See page 240.

SAPIR, EDWARD 1884–1939 *Culture, Language and Personality* (1956). Nine brilliant essays by a linguistic anthropologist. *Calif.*

TYRRELL, G. N. M. *The Personality of Man* (1947). A comprehensive though sometimes biased review of advances in psychic research, full of thoughtful observations and accounts of experiments. *Pen.*

G. Abnormal and Clinical Psychology

EHRENWALD, JAN 1900– (ed.) *From Medicine Man to Freud: A Treasury of Psychotherapy* (1956). Essays by experts on magic, religion, and science, furnishing sound background for the study of abnormal psychology. *Dell.*

FREEMAN, LUCY 1916– *Hope for the Troubled* (1953). Tells where to go for prevention and treatment of mental disorders. *PB.*

LINDNER, ROBERT 1914–1956 *The Fifty-Minute Hour* (1955). Fascinating case history, illustrating how therapeutic techniques are used. *Rinehart $3.50, Ban.*

———— *Rebel Without a Cause* (1957). An inspiring and illuminating case study of a psychopath helped by hypnoanalysis. *Ever.*

STRAFFORD-CLARK, DAVID *Psychiatry Today* (1952). A clear, interesting introduction to what psychiatry is and does. *Pen.*

WERTHAM, FREDERIC 1895– *The Show of Violence* (1949). Instructive case histories of neurotic killers. *Avon.*

H. Personality

BLUM, GERALD S. 1922– *Psychoanalytic Theories of Personality* (1953). Opinions of Freudians and neo-Freudians about the development of personality at various age levels. *McGraw-Hill $4.75.*

ELLIS, HAVELOCK 1859–1939 *Psychology of Sex* (2nd ed. 1938). The classical introduction to the subject. *Emerson $3, NAL.*

———— *On Life and Sex* (1957). A collection of essays for students of marriage and the family. *NAL.*

HADFIELD, J. A. 1882– *Dreams and Nightmares* (1954). Clear, readable, sound analysis of the meaning of dreams. *Pen.*

HORNEY, KAREN 1885–1952 *Our Inner Conflicts: A Constructive Theory of Neurosis* (1945). Sane, hopeful discussion of man's capacity and desire to be a decent human being and of the neuroses which arise from disturbed relationships. *Norton $4.50.*

HUMPHREY, GEORGE 1889– *Directed Thinking* (1948). How to organize one's thinking to solve daily problems. *Dodd, Mead o.p.*

MOTTRAM, V. H. 1882– *The Physical Basis of Personality* (1944). Explains how heredity, the nerves, and body chemistry help shape personality. *Pen.*

I. Psychoanalysis

BAKER, RACHEL 1903– *Sigmund Freud for Everybody* (1955). Popularized but accurate account of Freud's life, and summary of his major thought. *Pop.*

BRENNER, CHARLES 1913– *An Elementary Textbook of Psychoanalysis* (1957). A valuable introduction for the layman. *Anch.*

FORDHAM, FRIEDA *An Introduction to Jung's Psychology* (1953). A readable digest of an important thinker's concepts. *Pen.*

FREUD, SIGMUND 1856–1939 *Basic Writings* (1938). Comprehensive presentation of Freud's most important work. *MLG.*

_____ *A General Introduction to Psychoanalysis* (1920). An influential series of lectures by the famous founder of psychoanalysis. *Black, Perm.*

_____ *Psychopathology of Everyday Life* (1914). Freud's most popular book. *Macmillan $3.50, NAL.*

HALL, CALVIN S. 1909– *A Primer of Freudian Psychology* (1954). A comprehensive but nontechnical account of Freud's theory of personality. *World $2.50, NAL.*

JASTROW, JOSEPH 1863–1944 *Freud: His Dream and Sex Theories* (1940). Both summarizes and evaluates Freud's theories. *Perm.*

JONES *Life and Work of Sigmund Freud.* Monumental work. See page 160.

KNIGHT, JOHN (*pseud.*) *The Story of My Psychoanalysis* (1950). An often revealing account of a patient's feelings and thoughts during and after analysis. *PB.*

24. Anthropology and Sociology

H. WENTWORTH ELDREDGE, *Dartmouth College*

Anthropology, broadly speaking, is the comparative study of the beliefs and practices of all human societies, past and present. Its roots can be found in the reports written by explorers, missionaries, and traders who, after travels to little-known parts of the world, recorded the great differences they discovered between their own ways of life and those of other peoples. Ibn Batuta's descriptions of the peoples of West Africa, India, and China, and Marco Polo's reports on Asia are among the earliest such records available to the modern reader. In the 15th and 16th centuries, especially after the discovery of the New World, the number of these reports increased. Most, however, reflect the biases of their writers, who tended to be critical of the behavior of other peoples when it differed radically from their own.

Anthropologists have since discovered that what may seem to us unusual practices or beliefs are really only alternative ways in which different people have tried to solve real problems and answer basic questions that face men everywhere: how to cure illness, insure a good harvest, placate supernatural spirits, and so on. It was the search for understanding of the great variety of human practices and beliefs that shaped anthropology into a genuine "science of man." Anthropologists' studies of many different societies have contributed hundreds of specimens for analysis and comparison, and controlled comparisons among them have demonstrated the character and universal nature of the problems man faces, as well as the variety of solutions different societies have evolved to meet them.

The early studies of the anthropologist were confined for the most part to small, little-known peoples who lacked writing and had a simple technology; in recent years, however, anthropologists have begun to study larger and more complex societies. In this growing interest in modern nations it is possible to see anthropology and sociology drawing closer together.

In addition to its interest in the "designs for living" of various contemporary peoples, anthropology also includes the study of archeology, which attempts to reconstruct the history of ancient societies by examining their material remains; linguistics, which studies the growth and structure of language; and physical anthropology, which is concerned with man's biological diversity and physical evolution. Recently, studies of human personality in the context of the cultures which shape them have become important. Applied anthropology, another new direction in the science, deals with problems encountered in attempts to change and improve the lives of people in underdeveloped areas, problems resulting from the introduction of new tools, techniques, and values which may conflict with the traditional adjustments of the society.

Sociology, which has grown to its present position among the social sciences from roots in social philosophy, social reform, and social reportage, differs from its forerunners in the assumptions upon which it rests and in its manner of assembling and handling the evidence, rather than in the kind of problems it deals with. Current sociological writing is factual and mundane rather than intuitive and idealistic; but it has the virtue of showing more clearly how our own and other social institutions are actually constituted, how they relate to one another, and how they operate through time.

Sociologists have not yet reached any final decision about the boundaries and content of their subject, but most would agree that organized human behavior, especially in literate societies, is the focus of their study. Such behavior may be that of a juvenile gang in a big city, an extended family in a village of India, a community of crofters in a distressed area of Scotland, or an upper-income group in a metropolitan suburb. The sociologist's concern is to describe accurately and fully the human interactions and interrelationships which bind groups such as these into effective wholes. Although all of the basic institutions which together make up the life of a specific society—that is, economic, political, religious, familial, educational, etc.—are studied by sociologists in terms of their human and cultural components, in actual practice many parts of this material are normally left to specialists in other social sciences; and the intensive field investigations of preliterate cultures is still regarded as the proper province of anthropologists. But the time may well be approaching when one unified behavior science of man may take the place of the separate efforts of four or five isolated and traditionally competitive social sciences; many sociologists already take this wholistic point of view. The integration of sociology and anthropology, now well advanced toward a common goal in both theories and methods, may presage future developments on a broader front.

Meanwhile sociology continues to focus most of its attention upon aspects of the society and culture of modern, urban-industrial peoples and their problems. If the most important new fact of the past half-century is, as Julian Huxley suggests, "that the human species, for the first time in its history, has begun to take stock of its position in the world," then sociology has an important role in this stocktaking. The growth in size and complexity of contemporary societies creates new problems and underlines the indispensable need for wider public understanding of them. Sociological analysis of urbanism, industrial relations, population growth, and family organization—to name a few areas of effort—has added greatly to our deeper knowledge of the intricacies of modern life.

ARON, RAYMOND 1905– *The Century of Total War* (1954). The world revolution of our time viewed by the brilliant Sorbonne sociologist and commentator for *Figaro. Doubleday $5, Bea.*

ASHLEY MONTAGU, M. F. 1905– *Man's Most Dangerous Myth: The Fallacy of Race* (rev. ed. 1952). A critical re-examination of the concept of race. *Harper $5.*

BARBER, BERNARD 1918– *Science and the Social Order* (1952). A sociological investigation of the role of science in society today. *Free Press $5.*

———— *Social Stratification* (1957). An objective treatment of the form and function of social class. *Harcourt, Brace $6.50.*

BATES, MARSTON 1906– *The Prevalence of People* (1955). Lucid and wide-ranging summary of population trends in the world today and their implications for the future. *Scribner $3.95.*

BENEDICT, RUTH 1887–1948 *Patterns of Culture* (1934). Probably the most influential book of recent years about primitive societies, focusing on the theory that cultural values are relative, not absolute. Three primitive cultures are described and contrasted for the light they can throw upon our own society. Illuminating on the relation between culture and personality. *Houghton Mifflin $4, NAL.*

BOAS, FRANZ 1858–1942 *Primitive Art* (1927). A classic study. *Dov.*

BOWEN, ELENORE SMITH *(pseud.)* *Return to Laughter* (1955). Intriguing fictional account of an anthropological fieldworker's experience in a West African tribe. *Harper $3.50.*

CHASE, STUART 1888– *The Proper Study of Mankind* (rev. ed. 1956). An authoritative and extremely readable discussion of the principal social sciences—anthropology, sociology, social psychology, economics, politics—and their interrelations. *Harper $3.*

CHILDE *What Happened in History.* From human beginnings to the "Urban Revolution." See page 200.

COON *The Story of Man.* The growth and spread of human society. See page 200.

DAVIE, MAURICE R. 1893– *Negroes in American Society* (1949). Comprehensive and authoritative survey of the status of American Negroes from colonial times to the present. *McGraw-Hill $6.75.*

DAVIS, KINGSLEY 1908– *Human Society* (1949). Perhaps the best comprehensive textbook of sociology that has yet appeared. *Macmillan $5.50.*

ERIKSON, ERIK H. 1902– *Childhood and Society* (1950). A child psychiatrist who has done anthropological fieldwork examines the connection between child training and adult personality in a number of societies, both primitive and modern. *Norton $5.50.*

EVANS-PRITCHARD, EDWARD EVAN 1902– *Social Anthropology* (1954). Brief account by an Oxford professor of what anthropology is and does. Controversial and stimulating. *Free Press $3.*

The Exploding Metropolis (1958). Ed. by the staff of *Fortune* magazine. On the border line between city planning and sociology. An up-to-the-minute presentation. *Anch.*

GALBRAITH *The Affluent Society.* See page 217.

GORER, GEOFFREY 1905– *Exploring English Character* (1955). Report on changing English morals and behavior based on an elaborate questionnaire answered by over 11,000 persons. *Criterion $5.*

HOEBEL, E. A. 1906– *The Law of Primitive Man* (1954). An introduction to the methods of legal control in primitive societies. *Harvard Univ. $5.50.*

ANTHROPOLOGY AND SOCIOLOGY 239

HOLLINGSHEAD, AUGUST DE B. 1907– *Elmtown's Youth* (1949). Study of problems of adolescence in a Midwest community with special reference to its social class structure. *Wiley $5.50.*

HOMANS, GEORGE C. 1910– *The Human Group* (1950). Comparative study of the structure and function of small groups as the basic unit in all societies. *Harcourt, Brace $5.*

HOWELLS, WILLIAM W. 1908– *Back of History* (1954). The history of human achievement and the nature of human culture. *Doubleday $5, Random House $3.50.*

——————— *The Heathens* (1948). Primitive religions presented in a way which expresses the fundamental unity of human religious experience. *Doubleday $4.*

KLUCKHOHN, CLYDE 1905– and D. C. LEIGHTON 1908– *The Navaho* (1946). Describes the culture of a contemporary American Indian. *Harvard Univ. $3.75.*

LA FARGE, OLIVER 1901– *Laughing Boy* (1929). Story of a Navaho's struggle to maintain the integrity of his culture. *Houghton Mifflin $3, PB.*

LAPIERE, RICHARD 1899– *The Freudian Ethic* (1959). Devastating critique of Freudian negativism and "permissiveness" which the author views as undermining Western civilization. *Duell, Sloan & Pearce $5.*

LEE, ALFRED McCLUNG 1906– and ELIZABETH BRIANT LEE 1908– (eds.) *Social Problems in America* (rev. ed. 1955). Comprehensive collection of readings and interpretative essays on the whole range of social problems. *Holt $4.*

LERNER, MAX 1902– *America as a Civilization* (1957). This awesome tome is the most complete and readable modern analysis of our society and its culture in all its phases. *Simon & Schuster $10.*

LINTON, RALPH 1893–1953 *The Study of Man* (1936). One of the best introductions to anthropology. *Appleton-Century-Crofts $5.50.*

——————— *The Tree of Culture* (1955). Encyclopedic synthesis of the development of man's culture in time and space. *Knopf $6, Vin (abr.).*

LYND, ROBERT S. 1892– and HELEN M. LYND 1897– *Middletown* (1929) and *Middletown in Transition* (1937). Pioneer studies of culture patterns in a typical American city (Muncie, Ind.) before and during the depression. *Harcourt, Brace $3.50 ea., former in Harv.*

MALINOWSKI, BRONISLAW 1884–1942 *Magic, Science and Religion, and Other Essays* (1954). An examination of the religious life of man from the perspective of primitive society. *Anch.*

MAYER, KURT B. 1916– *Class and Society* (1955). Excellent brief survey of the phenomenon of social class in modern society. *Ran.*

MEAD, MARGARET 1901– *Male and Female* (1955). Biosocial survey of the differences between the sexes by a famous American anthropologist. *Morrow $5, NAL.*

_____ *Sex and Temperament in Three Primitive Societies* (1955). A series of studies concerned with the cultural definition of sex roles in different primitive societies. *NAL.*

_____ (ed.) *Cultural Patterns and Technical Change* (1955). Case studies of Western impact on societies in underdeveloped areas. *NAL.*

MEERLOO, JOOST A. M. 1903– *The Rape of the Mind* (1956). An evaluation of new techniques, both bureaucratic and psychological, for thought control. *World $5.*

MERTON, ROBERT K. 1910– *et al.* (eds.) *Sociology Today: Problems and Prospects* (1959). Exactly what the title says; complete and reliable. *Basic Books, $7.50.*

MILLS, C. WRIGHT 1916– *The Power Elite* (1956). Expansion of the provocative thesis that the United States is increasingly controlled (albeit only semiconsciously) by a small, interlocking group of big generals, big politicians, and big businessmen. *Oxford Univ. $6, GB.*

MOORE, WILBERT E. 1914– *Economy and Society* (1955). The interrelationships between economics and sociology. *Ran.*

MUMFORD, LEWIS 1895– *The Culture of Cities* (1938). The past, present, and hoped-for future of the city—and of civilization. *Harcourt, Brace $5.*

NELSON, LOWRY 1893– *American Farm Life* (1954). Brief, readable presentation of the salient features of farm life in the United States today. *Harvard Univ. $3.75.*

PACKARD, VANCE 1914– *The Hidden Persuaders* (1957). Explains how American public opinion today is manipulated, especially by specialists in motivational research. *McKay $4, PB.*

_____ *The Status Seekers* (1959). Colorful, challenging summary of the shifting American class pattern. *McKay $4.50.*

PETERSEN, WILLIAM 1912– (ed.) *American Social Patterns* (1956). Excellent examples of modern sociological monographs on interracial housing, bureaucracy, politics, and union democracy in modern America. *Anch.*

REDFIELD, ROBERT 1897– *The Little Community* (1955). A noted anthropologist suggests various ways of looking at the culture of peoples in small, technologically simple societies. *Univ. of Chicago $4.*

RIESMAN, DAVID 1909– *Individualism Reconsidered* (1954). Stimulating essays on various facets of modern life. *Free Press $6, Anch (abr.).*

_____, NATHAN GLAZER, and REUEL DENNEY 1913– *The Lonely Crowd* (1950). Provocative study of the changing social character of the American people—from innerdirected to otherdirected. *Yale Univ. $3.75, Anch (abr.).*

SANDOZ, MARI 1907– *Cheyenne Autumn* (1953). The tragic story of how the Cheyennes fought to remain on their ancestral lands. *McGraw-Hill $4.50.*

SAPIR *Language.* A classic account of man's primary device for "culture-building." See page 227.

SCHERMERHORN, RICHARD A. 1903– *These Our People* (1949). Lively, informative account of the principal minority groups— their history, problems, and contributions to American life. *Heath $6.*

SIMPSON, GEORGE G. 1902– *The Meaning of Evolution* (1949). A lucid account of organic evolution, with several chapters on man's place in nature and the potential utility of evolutionary theory in understanding modern society. *Yale Univ. $4, NAL (abr.).*

SPECTORSKY, AUGUSTE C. 1910– *The Exurbanites* (1955). How upper-bracket intellectuals and executives live in the outer suburbs of New York. *Lippincott $3.95, Berk.*

SUMNER, WILLIAM GRAHAM 1840–1910 *Folkways* (1907). Classic study in comparative sociology, showing how manners, morals, and customs vary according to time and place. *Ginn $7.50.*

SUTHERLAND, EDWIN H. 1883–1950 and DONALD R. CRESSY 1919– *Principles of Criminology* (5th ed. 1955). Standard text providing basic principles and modern practices in the control of criminal behavior. *Lippincott $6.75.*

THOMSON, SIR GEORGE P. 1892– *The Foreseeable Future* (1955). A Nobel physicist forecasts the probable advances in technology during the next 100 years and their social implications. *Cambridge Univ. $2.50.*

TRUXAL, ANDREW G. 1900– and FRANCIS E. MERRILL 1904– *Marriage and the Family in American Culture* (1953). The changing American family: its character, problems, and effects on personality development. *Prentice-Hall $6.95.*

UNDERHILL, RUTH 1884– *Red Man's America* (1953). The history and cultures of North American Indians. *Univ. of Chicago $6.50.*

WHITE, LESLIE A. 1900– *The Science of Culture* (1949). A group of essays dealing with such diverse subjects as the origins of the incest taboo, social evolution, the role of the individual in society, and the origins of culture. *Farrar, Straus & Cudahy $6, Ever.*

WHYTE, WILLIAM F. 1914– (ed.) *Industry and Society* (1946). Articles dealing with characteristics and problems of human relations in industry. *McGraw-Hill $4.75.*

————— *Street Corner Society* (rev. ed. 1955). Intimate study of adolescent gangs in city slums. *Univ. of Chicago $5.*

WHYTE, WILLIAM H., JR. 1917– *The Organization Man* (1956). Expansion of the thesis that in modern big-business America the individual, lost in huge bureaucracies, slides into the relaxed pattern of a "team member" incapable of developing independent personality. *Simon & Schuster $5, Anch.*

WIENER, NORBERT 1894– *The Human Use of Human Beings: Cybernetics and Society* (rev. ed. 1954). Presents a new approach to understanding society through the analysis of communications. *Houghton Mifflin $3.50, Anch.*

WOOD, ROBERT C. 1923– *Suburbia, Its People and Their Politics* (1959). The chief characteristic of our great urban sprawls thoroughly and interestingly analyzed. *Houghton Mifflin $4.*

25. Physical Sciences

PALMER W. TOWNSEND, Air Reduction Company

By constant travel and trade, the Ionian Greeks of the 6th century B.C. had freed themselves from the dead weight of custom and ritual fear—powerful inhibitors of scientific investigation and research. Greek scientists, moreover, had an impelling social motivation: the merchants of the ancient world needed the precision of science for their weighing and counting, for their manufacture and transportation. Science consequently flourished. But in the Middle Ages the return to a decentralized economy, rooted in and chained to the soil, eliminated the need for continuing technical development; and so science declined.

With the Renaissance, the merchants and scholars of Europe began to travel, to exchange goods and ideas and songs, to need new roads, new orientations, new processes. Then science was reborn. From the Renaissance to the 20th century, science and technology have progressed with ever-increasing impetus, discarding the dead, inaccurate, or inadequate in their literature, and rediscovering and reapplying out of original context their universal truths.

In today's complex civilization, the role of science and technology is often as dramatically obvious as a flaming sputnik in the sky; yet frequently it is well hidden—as the 300 chemical products involved in the manufacture of an automobile. Science continues to respond to the demands of the society in which it functions, whether the need be a new wonder drug or a new wonder weapon. Considering the scope of technological change experienced by our parents, who can predict what fantasies of our imaginations will be routine occurrences to our children?

But the contributions of science and technology are often mixed blessings. Automation may raise living standards but may also jeopardize economic and social balances. At the same time that technical problems are solved, baffling social, political, and philosophical disturbances may be created. To understand the role of science in our ever-changing society, to use constructively its wonders, and to forecast its ultimate effects, we need knowledge of its history and methods.

Many good books on science are written without technical jargon or involved mathematics. Indeed, many accounts of scientific discoveries have the dramatic excitement of a first-rate "whodunit." Fundamentally, the story of science—of its role in the biography of man—is the fascinating tale of the men and the forces reshaping our physical world to meet our human needs.

A. Main List

BARNETT, LINCOLN 1909– *The Universe and Doctor Einstein* (rev. ed. 1952). Brilliant, easy-to-grasp exposition of the quantum theory and relativity. *NAL.*

BERNHARD, HUBERT JAY 1916– *et al. New Handbook of the Heavens* (2nd ed. 1948). Guide to the stars for the amateur. *McGraw-Hill $4.95, NAL.*

BRIDGMAN, PERCY W. 1882– *The Logic of Modern Physics* (1927). A distinguished scientist discusses the operational approach to knowledge of the external world. *Macmillan $3.50, Dov.*

CERAM, C. W. (KURT W. MAREK) 1915– *Gods, Graves and Scholars* (1951). Dramatic narrative of the adventures and explorations of the great archeologists. *Knopf $5.75.*

———— *The March of Archaeology* (1958). Extensively illustrated description of the development of this science. *Knopf $15.*

CHAPIN, HENRY and F. G. WALTON SMITH 1909– *The Ocean River* (1952). The story of the Gulf Stream and its influence on the climate and history of the Atlantic Community. *Scribner $4.*

CLOOS, HANS 1885–1951 *Conversation with the Earth* (1953). A geologist's autobiography, the record of a life spent in search of the earth's secrets. *Knopf $5.75.*

COHEN, I. BERNARD 1914– *Science, Servant of Man* (1948). Case histories of great scientific achievements, showing how freedom of inquiry is necessary to the attainment of practical ends. *Little, Brown $5.*

CONANT, JAMES B. 1893– *Science and Common Sense* (1951). Reveals the scientist, not as mere experimenter, but rather as the investigator of speculative general ideas. *Yale Univ. $3.75.*

CURIE, EVE 1904–1956 *Madame Curie* (1937). Sympathetic portrayal of the spirit of pure science incarnate. *Doubleday $5, PB.*

DAMPIER, WILLIAM C. 1867–1952 *A History of Science* (rev. ed. 1949). An extremely satisfactory history, with special emphasis on philosophy and religion. *Cambridge Univ. $3.75, Mer (abr.).*

DANTZIG, TOBIAS 1884–1956 *Number, the Language of Science* (1956). Traces the evolution of mathematical thought. *Anch.*

EDDINGTON, SIR ARTHUR S. 1882–1944 *The Nature of the Physical World* (1932). Views of time-space, relativity, causation, and man's place in the world. *Cambridge Univ. $4.25, AA.*

FARRINGTON *Greek Science.* Relationship of culture to science. See page 29.

FINCH, JAMES K. 1883– *Engineering and Western Civilization* (1951). A general history of engineering, revealing the relationship between technology and the social and natural sciences. *McGraw-Hill $6.50.*

FRASER, SIR RONALD 1897– *Once Round the Sun* (1958). The story of the International Geophysical Year. *Macmillan $3.95.*

FRIEND, J. NEWTON 1881– *Man and the Chemical Elements* (1953). Absorbing narrative of the discovery and industrial application of the chemical elements. *Scribner $6.*

GAMOW, GEORGE 1904– *The Birth and Death of the Sun* (1940). Stellar evolution and the anatomy of matter. *Viking $4.75, NAL.*

———— *Biography of the Earth* (1941). Story of the earth—past, present, and future. *Viking $4.75, Comp, NAL.*

———— *One, Two, Three . . . Infinity* (1947). Facts and speculations of science. *Viking $5, NAL.*

———— *The Creation of the Universe* (1952). The origin and evolution of the universe, popularly told. *Viking $3.75, Comp, NAL.*

GARDNER, MARTIN 1914– *Fads and Fallacies in the Name of Science* (2nd ed. 1957). Pseudoscientists, cults, and human gullibility fascinatingly recounted. *Dov.*

JEANS, SIR JAMES 1877–1946 *The Growth of Physical Science* (2nd ed. 1951). Compact history of mathematics and physics from Bablyon to nuclear fission. *Cambridge Univ. $3.75, Prem.*

———— *The Universe Around Us* (4th ed. 1944). Relegating mathematics to the footnotes, the author tells what scientists are thinking about. *Cambridge Univ. $5.*

JUNGK, ROBERT 1913– *Brighter Than a Thousand Suns* (1956). A personal history of the atomic scientists. *Harcourt, Brace o.p.*

KILLEFFER, DAVID H. 1895– *Two Ears of Corn, Two Blades of Grass* (1955). Chemistry's answer to pessimism. A chemical engineer explains how scientific "know-how" can overcome the causes of war, depression, and human suffering. *Van Nostrand $4.*

KNAUSS, HAROLD P. 1900– *Discovering Physics* (1951). Profusely illustrated and nontechnical treatment of a basic science. *Addison-Wesley $6.50.*

KRAMER, E. E. 1902– *The Main Stream of Mathematics* (1951). The fundamental concepts of mathematics. Written for the layman, it includes many interesting anecdotes about the great mathematicians. *Oxford Univ.* $7.50.

LEY, WILLY 1906– *Satellites, Rockets and Outer Space* (1957). Rocket research from earliest times to the present by an authority and enthusiast. *NAL.*

LOW, ARCHIBALD M. 1888– *Electronics Everywhere* (1952). Completely nontechnical discussion of the wonders of electronics, past, present, and future. *Day* $2.75.

LUCRETIUS *On the Nature of Things.* Roman poet–philosopher defending science against superstition. See page 34.

MELVILLE, SIR HARRY 1908– *Big Molecules* (1958). Plastics and other high polymers described for the layman. *Macmillan* $3.95.

MOULTON, FOREST R. 1872–1952 and JUSTUS J. SCHIFFERES 1907– (eds.) *Autobiography of Science* (1945). The progress of science told in the words of the great men who made the significant discoveries. *Doubleday* $5.

NEWMAN, JAMES R. 1907– (ed.) *The World of Mathematics* (1956). An anthology of mathematical literature from the Greeks on, compiled for both layman and expert. *Simon & Schuster 4 vols.* $20.

ORR, CLYDE, JR. 1921– *Between Earth and Space* (1959). The atmosphere as it affects man. *Macmillan* $4.95.

PEARSON, KARL 1857–1936 *The Grammar of Science* (1892). A classic interpretation of the scientific point of view. *Evman-h, Mer.*

SAWYER, W. W. 1911– *Mathematician's Delight* (1943) and *Prelude to Mathematics* (1955). Mathematics as interesting mental exercise rather than forbidding science. *Pen.*

STEINMAN, DAVID B. 1886– *The Builders of the Bridge* (1945). Detailed study of the Roeblings, pioneer builders of suspension bridges. *Harcourt, Brace* $6.

STRAUS, MICHAEL W. 1897– *Why Not Survive?* (1955). Powerful argument for conservation of our natural resources by a leader in the fight for "public power." *Simon & Schuster* $4.

THIEL, RUDOLF 1899– *And There Was Light: The Discovery of the Universe* (1957). Story of adventure and discovery in the world of astronomy from ancient astrologers to modern astrophysicists. *Knopf* $6.95.

VITRUVIUS *On Architecture.* Roman civil engineering. See page 35.

WEINER, J. S. 1915– *The Piltdown Forgery* (1955). First-class detective yarn about one of the greatest hoaxes of modern science. *Oxford Univ.* $3.50.

WHITEHEAD *Science and the Modern World.* Philosophical interpretation. See page 188.

WIENER *Cybernetics.* Provocative correlations of electronic computers with mental processes, shedding light on individual and social neuroses. See page 241.

Additional Recommended Paperbounds

ABRO, A. D' *The Evolution of Scientific Thought; from Newton to Einstein.* Dov.

ALEXANDER, W. and A. STREET *Metals in the Service of Man.* Pen.

Anchor Science Study Series. Many volumes in preparation. Anch.

ANDRADE, E. N. daC. *An Approach to Modern Physics.* Anch.

ARCHIMEDES *Works.* Dov.

ARMITAGE, ANGUS *The World of Copernicus.* NAL.

BAGEHOT, WALTER *Physics and Politics.* Bea.

BORN, MAX *The Restless Universe.* Dov.

BURLINGAME, ROGER *Machines That Built America.* NAL.

CLIFFORD, WILLIAM *The Common Sense of the Exact Sciences.* Dov.

CONANT, J. B. *On Understanding Science.* NAL.

COUZENS, E. G. and V. E. YARSSLEY *Plastics in the Service of Man.* Pen.

FEARNSIDES, W. G. and O. M. B. BULMAN *Geology in the Service of Man.* Pen.

GALILEO *Dialogues Concerning Two New Sciences.* Dov.

HATFIELD, H. S. *The Inventor and His World.* Pen.

HOYLE, FRED *The Nature of the Universe.* NAL.

HUXLEY, JULIAN *Man in the Modern World.* NAL.

JAFFEE, BERNARD *Crucibles: The Story of Chemistry.* Prem.

JEANS, SIR JAMES *The Mysterious Universe.* Evman.

———— *The New Background of Science.* AA.

LEONARD, J. N. *Flight into Space.* NAL.

NEWTON, SIR ISAAC *Opticks.* Dov.

POINCARE, HENRI *Science and Hypothesis.* Dov.

———— *Science and Method.* Dov.

———— *The Value of Science.* Dov.

RAPPORT, SAMUEL and HELEN WRIGHT *The Crust of the Earth.* NAL.

REICHENBACH, HANS *From Copernicus to Einstein.* WL.

SCHRODINGER, ERWIN C. *Science, Theory, and Man.* Dov.

SCIENTIFIC AMERICAN, Editors of. *Atomic Power.* S&S.

———— *Automatic Control.* S&S.

———— *Lives in Science.* S&S.

———— *The New Astronomy.* S&S.

———— *New Chemistry.* S&S.

_____ *The Planet Earth. S&S.*

_____ *The Universe. S&S.*

SOULE, GEORGE *The Shape of Tomorrow. NAL.*

SOUTHWORTH, JOHN V. D. *The Story of the World. PB.*

STRUIK, DIRK *Concise History of Mathematics. Dov.*

SULLIVAN, J. W. N. *The Limitations of Science. NAL.*

SUTTON, O. G. *The Science of Flight. Pen.*

TITCHMARSH, E. C. *Mathematics for the General Reader. Anch.*

WADDINGTON, C. H. *The Scientific Attitude. Pen.*

B. Science Fiction

Science fiction concerns developments in science and society that seem improbable if not impossible to us. Yet some of its predictions are bound to be realized, as were Jules Verne's rockets to the moon and submarines under the Arctic ice. In the tradition of Swift, Verne, and Wells, it is fascinating and challenging to examine the technical, social, and moral consequences of possible future developments of science and technology as creative writers envision them. The following titles are among the best in an ever-growing field.

ASIMOV, ISAAC 1920– *The Caves of Steel* (1954). *NAL.*

_____ *The End of Eternity* (1955). *Doubleday $2.95, NAL.*

_____ *The Martian Way and Other Stories* (1955). *NAL.*

_____ *Naked Sun* (1957). *Doubleday $2.95, Ban.*

BALMER, EDWARD 1883– and PHILIP WYLIE 1902– *When Worlds Collide* (1932) and *After Worlds Collide* (1950). *Lippincott $3.95.*

BESTER, ALFRED *Starburst* (1958). *NAL.*

_____ *Demolished Man* (1953). *NAL.*

BOUCHER, ANTHONY 1911– (ed.) *Best from Fantasy and Science Fiction* (7th series) (1958). *Doubleday $3.75.*

BRADBURY, RAY 1920– *The Martian Chronicles* (1950). *Doubleday $2.95.*

_____ (ed.) *Circus of Dr. Lao and Other Improbable Stories. Ban.*

CAMPBELL, J. W., JR. 1910– (ed.) *Astounding Science Fiction Anthology* (1952). *Berk.*

_____ (ed.) *Astounding Tales of Space and Time. Berk.*

CAPEK *War with the Newts.* See page 97.

CLARKE, ARTHUR C. 1917– *The Deep Range* (1957). *Harcourt, Brace $3.95, NAL.*

_____ *The Sands of Mars* (1952). *Gnome $2.75, PB.*

HEINLEIN, ROBERT A. 1907– *Assignment in Eternity* (1953). *NAL.*

_____ *The Day After Tomorrow. NAL.*

_____ *The Door into Summer* (1957). *Doubleday $2.95, NAL.*

_____ *The Green Hills of Earth* (1951). *NAL.*

_____ *The Puppet Masters* (1951). *NAL.*

RUSSELL, ERIC FRANK *Wasp* (1957). *Perm.*

SWIFT *Gulliver's Travels*. See page 70.

28 Science Fiction Stories (1952). *Dov.*

VAN VOGT, A. E. 1912– *Destination: Universe! NAL.*

_____ *The Mind Cage* (1957). *Simon & Schuster $3.50, Avon.*

VERNE, JULES 1828–1905 *From the Earth to the Moon* (1865). *Lippincott $1.95, Prem.*

_____ *Journey to the Center of the Earth* (1864). *Longmans, Green 50¢, Wyn $2.95, Ace.*

_____ *Omnibus* (1951). Includes *20,000 Leagues Under the Sea, Around the World in 80 Days, Blockade Runners,* and *From the Earth to the Moon. Lippincott $3.45.*

_____ *20,000 Leagues Under the Sea* (1869). *Grosset $1.49, Heritage $6, Rand McNally $2.60, Evman-h, GtIl.*

WELLS, H. G. 1866–1946 *Seven Science Fiction Novels* (1950). Includes *Men Like Gods* (1923), *The Time Machine* (1895), *The War of the Worlds* (1898), and *The World Set Free* (1914). *Dov.*

26. Biological Sciences

RACHEL CARSON

The scope of biology can be truly defined only in broad terms as the history of the earth and all its life—past, present, and future. Any definition of lesser scope becomes narrow and academic and fails utterly to convey the majestic sweep of the subject in time and space, embracing all that has made man what he is, and holding a foretaste of what he may yet become. For it has dawned upon us in these recent years of the maturing of our science that neither man nor any other living creature may be studied or comprehended apart from the world in which he lives; that such restricted studies as the classification of plants and animals or descriptions of their anatomy and physiology (upon which the early biologists necessarily focused their attention) are but one small facet of a subject so many-sided, so rich in beauty and fascination, and so filled with significance that no informed reader can neglect it.

In the truest sense, there is no separate literature of biology or of any science. Knowledge of the facts of science is not the prerogative of a small number of men, isolated in their laboratories, but belongs to all men, for the realities of science are the realities of life itself. We cannot understand the problems that concern us in this, our particular moment of time, unless we first understand our environment and the forces that have made us what we are, physically and mentally.

Biology deals with the living creatures of the living earth. Pleasure in color, form, and movement, awareness of the amazing diversity of life, and the enjoyment of natural beauty are part of man's heritage as a living creature. Our first conscious acquaintance with the subject should come, if possible, through nature—in fields and forests and on the shore; secondarily, and by way of amplification and verification, we should then explore its laboratory aspects. Some of the most gifted and imaginative biologists have first approached their subject through the medium of sensory impression and emotional response. The most memorable writings—though they be addressed to the intellect—are rooted in man's emotional reaction to that life stream of which he is a part. The writing of the great naturalists such as Hudson and Thoreau, most easily sampled in some of the excellent anthologies now available, has a valid place in one's reading in the field of biology.

As the frontiers of science expand, there is inevitably an increasing trend toward specialization, in which all the mental faculties of a man or group of men are brought to bear upon a single aspect of some problem. But there is fortunately a counter tendency, which brings different specialists together to work in cooperation. Oceanographic expeditions commonly include biologists, chemists, physicists, geologists, and meteorologists—so diverse are the problems presented by one aspect of the earth's surface. Atomic physicists, by discovering that radioactive elements in fossils and minerals disintegrate at a rate that may be determined, have provided biologists with a tool that has already revolutionized our concept of the age of the earth and permits a far more accurate approach than ever before to the problem of the evolution of man himself. Chemists and geneticists, by joining forces, seem to be solving the riddle of the gene and the actual means by which it produces hereditary characteristics.

Only within the 20th century has biological thought been focused on ecology, or the relation of the living creature to its environment. Awareness of ecological relationships is—or should be—the basis of modern conservation programs, for it is useless to attempt to preserve a living species unless the kind of land or water it requires is also preserved. So delicately interwoven are the relationships that when we disturb one thread of the community fabric we alter it—perhaps almost imperceptibly, perhaps so drastically that destruction follows.

If we have been slow to develop the general concepts of ecology and conservation, we have been even more tardy in recognizing the facts of the ecology and conservation of man himself. We may hope that this will be the next major phase in the development of biology. Here and there awareness is growing that man, far from being the overlord of all creation, is himself part of nature, subject to the same cosmic forces that control all other life. Man's future welfare and probably even his survival depend upon his learning to live in harmony, rather than in combat, with these forces.

The books listed below have been chosen to reflect the richness and diversity of biology. Almost any of them, excellent in itself, leads on to even wider vistas that the reader, according to his taste, may explore through still other books.

ALLEN, DURWARD L. 1910– *Our Wildlife Legacy* (1954). A clear, forceful account of wildlife as a natural resource and a statement of the basic principles of modern conservation. *Funk & Wagnalls $5.*

BARNETT, LINCOLN 1909– *The World We Live In* (1955). The richly illustrated dramatic story of how the earth, atmosphere, and oceans were formed and how life arose and evolved. First appeared in *Life. Simon & Schuster $13.50.*

BEEBE, WILLIAM 1877– (ed.) *The Book of Naturalists* (1944). Well-chosen anthology containing many of the classics of natural history from Aristotle to modern writers. *Knopf o.p.*

———— *High Jungle* (1949). The marvelously interwoven life of a tropical jungle, with its strangeness and beauty, re-created by a gifted naturalist. *Duell, Sloan & Pearce $6.*

BERRILL, N. J. 1903– *Man's Emerging Mind* (1955). A fresh, thought-provoking discussion of man's development and evolution with speculation on his future. *Dodd, Mead $4, Prem.*

———— *You and the Universe* (1958). The nature of the universe and of life, and the interrelations between man and outer space. *Dodd, Mead $4.*

CARHART, ARTHUR H. 1892– *Timber in Your Life* (1955). Shows basic relations of forests, land, and water, stressing the need of concerted social effort for conservation. *Lippincott $4.50.*

———— *Water—Or Your Life* (1951). A plea for coordinated effort to conserve one of our most vital, least appreciated resources. *Lippincott $4.50.*

CARSON, RACHEL 1907– *The Edge of the Sea* (1955). Interprets the life of the shore as governed by its environment: the geology of the coast, tidal range and rhythm, surf, climate, and interrelations of species. *Houghton Mifflin $3.95, NAL.*

———— *The Sea Around Us* (1951). The origin, history, and dynamic nature of the sea as the original home of life. *Oxford Univ. $4, NAL.*

CHEESMAN, EVELYN 1881– *Insects: Their Secret World* (1953). Insect habits, activities, and relationships described clearly and with attractive style by an entomologist of the British Museum. *Sloane $3.50.*

COON *The Story of Man.* From ape men to the atomic age. See page 200.

CRISLER, LOIS *Arctic Wild* (1958). Written with beauty, honesty, and rare perception, this book is almost unique in the understanding it gives of one of the few examples of true wilderness remaining on earth. *Harper $4.95.*

DARWIN, CHARLES 1809–1882 *The Origin of Species* (1859) and *The Descent of Man* (1871). The basic writings of Darwin now available in one volume: *The Origin* is a milestone in human progress as an explanation of evolution through natural selection; *The Descent* provides a sequel and amplification. *MLG. Origin of Species* only: *Evman-h, NAL, Ungar, WoC.*

————— *Voyage of the Beagle.* Notes from the actual journal of Darwin's historic voyage. See page 159.

DUNN, L. C. 1893– and THEODOSIUS DOBZHANSKY 1900– *Heredity, Race, and Society* (rev. ed. 1952). Group differences and how they arise; influences of heredity and environment on mankind. *NAL.*

EKMAN, SVEN P. 1876– *Zoogeography of the Sea* (1953). A technical but basic account of the effect of environment on the physiology of marine fauna. *Macmillan $6.50.*

HASKINS, CARYL P. 1908– *Of Societies and Men* (1951). Important scholarly discussion of the relationships between man the animal and man the "capstone of creation." *Norton $6.*

HESSE, RICHARD 1868–1944 *et al. Ecological Animal Geography* (1951). This second edition of a classic volume presents the ecological aspects of marine, fresh water, and terrestrial life. *Wiley $9.50.*

HUDSON, W. H. 1841–1922 *The Best of W. H. Hudson.* Ed. by Odell Shepard. A sampling of the writings of the great naturalist, in whose pages the world of biology comes to life. *Dutton $5.*

HUSSEY, RUSSELL C. 1888– *Historical Geology* (2nd ed. 1947). Describes the changing shapes of continents and seas throughout geologic time, with accounts of the life characteristic of each period. *McGraw-Hill $6.75.*

HUXLEY, JULIAN 1887– *Man in the Modern World* (1948). Thirteen philosophic essays by a distinguished biologist on such topics as the uniqueness of man as an animal, climate and human history, eugenics and society. *NAL.*

HYLANDER, C. J. 1897– *The World of Plant Life* (2nd ed. 1956). Readable, comprehensive, illustrated survey of plant life from the simplest to the most complex. *Macmillan $10.95.*

JONES, SIR H. SPENCER 1890– *Life on Other Worlds* (1954). Pictures the universe in terms of modern astronomy and concludes there are other worlds where conditions necessary for life may exist. *Macmillan $3, NAL.*

KLINGEL, GILBERT *The Bay* (1951). The "universe of life" above and below the surface of Chesapeake Bay, written with perception and charm by a naturalist of rich experience. *Dodd, Mead $4.*

KRUTCH, JOSEPH WOOD 1893– *The Voice of the Desert* (1955). The extraordinary ways life meets the demands of the desert environment. The author's philosophic conclusions are significant for all life, in all surroundings. *Sloane $3.75.*

LEOPOLD, ALDO 1886–1948 *Sand County Almanac* (1949). A deep understanding of the essential relation of life to the land is revealed in this series of essays and sketches. *Oxford Univ. $4.*

MacGINITIE, G. E. 1889– and NETTIE MacGINITIE *Natural History of Marine Animals* (1949). An authoritative work on the behavior of a large number of marine animals representing all major groups. *McGraw-Hill $8.50.*

MOORE, RUTH 1903– *Man, Time, and Fossils* (1953). Fascinating story of how the concepts of man's evolution have developed, from Lamarck and Darwin down to atomic-age methods of dating the past. *Knopf $6.50.*

MORGAN, ANN H. 1882– *Field Book of Animals in Winter* (1939). Describes the adaptations to winter life made by a great variety of creatures. *Putnam $5.*

———— *Field Book of Ponds and Streams* (1930). A standard guide to fresh-water biology. *Putnam $5.*

OSBORN, FAIRFIELD 1887– *The Limits of the Earth* (1953). A study of increasing populations set against the decline of the world's natural resources. *Little, Brown $3.50.*

———— *Our Plundered Planet* (1948). Effectively presents the thesis that if man continues to prey on nature, nature will destroy him. *Little, Brown $3.50.*

PEATTIE, DONALD CULROSS 1898– *A Natural History of the Trees of Eastern and Central North America* (1950). By writing engagingly of the habits and characteristics of all the common trees, the author makes them more easily recognized and remembered. *Houghton Mifflin $6.*

RAYMOND, PERCY E. 1879– *Prehistoric Life* (1950). Readable, well-illustrated survey of the forms of life that preceded man. Explains the role of environment in evolution. *Harvard Univ. $5.*

SCIENTIFIC AMERICAN, Editors of, *Twentieth-Century Bestiary* (1955). Samples the curious and wonderful inventions of life: flight, navigation, parasitism, social organization. Based on articles in *Scientific American. S&S.*

———— *The Physics and Chemistry of Life* (1955). Current views on such topics as the origin of life, structure of the protein molecule, chemical basis of transmission of hereditary characters. Based on articles in *Scientific American. S&S.*

SIMPSON, GEORGE GAYLORD 1902– *The Meaning of Evolution* (1949). The important attainments of modern evolutionary thought and its effect on philosophy and ethics. *Yale Univ. $4, NAL (abr.).*

_____ *et al. Life: An Introduction to College Biology* (1958). Although a text, this readable and fascinating book will give any inquiring mind an excellent conception of the modern field of biology. *Harcourt, Brace $7.50.*

SINNOTT, EDMUND W. 1888– *Biology of the Spirit* (1955). An eminent biologist finds a basis for human aspirations and "the reality of the spirit of man" in the properties of protoplasm. *Comp.*

STILLSON, BLANCHE 1889– *Wings* (1954). The story of flight as achieved by insects, birds, and men, told with charm and fascinating detail. *Bobbs-Merrill $3.50.*

STORER, JOHN H. 1888– *The Web of Life* (1953). The balance of nature and the vital relation of living things to their environment, expressed clearly and simply for laymen. *Devin-Adair $3, NAL.*

TEALE, EDWIN WAY 1899– (ed.) *Green Treasury: A Journey Through the World's Great Nature Writing* (1952). A delightful introduction to the literature of earth, sea, and sky, the life of the earth, and man's place in nature. Among its 150 selections are the classics of Hudson, Thoreau, Muir, and Jefferies as well as others almost equally deserving to be read. *Dodd, Mead $5.*

_____ *The Lost Woods* (1945). Excursions into nature's wonders: the beauty of snowflakes, the insect world on a single leaf, the grandeur of the redwoods. *Dodd, Mead $5.*

THOREAU, HENRY DAVID 1817–1862 *Journals.* Ed. by Francis H. Allen and Bradford Torrey. Walden Edition, 14 vols. (1949). Containing the materials from which Thoreau constructed most of his books, the *Journal* entries cover the period 1837–1861 and are rich in observations on nature and reflections on its meaning. *Houghton Mifflin $35.*

_____ *Walden.* Living close to nature. See page 169.

VOGT, WILLIAM 1902– *Road to Survival* (1948). Summarizes world-wide evidence that man is decimating natural resources at a rate that threatens his own extinction. *Sloane $4.*

WORTH, C. BROOKE 1908– and ROBERT K. ENDERS 1899– *The Nature of Living Things* (1955). A highly readable introductory account of the plant and animal life of the earth, with discussions of evolution, genetics, conservation, etc. *NAL.*

ZINNSER, HANS 1878–1940 *Rats, Lice and History* (1935). Absorbing account of the interrelations of insects, disease, and social evolution. *Little, Brown $6.*

For those who wish to observe nature at first hand, two excellent series of guide books are available, containing practical identification aids for most groups of plants and animals, as well as for rocks and minerals and the stars. These are the Field Book series published by Putnam and selling at between $2.95 and $7.50 per volume, and the Field Guide series of Houghton Mifflin, priced at $3.95 per volume.

SPECIAL SECTION

---

27. Reference Books

CHARLES B. SHAW, Swarthmore College Library

Any book can be a reference book. If you want to decide whether there were two or three kittens that lost their mittens, a collection of Mother Goose rhymes becomes for the moment a reference book. One way to define a reference work is to say that it is a volume or set of volumes not intended to be read through, though probably some persevering souls have read from cover to cover the *World Almanac,* or an unabridged dictionary, or the *Encyclopaedia Britannica,* or the *New York Times Index,* or the *United States Catalog of Books in Print.* These titles are examples of the fundamental reference books.

Few individuals can afford to purchase many reference works, but nearly everyone wants some such books at hand—a dictionary, the *World Almanac,* an atlas, perhaps a garden encyclopedia. No library can have all the reference books in existence, but most libraries have an extensive, varied, useful assortment.

An example will show the time-and-energy savings assured by knowing reference books. A student, writing a paper on novels inspired by World War I, first compiled a list of such novels by turning page after page in volume after volume of reviewing journals of the 1920's. By consulting the indexes and citations in the *Book Review Digest* he could have made a better list in much less time.

As short cuts to hiding places of recorded facts, bibliographical guides and reference books of all sorts lead to desired information without lost motion or waste of time. The latent riches of scholarship, the recorded thoughts and observations of mankind's thinkers and doers lie at hand on printed pages. Awareness of reference books constitutes an easily remunerative way of prospecting among these riches. Such books are literally the keys that quickly unlock the doors to the golden store of the world's wisdom.

The following half-dozen pages name and briefly describe more than 100 of the major reference titles.

A. Bibliographies and General Indexes

Nearly every library will have the *United States Catalog* and *Cumulative Book Index*. These volumes bring up to date (with information about publisher, price, date, number of pages, etc.) the immense array of books published in this country. Information about almost any wanted book can usually be found under any of three or more entries: (1) author's name, (2) title of the book and (3) subjects with which the book deals. These last entries assemble lists of books on all subjects.

Libraries also have files of publications that analyze, usually in the same three ways, the contents of magazines. Material on any subject can thus be found in files of hundreds of thousands of volumes of periodicals. Representative analyses are *Poole's Index*, *Readers' Guide*, *International Index*, and *P.A.I.S.* (Public Affairs Information Service). There are additional indexes for special and limited fields: art, bibliography, biography, education, the industrial arts, music, etc.

Abstracts are another kind of helpful analysis of the literature of a given subject: *Chemical Abstracts*, *Historical Abstracts*, and *Psychological Abstracts* are three of many such publications.

The *Essay and General Literature Index* (from 1900 on), a subject analysis of thousands of miscellaneous books, gives citations of important writings. Almost any published poem, play, short story, or song can be found through special indexes: EDITH GRANGER'S *Index to Poetry* (Columbia Univ. 4th ed. 1953 $35), and its *Supplement, 1951–55* (Columbia Univ. 1957 $20); D. H. WEST & D. M. PEAKE'S, *Play Index* (Wilson 1953), and in earlier allied publications by I. T. E. FIRKINS and HANNAH LOGASA and J. H. OTTEMILLER; D. E. COOK & I. S. MONRO'S *Short Story Index* (Wilson 1953) and its *Supplement, 1950–54* (Wilson 1956); and M. E. SEARS' *Song Index* and *Supplement* (Wilson 1926 & 1934).

Paperbound Books in Print, first issued in the summer of 1955, is a quarterly statement of the growing array of inexpensive texts, minus "hard" binding, available from many publishers (Bowker $2).

The *Book Review Digest* since 1906 has quoted from reviews and assembled appraisals of thousands of new books each year.

Full and helpful lists of all sorts of reference books on every subject (these pages give only a tiny sampling) are LOUIS SHORES' *Basic Reference Sources (American Library Assn. 1954 $6.25)* and C. M. WINCHELL'S *Guide to Reference Books (A.L.A. 7th ed. 1951 $10); Supplement 1950-52 (A.L.A. 1954 $3.25)* and *Second Supplement (A.L.A. 1956 $3.50).* Also useful is R. W. MURPHEY'S *How and Where to Look It Up (McGraw-Hill 1958 $15).*

B. Encyclopedias

Standard, frequently revised general encyclopedias with helpful index volumes are *Encyclopedia Americana* (30 vols.) and *Encyclopaedia Britannica* (24 vols.). Good single-volume works for an individual's desk are *Columbia Encyclopedia* with *Supplement (Columbia Univ. 1956 $35)* and *Lincoln Library of Essential Information (Frontier 23rd ed. 1957 $22).*

C. Fact Books

One of these small single volumes, each including an amazing array and variety of information, is a helpful companion near one's desk. Annually revised titles include *Information Please Almanac (Macmillan vol. 13 1959 $1.25); World Almanac (N.Y. World-Telegram vol. 74 1959 $1.35);* and the *Statistical Abstract of the United States,* compiled by the U.S. Bureau of the Census *(Govt. Ptg. Off. 79th ed. 1958 $3.75).*

D. Dictionaries

Outstanding comprehensive authorities are SIR JAMES MURRAY'S *New English Dictionary*—"The Oxford Dictionary" *(Oxford Univ. 1888-1933 13 vols. $300); New Standard Dictionary (Funk & Wagnalls)* and *Webster's New International Dictionary (Merriam).* Smaller works for an individual's desk include C. L. BARNHART'S *American College Dictionary (Random House 1959 $5); New College Standard Dictionary (Funk & Wagnalls $5.50);* and *Webster's New Collegiate Dictionary (Merriam $5).*

Other useful books in this category include H. W. FOWLER'S *Dictionary of Modern English Usage (Oxford Univ. 1937 $3.75);* W. H. PHYFE'S *20,000 Words Often Mispronounced (Putnam new ed. 1937 $4);* L. V. BERREY & MELVIN VAN DEN BARK'S *American Thesaurus of Slang (Crowell 2nd ed. 1953 $8.50); Webster's Dictionary of Synonyms (Merriam 1951 $6);* and PETER ROGET'S *Thesaurus of English Words and Phrases (Evman-h, PB).*

E. Biography

Who's Who in America (Marquis vol. 30 1958-59 $25) is a biennial list of prominent living Americans. *Who's Who (Macmillan vol. 111 1959 $19.50)* is an annual similar list, chiefly of British citizens. *International Who's Who (Europa vol. 22 1958 £6)* and *Current Biog-*

raphy (Wilson 1940 on; annual vols. $6 each)—a monthly publication, annually cumulated—give sketches of prominent people of various nationalities.

Dictionary of American Biography (Scribner new rev. pop. ed. 22 vols. incl. Supplement & Index 1943–5 $220; Supplement 2 through 1940 Scribner 1958 $25) contains authoritative biographies of Americans no longer living. *Dictionary of National Biography (Oxford Univ. 1938 reprint incl. 1st Supplement 22 vols. $192; 2nd–5th Supplements, 1910–40 Oxford Univ. $8.80 each)* is the corresponding set for British lives.

New Century Cyclopedia of Names (Appleton-Century-Crofts 1954 3 vols. $39.50) and *Webster's Biographical Dictionary (Merriam 1956 $8.50)* are more general and widely inclusive but with far briefer information.

Biographical reference books abound for nearly every area of human effort, from art to zoology. Here are a sample few concerning authors, all by S. J. KUNITZ & HOWARD HAYCRAFT: *American Authors, 1600–1900 (Wilson 1938 $5); British Authors of the Nineteenth Century (Wilson 1936 $5)* and *Twentieth Century Authors (Wilson 1942 $8.50)* and its *First Supplement (Wilson 1955 $8).*

F. Atlases

Good and not too cumbersome general volumes are *Cosmopolitan Atlas (Rand McNally rev. ed. 1958 $13.95)* and JOHN BARTHOLOMEW'S *The Columbus Atlas (McGraw-Hill 1954 $10)*. A more limited and specialized volume is C. L. & E. H. LORD'S *Historical Atlas of the United States (Holt rev. ed. 1953 $5.50)*. Allied to atlases are such books as *The Columbia Lippincott Gazetteer of the World (Columbia Univ. 1952 $65)* and *Webster's Geographical Dictionary (Merriam rev. ed. 1955 $8.50)*.

G. History

OSCAR HANDLIN and others have compiled a helpful bibliography of historical materials: *Harvard Guide to American History (Harvard Univ. 1954 $10)*. H. R. KELLER'S *Dictionary of Dates (Macmillan 1934 2 vols. $17.50)* is a useful compilation. W. L. LANGER'S *Encyclopedia of World History (Houghton Mifflin 3rd ed. 1952 $8)* is a compact volume for an individual's desk. Limited to our own history, there is a similar range in scope and fullness in J. T. ADAMS & R. V. COLEMAN'S *Dictionary of American History (Scribner 1942 6 vols. $60)* and R. B. MORRIS' *Encyclopedia of American History (Harper 1953 $6.95)*. G. E. SHANKLE'S *American Nicknames (Wilson 2nd ed. 1955 $7.50)* also illuminates American history.

H. Social Sciences

A no longer new but still authoritative and useful publication in these fields, first issued (1930–5) in 15 vols. and reprinted as a "popular edition" in 1948 in 8 vols., is E. R. A. SELIGMAN & ALVIN JOHNSON'S *Encyclopedia of the Social Sciences (Macmillan $100)*.

For economics, useful volumes include two titles by H. S. SLOAN & A. J. ZURCHER: *Dictionary of Economics (Barnes & Noble 3rd ed. rev. 1957 $3.50)* and their *Dictionary of Business (Barnes & Noble rev. ed. 1957 $3.50).* A useful series of annual volumes of statistics has been issued by the National Industrial Conference Board: *Economic Almanac (Crowell vol. 14 1958 $5).* For general coverage there are G. G. CHISHOLM'S *Handbook of Commercial Geography (Longmans, Green 15th ed. 1956 $16)* and W. S. & E. S. WOYTINSKY'S *World Population and Production (20th Century Fund 1953 $12); Oxford Economic Atlas of the World (Oxford Univ. 1956 $6.75);* and, for information about our own country, both *Historical Statistics of the United States, 1789–1945* issued by U.S. BUREAU OF THE CENSUS *(Govt. Ptg. Off. 1949 $2.50)* and its *Continuation to 1952 (Govt. Ptg. Off. 1954 55¢)* and—edited by J. F. DEWHURST—*America's Needs and Resources (20th Century Fund 1955 $10).*

For government or political science there is WALTER THEIMER'S *Encyclopedia of Modern World Politics (Rinehart 1950 $5.50);* UNITED NATIONS DEPARTMENT OF PUBLIC INFORMATION'S *Everyman's United Nations (Columbia Univ. 5th ed. 1956 $1.50);* and, since 1927, the annual *Political Handbook of the World (Harper 1959 $3.95).* For information about state government there has been issued since 1935 the biennial *Book of the States (Chicago Council of State Governments vol. 12 1958–9 $9);* and, since 1934, for matters on the local level, the annual *Municipal Year Book (Chicago International City Managers Assn. vol. 25 1958 $10).*

I. Philosophy and Religion

In these fields the monumental standard works are both old: J. M. BALDWIN'S 1910 *Dictionary of Philosophy and Psychology (Peter Smith reprint ed. 3 vols. in 4 $50)* and JAMES HASTINGS' *Encyclopedia of Religion and Ethics (Scribner 1908–26 13 vols. $140).* Useful recent works include M. S. & J. L. MILLER'S *Harper's Bible Dictionary (Harper 1958 $7.95)* and R. D. HITCHCOCK'S *Topical Bible and Cruden's Concordance (Baker 1952 $9.95).*

J. Literature

Cassell's Encyclopedia of World Literature (Funk 1954 2 vols. $25), the *Columbia Dictionary of Modern European Literature (Columbia Univ. 1947 $10),* SIR PAUL HARVEY'S *Oxford Companion to*

Classical Literature (Oxford Univ. 2nd ed. 1937 $3.75), and SIR
PAUL HARVEY & J. E. HESELTINE'S *Oxford Companion to
French Literature (Oxford Univ. 1959 $12.50)* are helpful in pro-
viding information about non-English books and authors.

The *Cambridge History of English Literature (Macmillan 1949–
53 reissue 15 vols. $45)* and *Literary History of the United States
(Macmillan rev. ed. in 1 vol. 1953 $11.50)* are the standard historical
reference works.

General books, so miscellaneous and widely varied in the information they include as to be miniature encyclopedias, include, in addition to those already cited, others in the series of "Oxford Companions," all published by Oxford Univ.: SIR PAUL HARVEY'S
Oxford Companion to English Literature (3rd ed. 1946 $10), J. D.
HART'S *Oxford Companion to American Literature (3rd ed. 1956
$10)*, and PHYLLIS HARTNOLL'S *Oxford Companion to the
Theatre (2nd ed. 1957 $11.50)*. W. R. BENET'S *The Reader's Ency-
clopedia (Crowell 1955 $6.50)* and *Brewer's Dictionary of Phrase and
Fable (Harper rev. ed. 1953 $5)* are other useful volumes of this
sort.

Who said it? Books of quotations will give the answer. The best
book in this category is the one in which you find the desired
quotation. Among a great many, the following five are particularly
helpful: F. P. ADAMS' *F.P.A. Book of Quotations (Funk 1952 $5.95)*;
JOHN BARTLETT'S *Familiar Quotations (Little, Brown 13th ed.
1955 $10)*; H. L. MENCKEN'S *New Dictionary of Quotations
(Knopf 1942 $10)*; *Oxford Dictionary of Quotations (Oxford Univ.
2nd ed. 1953 $10.50)*; and B. E. STEVENSON'S *Home Book of
Quotations (Dodd, Mead 9th ed. 1959 $20)*.

K. Art and Music

In the fine arts (except for music) many of the still standard refer-
ence books are old and out of print: for example, MICHAEL
BRYAN'S *Dictionary of Painters and Engravers (1903–5 5 vols.)*;
J. D. CHAMPLIN'S *Cyclopedia of Painters and Paintings (1887 4
vols.)* and RUSSELL STURGIS' *Dictionary of Architecture (1901–2
3 vols.)*. Recent smaller publications of this sort include B. S.
MYERS' *Encyclopedia of Painting (Crown 1955 $11.95)*; F. HAZAN'S
Dictionary of Abstract Painting (Tudor 1957 $6.95) and HELEN
GARDNER'S *Art Through the Ages (Harcourt, Brace 4th ed. 1959
$8.95)*. Other recent good books in their respective fields are A. E.
BURKE'S *Architectural and Building Trades Dictionary (Amer.
Technical Soc. 2nd ed. 1955 $6.50)*; L. A. & H. B. BOGER'S *Dic-
tionary of Antiques and the Decorative Arts (Scribner 1957 $13.95)*
and J. L. STOUTENBURGH'S *Dictionary of Arts and Crafts
(Philosophical Library 1956 $6)*.

In music the standard monumental work is SIR GEORGE
GROVE'S *Dictionary of Music and Musicians (St Martin's 5th ed.
1954 9 vols. $127.50)*. Less inclusive but useful general compendiums
include WILLI APEL'S *Harvard Dictionary of Music (Harvard*

Univ. 1944 $9.50); W. S. PRATT'S *New Encyclopedia of Music and Musicians (Macmillan rev. ed. 1951 $9.50);* P. A. SCHOLES' *Oxford Companion to Music (Oxford Univ. 9th ed. 1955 $21.50);* and OSCAR THOMPSON & NICHOLAS SLONIMSKY'S *International Cyclopedia of Music and Musicians (Dodd, Mead 8th ed. 1959 $20).* For information about opera there are GUSTAV KOBBE'S *Complete Opera Book (Putnam rev. ed. 1954 $10)* and J. W. McSPADDEN'S *Operas and Musical Comedies (Crowell 3rd ed. 1955 $4.50).* Contemporary music is well covered in three books by DAVID EWEN: *American Composers Today (Wilson 1949 $4); European Composers Today (Wilson 1954 $4);* and *Complete Book of Twentieth Century Music (Prentice-Hall 1952 $7.50).* Information about recordings will be found in a fourth book by DAVID EWEN: *Musical Masterworks (Arco 2nd ed. 1955 $3.95)* and in DAVID HALL & ABNER LEVIN'S *The Disc Book (Long Player Publications 1955 $7.50).*

L. Science

A representative work of general inclusiveness is *Van Nostrand's Scientific Encyclopedia (Van Nostrand 3rd ed. 1958 $30).* Also general in scope are I. F. & W. D. HENDERSON'S *Dictionary of Scientific Terms (Van Nostrand 6th ed. 1957 $12.50)* and W. E. FLOOD & MICHAEL WEST'S *Explaining and Pronouncing Dictionary of Scientific Words (Longmans, Green 2nd ed. 1955 $3.25).*

For astronomers there are E. A. BEET'S *Guide to the Sky (Cambridge Univ. $3),* H. C. MACPHERSON'S *Guide to the Stars (Philosophical Library new rev. ed. 1955 $2.75),* and SIR HAROLD S. JONES'S *Space Encyclopedia (Dutton $6.95).*

Botanists will find useful B. D. JACKSON'S *Glossary of Botanic Terms (Hafner 4th ed. 1949 $4);* L. H. & E. Z. BAILEY'S *Hortus Second (Macmillan 1951 $13.50);* and a dictionary, J. C. WILLIS' *Flowering Plants and Ferns (Cambridge Univ. 6th ed. 1931 $5.50).*

In chemistry the encyclopedias and dictionaries range from such a monumental work as SIR T. E. THORPE'S *Dictionary of Applied Chemistry (Longmans, Green 4th ed. 1937–56 12 vols. $234.50)* to C. T. KINGZETT'S *Chemical Encyclopedia (Van Nostrand 8th ed. 1952 $18.50);* G. L. CLARK'S *Encyclopedia of Chemistry (Reinhold 1957 $19.50);* STEPHEN & L. M. MIALL'S *New Dictionary of Chemistry (Longmans, Green 2nd ed. 1949 $14.50);* and HARRY BENNETT'S *Concise Chemical and Technical Dictionary (Chemical Pub. Co. 1947 $10).* Additional volumes for the chemist include A. A. HOPKINS' *Standard American Encyclopedia of Formulas (Grosset 1953 $3.50)* and *Handbook of Chemistry and Physics (Chemical Rubber Co. 39th ed. 1957 $12).*

For those seeking information about physical and mental health there are W. A. N. DORLAND'S *Illustrated Medical Dictionary (Saunders 23rd ed. 1957 $12.50)* and LELAND HINSIE & JACOB SHATZKY'S *Psychiatric Dictionary (Oxford Univ. 2nd ed. 1953 $15)* and its *Supplement (Oxford Univ. $7).*

M. Miscellaneous

To pick, from the vast and varied array of reference books, only half a dozen more that will give some idea of the range and scope and helpfulness of this kind of publication is like trying to choose from a binful of mixed seeds the exact six that one wants in order to grow a white aster, an angel-wing begonia, an orange cosmos, a light-blue delphinium, an elm, and a forget-me-not. (Fortunately, reference books are not in unclassified and unsorted bins.) Here, in an attempt to hint further at the availability of wide-ranging aid in this imposing quantity of books, is a miscellaneous selection of six titles that have demonstrated their usefulness. (1) For the traveler: *Hotel Red Book (Amer. Hotel Assn. Directory Corp. vol. 72 1958 $5)*. (2) For the sports enthusiast: F. G. MENKE'S *Encyclopedia of Sports (Barnes & Noble rev. ed. 1953 $10)*. (3) For the handyman: R. E. KINGERY'S *How-To-Do-It Books (Bowker 2nd ed. 1954 $4.50)*. (4) For the writer: *Manual of Style (Univ. of Chicago 11th ed. 1949 $5.50)*. (5) For the job-seeker: GERTRUDE FORRESTER'S *Occupational Literature (Wilson 1958 $6.50)*. (6) For the socially perplexed: EMILY POST'S *Etiquette (Funk 9th ed. 1950 $5.50)*.

Librarians at schools, colleges, and universities and in public libraries are trained and experienced in aiding individuals to find their way about in the forest of reference books. In nearly any library you will find a librarian whose obligation and pleasure it will be to help you find and consult the book you need.

Author, Title, and Subject Index to the *Good Reading* Book Lists

266

278

284

For your permanent library . . .
a durable, hardbound edition of

GOOD READING

Once you've taken this "guided tour through the world of books," you may want a hardbound edition on your shelves to serve you in the years to come. When a new field piques your interest, next year or several years from now . . . you'll be able to turn to your permanent edition of GOOD READING for suggestions on the most significant titles. And, when you're looking for an unusually thoughtful gift, here's one that will be appreciated by many of the friends on your list.

You'll see the same stimulating selection of books, the same helpful and authoritative introductions to each list—presented in a larger type face on bigger, permanently durable paper. The clothbound edition, published in February 1960—and identical in content to this paperback edition—sells for $4.00 postpaid.

Order your copy of the hardcover edition of *Good Reading* either from your bookstore or direct from RRB, New American Library of World Literature, 501 Madison Ave., New York 22, N.Y. If you order through New American Library, please make checks payable to: R. R. Bowker Company. Price is $4.00 pre-paid.